DATE DUE

MAY 2 0 1976			
MAY 2 0 1976 DEC 2 '76			
DEC 2 '76			
MAR 4 '77			
NOV 1 8 1977			
SEP 1 5 1980			
30 505 JOSTEN'S			

BEYOND WEAVING

BEYOND WEAVING

BY MARCIA CHAMBERLAIN
AND CANDACE CROCKETT

PHOTOGRAPHS BY DAVID DONOHO

WATSON-GUPTILL PUBLICATIONS, NEW YORK

PITMAN PUBLISHING, LONDON

Copyright © 1974 by Watson-Guptill Publications

First published 1974 in the United States and Canada by Watson-Guptill Publications,
a division of Billboard Publications, Inc.,
One Astor Plaza, New York, N.Y. 10036

Published simultaneously in Great Britain by Sir Isaac Pitman & Sons Ltd.,
39 Parker Street, Kingsway, London WC2B 5PB
ISBN 0-273-00811-0

Manufactured in U.S.A.

Library of Congress Cataloging in Publication Data
Chamberlain, Marcia
  Beyond weaving.
  Bibliography: p.
  1. Handicraft. I. Crockett, Candace, 1945–
joint author. II. Title.
TT699.C47   1974   746   74-1110
ISBN 0-8230-0486-4

First Printing, 1974

CONTENTS

ACKNOWLEDGMENTS

The ease with which all our demonstration sections came together was due in large part to David Donoho's excellent photographic work, and to his personal interest—as friend and colleague—in *Beyond Weaving*. We feel especially fortunate to have been able to work with David. Many of our students at California State University at San Jose also assisted in the preparation of step-by-step examples, especially Bonnie Britton, Jennifer Cooper, and Edwin Geer, Jr. Nora Fisher and Carol Stiero of the Museum of International Folk Art, in Santa Fe, New Mexico, gave unhesitatingly of their time and knowledge, as did Curator Yvonne Lange. Margery Anneberg of the Anneberg Gallery in San Francisco encouraged our free use of her collection. Ann Blinks and Paula Simmons cheerfully shared their knowledge of wool and spinning learned from years of experience and serious study.

We are most appreciative of the discernment shown by Ted Hallman, Freda Koblick, Mary Jane Leland, and Arthur Sandoval in their selection and procurement of photographs from craftsmen and museum collections. The staff of the American Crafts Council contributed their time, services, and resources very freely. Bernard Kester, chairman of the art department at UCLA, and Eudorah Moore, curator of California Design Incorporated, were responsible for the Fiber Symposium of 1971 and were generous in allowing us to quote excerpts from videotapes of interviews made during that landmark event. Helen Pope and Carol Beadle each contributed in many ways to the development of this book. Peggy Stephenson assisted in all phases of the preparation of the manuscript, and has helped in the many ways that count so much.

Special thanks also go to the craftsmen and the museums who so freely contributed photographs of work for inclusion in this book, and to the many who helped, but whose names do not appear here.

INTRODUCTION

An important part of the current renewal of interest in woven forms and fabric construction has to do with non-loom or off-loom techniques. This volume is designed to present both information and instruction for those techniques—information and instruction we consider to be beyond weaving.

As we gathered the materials necessary for this book, we worked and talked with fellow craftsmen, and we were constantly reminded of the enormous energy, concern, integrity, and workmanship being put into the fiber arts today.

We were also brought to understand, more clearly than ever before, our debt to past craftsmen. We examined evidence from prehistoric times, and were able to appreciate the changes that early man experienced as he evolved through his nomadic and pastoral days. We were able to see him develop from being a user of found tools to being a maker of tools, and we were able to see him develop increasingly greater sophistication in the manufacture and use of those tools. Throughout his development, early man used what chance and his own developing knowledge provided him in the way of "fibers"—strips, sinews, plant fibers, hair. . . . He concurrently developed ways to treat and color his materials so they would be more permanent or more comfortable, and so they would bring greater esthetic joy into his life. We were impressed throughout our study with the parallels between the ancient craftsman and his modern followers. Both have been able to use fiber crafts in clearly functional and practical ways, and both have used their crafts to make observations on life's mysteries. The human life that is worked into a hand-fashioned fiber form, whether an ancient fetish or a modern fiber sculpture, stays with the piece forever.

WHATEVER MAN MAKES

"Whatever man makes and makes it live
lives because of the life put into it.
A yard of India muslin is alive with Hindu life.
And a Navajo woman, weaving her rug in the pattern of her dream
must run the pattern out in a little break at the end
so that her soul can come out, back to her.

But in the old pattern, like snake-marks on the sand
it leaves its trail."

D. H. Lawrence

Dearly Beloved We Are Gathered Together (detail) by Robert J. Mills, 1973. Polypropylene fibers, 84″ high. This piece is of special interest because of the select use and control of new synthetic fibers. It shows a combination of wrapping and knotted half-hitches. Photo by Sharyn Amii Mills.

CHAPTER ONE

FIBER PROPERTIES

"A true craftsman takes that quality which sets his medium apart from any other and by emphasizing it, becomes its master."

from *Heritage: An Illustrated History of Western Culture* by Allison Travis Brown

A large portion of this chapter is based on techniques traditionally associated with textile manufacturing. There should be no limit on their translation, however, into techniques for use with other linear elements. The governing consideration is your understanding of the properties of the material and exploring them to the utmost.

Natural fibers are more accessible to you as an artist and more easily processed into workable form than synthetics. Let us then consider some of the general properties of natural fibers before we explore the specific characteristics of each—cotton, flax, silk, and wool.

PROPERTIES OF NATURAL FIBERS

The general properties of fibers are determined by the nature of their external structure, their internal structure, and their chemical composition. Natural fibers, except for silk, have three distinct parts: an outer covering, an inner area, and a central core that may be hollow.

The outer covering of a fiber determines, for example, its resistance to abrasion. Another characteristic, which may be modified by fiber length, is luster. Each of the natural fibers—cotton, flax, silk, and wool—has select advantages and disadvantages in these and other properties.

Consider the relative relationships between the four types of fiber in the areas of moisture absorption, stretch and recovery, stiffness, abrasion, strength, and heat tolerance.

The chart below does not take into consideration the relative position of man-made fibers for each classification. Some would fall above and some below depending on their individual chemical engineering.

In the spinning of all filament, there are four general properties to consider: length of fiber, its pliability, its relative strength, and its cohesiveness. Spinning will increase the strength of a filament, and the success of spinning is interrelated to the other three properties. Let us see what makes the

	Moisture absorption	Stretch and recovery	Stiffness	Abrasion	Strength	Heat tolerance
Cotton	L	L	H–M	M	M	H–M
Flax	H	L	H	H	H	H
Silk	M	M–H	M–L	M	H–M	M–L
Wool	H–M	H	L	L	L	M
	H = Highest		M = Medium		L = Lowest	

most widely used natural fibers different from one another.

Cotton. Vegetable fibers were the earliest to be spun into yarns, with cotton probably predating flax. We know that cotton was cultivated and used in the Tehaucan Valley of Mexico 7,000 years ago, and cotton fabrics woven as early as 3500 B.C. have been found at Moheijo-Daro in the Indus Valley. The fragile nature of the material contributes to its rarity, but because of clear "fossil" impressions of woven cloth in more durable materials such as clay and metal, we know that cotton spinning predates this Indus Valley find.

Under a microscope, cotton fibers appear as flattened tubes with twists or spirals both to the left and right. Actually the tube is a hair filament that grows clustered around a seed. On the outside is a waxy cuticle. The inner area is made up of successive layers of reversing cellulose spirals. The central core appears as a collapsed tube.

The outer covering repels moisture, but the inner structure is very absorbent. Cotton fibers therefore stretch, shrink, swell, and contract with changes in humidity, and these characteristics make it one of the easiest filaments to spin. The only shortcoming is its relative strength due to the reverse spiral, or twist, of the inner area.

Flax. Principally grown first in Egypt, flax is a vegetable fiber that might well be as old as cotton in its use. Mostly cellulose, it is a bast (inner bark layer) fiber, not a seed hair, and is woody in nature.

Flax, from which linen is spun, is actually a processed layer from the stem of a plant. The plant grows to about 3 feet with blue flowers and bolls containing linseed. A number of processes extract the usable fibers found between the pith and the skin of the stem, and these processes are discussed in detail in Chapter 3.

What is of special interest here is the interior structure of the extracted flax fibers. These fibers carry water through the stems. Under the microscope a flax fiber has traverse nodes or joints at intervals and there is no twist in the filament. These properties give linen fiber two of its major characteristics: it holds and carries water in the closely ordered fibers and it has poor flex-abrasion resistance. The latter means that the fibers will break quite easily.

Because vegetable fibers are responsive to moisture, they are best spun when wet. The toughness of fiber and brittle quality of flax are present in other bast fibers. These may be used in the same manner as flax although they cannot be as finely spun.

Ramie, Hemp, and Jute. Ramie has its origins in Asia. Sometimes referred to as grasscloth, it is actually a member of the nettle family and grows as a shrub. Ramie is used for the same type of products as linen and can be mistaken for linen. It has a silklike sheen and is one of the strongest fibers, increasing in strength when wet.

Hemp is as old as flax, but lacks the fineness of linen. It is a member of the mulberry family and hemp, like ramie, finds its origins in Asia. Very strong, therefore predominantly used for cordage and twine, its use has declined with the introduction of synthetics.

Geographically, the incidence of mulberry for the production of hemp and its leaves for the nurturing of the silkworm seem to center in areas of China: central and southeast Honan, south Hopei, and southwest Shantung. Hemp cloth was, of course, a base for their lacquer ware. It was called *chia chu* (lined with hemp cloth) and long predates the use of wood and silk in this technique.

Jute is the second most widely used vegetable fiber, next to cotton. Its origin is Eastern India and it is a member of the linden family. Because the individual fibers are both short and brittle, it is the weakest of the fibers in this group.

Other Vegetable Fibers. Indian mallow from Southern Asia, a member of the same family as cotton, and kenaf or ambary from East India are both used for bulk textile production. Leaves from plants such as sisal, maguey, and yucca yield other workable fibers. Sisal and hemp come from the agave plant, a native of Yucatan. Maguey, another member of the agave family, yields not only fibers for twisting strong rope, but the outer skin may be used as paper. It is probably one of the few plants which produces a needle already threaded, for when you pull the needle from the tip of a leaf it brings with it a group of fibers ready for stitching. The yucca, a member of the lily family, yields similar fibers for making cordage.

Silk. Chinese legend dates sericulture at about 2640 B.C. when a controlled agriculture for raising silkworms was started by the Empress Si-Ling-Chi. Wild silk was known before this date, but it was the control in harvesting that was most important to the advancement of silk fibers. The life cycle of the silkworm is 8 to 10 days, when the chrysalis is inactive within the cocoon. At the end of this period the moth emerges and breaks the continuous silk filament that makes up the cocoon. We can assume that until controlled conditions in sericulture were developed, silk was carded and spun from broken cocoons.

Silk has always been a luxury fiber because its production is limited and the processing of the filament is tedious. However, the natural luster, brilliance of dyed color, dry tactile hand, good covering power, and the crisp draping qualities when woven are all most desirable.

Actually, there are filaments from some 70 varieties of silk moths. Silkworms feed primarily on mulberry and oak, therefore it is feasible that sericulture developed where these two trees are native. India, Persia, Greece, Sicily, Italy, Spain, France, England, and Ireland have all attempted sericulture at some time in history. The latter two failed, primarily due to climate. However, silk did become one of the crops for the American Colonies under James I.

The bombyx (silkworm) mori (belonging to the mulberry tree) is the most useful species for producing silk filament. The silk for the cocoon comes from a secretion formed and stored within the body of the silkworm in two symmetrically located glands. This liquid flows through two spinnerets to a common exit in the head of the worm. This first secretion is called febroin. As the febroin exits, it is joined by a second secretion called sericin, which glues the two filaments of febroin together into one. The Chinese found that sericin can be softened by hot water, making it possible to unwind the cocoon and at the same time keep a continuous filament of silk intact.

This spinneret—the principle of secretions and binders under pressure and heat—forms the base for contemporary industrial practices used to make synthetic threads. Silk is reeled rather than spun (see Chapter 3). The nature of silk, a continuous filament, provides all the natural and desired elements of a strong filament, while shorter fibers—cotton and wool—have to be joined by spinning.

Wool. Wool and silk are protein fibers, both animal products. Wool-bearing animals—such as sheep, goats, and camels—were providing personal warmth, shelter, and food long before mankind decided to fleece them.

Historically, while sheep were among the first animals to be domesticated, they were the last to have their wool spun—for several reasons. First, the

Untitled by Arthur A. Sandoval, 1973. Belgian linen, polished linen, cow and horse tails, jute, excelsior, raffia, 72" x 30" x 15". Simple finger knitting is just one of many techniques used by the artist to allow as much of the bundled material to show as possible. The piece shows a free and spirited use of both materials and techniques. Photo courtesy of the artist.

Figure 1. *This photo illustrates the parts of a rope and the direction in which each part lays (one strand has been unraveled to show two parts). First, many fibers are spun or twisted together to form yarns. These yarns are plied to form strands; the strands are then twisted to form rope. Notice that the strands have a right-hand twist, and the rope is formed of three strands with a reverse twist. It is this reverse twist that helps keep rope straight.*

hair was already firmly embedded in a fabric (skin). Plucking it was neither productive nor necessary to make body coverings. One needed shearing instruments to get sufficient fleece and such shearing instruments were not available until the Iron Age. A third reason is that the techniques used for spinning wool are derivatives of those for spinning vegetable matter.

Wool is, however, the easiest fiber to spin, having a number of characteristics all conducive to its successful use. In fact, the very characteristics that make it successful as a felting material are the same ones that make it successful for spinning. These characteristics are so desirable that many synthetic filaments are manufactured with the prime interest of imitating one or more combinations of them.

Microscopically, the wool fiber is made up of the cuticle, a cortex, and a medulla. The outer layer, or cuticle, is composed of slightly overlapping scales that encircle the hair shaft. The free edges of the scales project outward toward the tip of the hair. It is these scales that make some people itch when they wear wool. The cortex is the main part of the fiber and is made up of long cigar-shaped cells that move when exposed to moisture. In the center of the hair is the medulla, or core, which is similar in appearance to a honeycomb. It contains air spaces that can increase the insulating power of the fiber.

Crimp is one of the terms often used in describing one of the most desirable characteristics of wool. A combination of twist and wave in a wool filament, crimp is a dominant result of the ability of the cortex to react to moisture. The crimp straightens when wool is subject to moisture and recrimps when it dries. The straightening of the natural twist and wave is, in a sense, elastic and can give the wool as much as 30% stretch or shrink.

When wool fibers are rubbed against each other, the outer scales of the cuticle can interlock. This property of interlocking combined with elasticity and crimp make wool easier to spin and felt. Both are discussed in more detail in the following chapters. Wool combines very well with synthetics because the straight man-made filament has a tendency to automatically hide under the wool springs.

Spinning and Plying

Spinning is an auxiliary technique basically employed to extend the length of a short fiber into a long filament. A spun fiber is characterized by

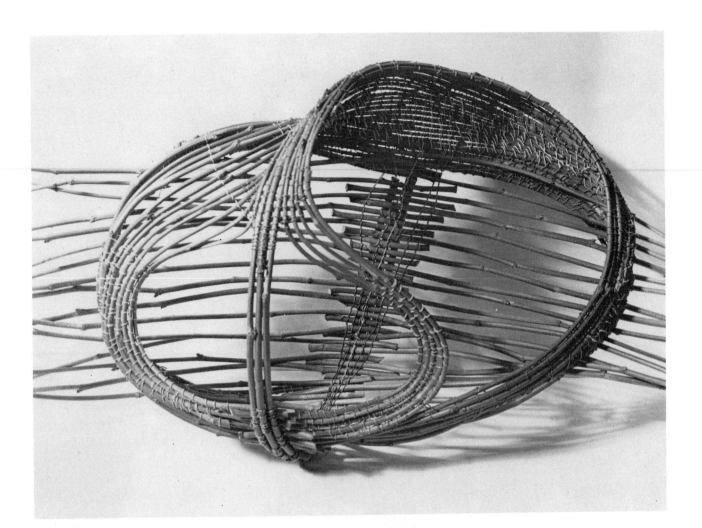

Open Basket (Above) by Gyongy Laky, 1973. Coiled California Sycamore and plastic-coated wire, 26″ x 20″ with 36″ twig projections. The flexibility of the Sycamore (cut in winter) obviously determined much of the basket's form. The whips, which are long, also dictated the basket's size to some extent. Photo by Candace Crockett.

Coiled Form by Gyongy Laky, 1973. Wild Boston fern and mosses, 7″ in diameter. Units of natural materials have always been adapted by peoples for practical purposes. Only after refining such materials were symbolism and abstract concepts such as decoration included. Here the artist is saying that the dictum of process art is also true in the simplest of expression and, more particularly, in the simplest of found materials. Photo by Candace Crockett.

Sculptured Forms by Ruth Asawa, 1952-62. Copper, brass, aluminum, iron, and Monel wires. The artist has worked on the esthetic problems of interwoven and continuous surface forms for ten years, and this grouping is only a sample of the possibilities she found. Each type of wire had its own qualities that contributed to the resolution of the form. Photo by Laurence Cuneo.

protroding fiber ends, making it fuzzy. The natural strength of the fiber is also increased because several fibers are joined together. When more than one filament is joined it is called plying. Generally spinning and plying once constitutes a yarn. When there is a second plying, it is sometimes referred to as a rope (see Figure 1).

Letters have been assigned to better identify the directional twist from spinning. You can see for yourself which way a yarn is spun by suspending a paper clip from the end of a yarn length. If it rotates in a counterclockwise direction when viewed from above, it is an S-twist; if it rotates clockwise, it is a Z-twist.

MINERAL FIBERS

Asbestos and precious metals such as gold and silver often appear in textiles. The toxicity of asbestos, as well as its nearly unspinnable character, limits its appeal to the artist. If it is spun, it is necessary to combine it with at least 5% cotton.

Gold and silver have historically enhanced fabrics, and two processing methods have been used to produce a pliable metallic thread. One is to hammer the metal into foil form and lay it as a flat strip into the web. It may also be wrapped around a cord of silk, linen, or cotton. Occasionally, animal skin is used as a core for either gold or silver gilt. There are also examples of gilded mulberry paper from China.

As the processing of metals changed, they were drawn into thin threads or wire without a foundation core. Today, we have many types of metals to call on when using textile techniques.

MAN-MADE FIBERS

Rayon was the first in a long line of continuing experiments within the textile industry to produce man-made fibers. In the beginning, this experience was based on a knowledge of natural fibers and centered mainly on the intent to imitate. First the textile industry took the idea of a spinneret from silk to produce a monofilament; then they chopped it up into lengths that corresponded to wool and cotton. To these short lengths they artificially added various surface contours as well as a crimp or twist. Each chemical combination produced an artificial filament with its own characteristics as well as increasing the possible usefulness beyond those found in natural fibers. Blends are made using both man-made and natural fibers, thus gaining the positive qualities of each.

DYEING

Natural fibers respond to dyeing in direct ratio to their affinity to moisture and their surface configurations. Therefore, linen will take dye very well but it will discharge dye equally rapidly. The primary purpose of the bast fiber in flax is to conduct water, and it will continue to do so even after spinning.

Another major consideration is the number of available dye sites within each fiber. Wool has numerous ones in its scaly outer surface that can be opened up with moisture and closed with drying. Synthetics are very difficult to dye and any color is usually added during the filament processing, either while it is in solution or immediately after—but always before it is spun into yarn. There are eleven classifications of dyes used in industrial dyeing. The major dyes used on cotton, linen, and wool are called fiber reactives and give bright colors with excellent fastness. Others are mordant and acid dyes.

New chemical treatments of yarn surfaces have changed these dye responses. Many prepared yarns now have dirt and moisture repellents incorporated in their manufacture. These may hinder any dye processing you are doing and they may also modify expected results.

OUR NEXT CHALLENGE

The next challenge for industry is to look beyond imitation and to recognize the intrinsic possibilities of synthetics for a new plastic form and new methods of fabrication. The challenge for artists is to entice industry into "raiding" their vision. Think what you could do if, instead of relying on what is already produced, you could produce your own yarns. Maybe that is why today and tomorrow you are going to be spinning and dyeing your own natural yarns.

FIBER CLASSIFICATION

Fibers are broadly classified into "natural" and "man-made." Natural fibers are as they exist in nature and may be used after relatively simple processing. Vegetable fibers are classified as cellulose; animal fibers as protein.

Man-made fibers are divided into two generic groups: cellulose and non-cellulosic. Rayon and acetate are the only two cellulose fibers, and they are partially derived from vegetable wastes.

The charts that follow identify the primary textile fibers and their select generic names.

Fiber Classification Charts

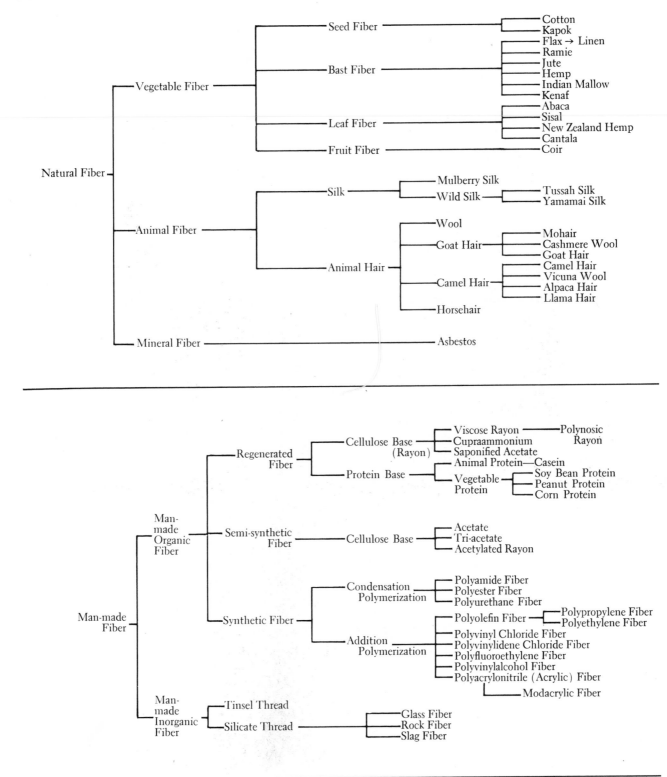

Paper Bag (Left) *by Judyth Dreiger. Paper shopping bags, 12" x 4". Twining a bag from paper bags that would ordinarily be discarded is an inventive use of found materials. Photo by David Donoho.*

Raincoat. This handsome Korean raincoat is made in two sections that are attached at the shoulders with twisted palm rope. The material is overlapping layers of handsewn coconut palm. Photo courtesy of the Museum of International Folk Art, Santa Fe, New Mexico.

CHAPTER TWO

FELTING

True felting, one of the oldest methods of making fabric, is constructed of wool, hair, or fur that is matted or webbed together. A random arrangement of fibers is subjected to moisture, heat, and pressure, and this treatment produces a felt fabric.

A true felt is made with wool fibers; however, other fibers may be added to it. The degree of this mix establishes both the felt quality and its eventual use. The more wool in felt, the better the quality. Actually, as little as 10% wool in a blend can be felted, such is its felting power. The wool fibers work best when they are between 1″ and ½″ in length.

Felting is essentially a kinetic phenomenon. As the wool fibers are laid at random and "shocked" by moist heat and pressure, the scales on the filaments lock or crimp together. The scales act almost as fishhooks, allowing the fiber to move in only one direction. Felt, then, is not interworked in any regular order but relies exclusively on the intrinsic structure of the material used and the external and natural conditions of heat, moisture, and pressure.

History and Lore of Felt

The earliest felt came from Central Asia, although it was also made in ancient Europe. We have no record of felt in the Americas or Africa. Felt lore is not too extensive but certainly has an interesting gamut. Lewis Carroll's writings provide a timely commentary on society in the fact that mercury poisoning did indeed send hatters mad. Popular also among the trade is the story that Noah discovered felted wool after the animals departed the Ark. Noah used sheep's wool to make the animals' travels more comfortable; they provided the other natural conditions.

Matting

One of the major differences between felting vegetable and animal fibers is that the former are truly matted in the initial process. Matting can be accomplished by packing fibers into a limited space without chemical swelling or agitation. The surface characteristics or entangling tendencies of vegetable fibers contribute to the success of matting. Cotton or kapok mat and wool felts are good examples.

Cotton, as discussed in Chapter 1, has a random countermovement within each cotton filament. It is this recurring countermovement that makes it cling together in a mat. The only vegetable fiber used in animal felting is redwood bark, which is added to rabbit fur felts.

Natural Mats and Felts

There are other fibrous structures made of plant material that, by their nature, fall into the classification of being felted or matted. These are, in a sense, already matted. Having a natural random and interlaced arrangement of tough fibers, the plant material needs only to be softened and flattened smooth.

Beaten bark-cloth is most notable in this category. It is made from the inner bark of suitable trees and shrubs. Of these, the wild fig, mulberry, and breadfruit are the most suitable and widely used. Bark-cloth is found throughout the tropical and subtropical land belts with very little variation in its processing or the tools used.

Bark-Cloth and Paper

Different locales often give individual names to the bark-cloth, the most popular being tapa. As the numerous bark-cloths are made with such similarity, one can only speculate on the popularity of calling all those from Oceania "tapa." Lore has it that its name came from the tap, tap, tap of the native beaters. Perhaps it is the onomatopoeic appeal of the word. In any event, tapa specifically is made from the inner bark of the mulberry and is designated as Polynesian.

In making bark-cloth, the inner bark is stripped, soaked, and beaten. This removes the softer material and leaves the stronger fibrous structure, resulting in a matte fiber-cloth. Sections of bark may be overlapped to either enlarge the cloth area or reinforce naturally weak sections. Gum, paste, or glue is sometimes used to bond these reinforcements. The pieces may also be sewn together.

Paper is another material that has a similar structure to felting and matting. The manufacturing processes often correspond to those of felting and the nomenclature parallels it. Essentially, the short or chopped raw materials are subject to moisture, heat, and pressure before emerging as paper. One of the most circular instances of use takes place in paper manufacturing in that heavy industrial felt fabrics are used for the dewatering process.

SYNTHETICS IN FELTING

Many of the synthetic filaments in use today have been combined with wool in felted products. One drawback, however, is a stiff harshness, or "hand," to the fabric after the heat treatment. Other non-woven techniques have been developed for the new bonded textiles. Adhesives that set the crosspoints of the fibers are added in the same way as they are to some commercial felts with low wool content. These non-woven textiles, while loosely related to felting and matting, do not include wool in their manufacture.

The non-woven fabrics using webs or batts of fibers are treated by mechanical, chemical, or thermal processes. Generally, these new industrial products are classified into four types: paper, bonded

Ceremonial Suit. This two-piece suit from Panama is made of palm bark-cloth. The fragile nature of the material and the decorative quality of the painted designs indicates that it is for a special occasion. It is in excellent condition, still showing brightly painted designs in light blue, red, and yellow. Collection of the Museum of International Folk Art, Santa Fe, New Mexico. Photo by Candace Crockett.

fiber webs and fusibles, spun-bonded webs, and needle-punched fabrics.

FELTING LOOMS

Needle-punched fabrics are of particular relevance to felting. Essentially, the textile is prepared by passing a batt over a needle loom as many times as is necessary to produce strength and texture in the fabric. The needle loom is made up of a series of boards with barbed needles set at close intervals. The barbs catch a few fibers as they pass back and forth through the web and thus mechanically interlock them. It parallels the natural action of wool scales in felting or cotton twisting in matting.

Adaptations of knit-sew machines can do the same thing. One of these is the Arachne system developed in Czechoslovakia. By eliminating the stitching thread from the knit system and having the needles pass through the web closed, then open, then pulling back through the web acting as a barb, the batt fibers are interlocked.

Czechoslovakia has pursued other experimental programs in non-woven and felted products. One of major interest, Art Protis, is described here by Robert Freimark. He is the only American artist who has been invited to work with the process. His first visit to Czechoslovakia was in 1970, and he has returned on four occasions to create a total of 48 tapestries. His work is shown in the color section.

"Art Protis is one of the most recent of techniques, having been developed at the Wool Research Institute in Brno, Czechoslovakia. Though its full range of capabilities may not yet have been fully explored, so far its primary characteristic has been the use of carded, non-spun dyed wool batts superimposed on a basic foundation. These strands may vary in length and end either in gradation or abruptly —as hard edge. They may range from a dense opaque to something completely transparent, or they may float over solid areas or lines as does a film or haze, thus creating illusionary depth. There are seemingly endless variations in lamination, affording soft color

Croatian Jacket (back view). *A rich and traditional use of felt for clothing is shown in this long jacket from Yugoslavia. It was first tailored, then embellishments were cut and appliquéd to it. Collection of the Museum of International Folk Art, Santa Fe, New Mexico, Photo by Candace Crockett.*

nuances as well as impenetrable depth, some of which is achieved also by the direction of the fiber strand.

"When all the fibers have been arranged to the artist's approval, the entire assemblage passes through a patented textile machine which presses and then attaches every fiber to the backing. However, this part of the process accounts for no more than 5% of the manual and artistic work contributing to the creation.

"The fibers are carded and tedded out in thin sheets. Art Protis has over 120 different shades of color for the artist to choose from. A tapestry or mural hanging is created by superimposing a skein of these strands of various color, direction and density upon a select backing. He may also choose to add other materials, pre-woven, printed or cut to shape, to mention possibilities. The range of non-conventional tapestry materials which may be included is ever-expanding (as more and more artists experiment), including such diverse products as rope, recording tape, commercial felt, lace, and even gold leaf. Some of the more recent editions have introduced photographic elements, by coating certain areas with photo emulsion and later relating adjacent areas to the positive print exposed on this portion.

"Each work of art thus produced is an original, although some have been produced in small editions. Each work is registered in Czechoslovakia and signed on the reverse side. It is also accompanied by a certificate of originality. Assistants at Art Protis complete the works by adding a dust backing and equipping hangers. It is to the credit of Art Protis that they have fought to keep the standards at a high level.

"The atmosphere and influence of Art Protis tapestries cannot be duplicated by any other media. They seem especially suited to the enhancement of cold or distant architectural elements, so characteristic of much contemporary metal and concrete, for which they are a natural complement. The addition of warm textiles serves to re-relate such structures to human adaptation."

The soft feathered edge described by Bob Freimark is not usually asociated with the artist's use of felt. This is due to our having to use a manufactured material instead of becoming the artist-manufacturer. The results are always hard-edged with applied layers—decorative but reflecting little of the process of making felt. Because felting wool requires only time and minimum equipment, let us follow the steps necessary in making felt.

MAKING WOOL FELT

All wool is conducive to felting. However, the breed and certain portions of the fleece, as you will learn in Chapter 3, offer a great choice and variety in wools. We have found that fine, short fleece responds best for felting because it contains the greatest number of possibilities in both crimp and scale content.

Felting will occur with both natural and scoured wool. The natural fleece contains lanolin, but this decreases as you repeat the wetting and only helps hold the webs together in the beginning. You may use natural or dyed fleece.

Layering and Basting. Ted, or spread out, the batts of carded wool. As the carding has placed most of the fibers in one direction, you may find it to your advantage to alternate the direction in stacking the layers. In so doing, you can pull open one layer to expose the previous layer, thin the edges of one batt as it lies over the previous one, or lay in smaller, different colored sections.

In Step 2 we added some uncarded locks to the carded wool. These long locks are already naturally matted at the base, and they will join with the combed wool sections as the shocking takes place.

Baste the loosely assembled fleece to a temporary backing. We use an old muslin sheet that is removed after the felting is complete. The wool will float and separate during the wetting if you do not anchor the fleece in some manner after you have arranged the design. The muslin also serves as a handy way to roll the wool tightly in the next step.

Preparing the Fleece. Select wool fleece that is short and fine in character. Remove the vegetable matter by teasing (picking out the dirt and plant debris that may still be in the wool). Then spread the locks into a more open batt.

Comb the wool with hand carders or use a carding machine. Both teasing and carding are shown in Chapter 3. Up to this point, the preparation of wool is the same for both felting and spinning.

The sample shown in the photograph nearby was prepared on the carding machine. As the drum turns, the teased wool builds a thin batt of filaments, all generally lying in one direction. Each batt is pulled from the drum and will measure about 8″ x 12″. Prepare as many batts as you want; the more batts, the thicker and denser the felt will be. The example has eight layers of different colors of natural fleece.

Shocking the Fleece. Shocking means subjecting the

Felting: Step 1. First comb the wool (or wool mixture). The sample shown here was combed on the small carding machine shown in Chapter 3. Lift the wool from the drum and lay it on a flat surface. Our example uses eight layers of natural, unwashed wool from different colors of fleece. Some of the layers are thinner than others; other have openings made to allow the color variations to come through.

Step 2. Here are several types of prepared wool ready for felting. The center portion is the wool that was carded in Step 1. It is adjusted to a given design area. The light area contains naturally felted locks from the fleece. The longer locks are matted or felted at the base. All three types of fleece have been basted to a piece of muslin to hold them firm so the wool will not separate and float apart during the shocking process.

Step 3. Pour boiling water over the fleece (it can be submerged, but this is harder to handle) and immediately follow this with a cold-water bath. Roll the work tightly and let it rest for an hour or so. Repeat this process until the desired degree of felting is achieved. The hot and cold shock combines with the pressure to achieve a felted surface. This entire step can also be done by placing the firmly-basted fleece in a washing machine and setting the wash cycle to warm.

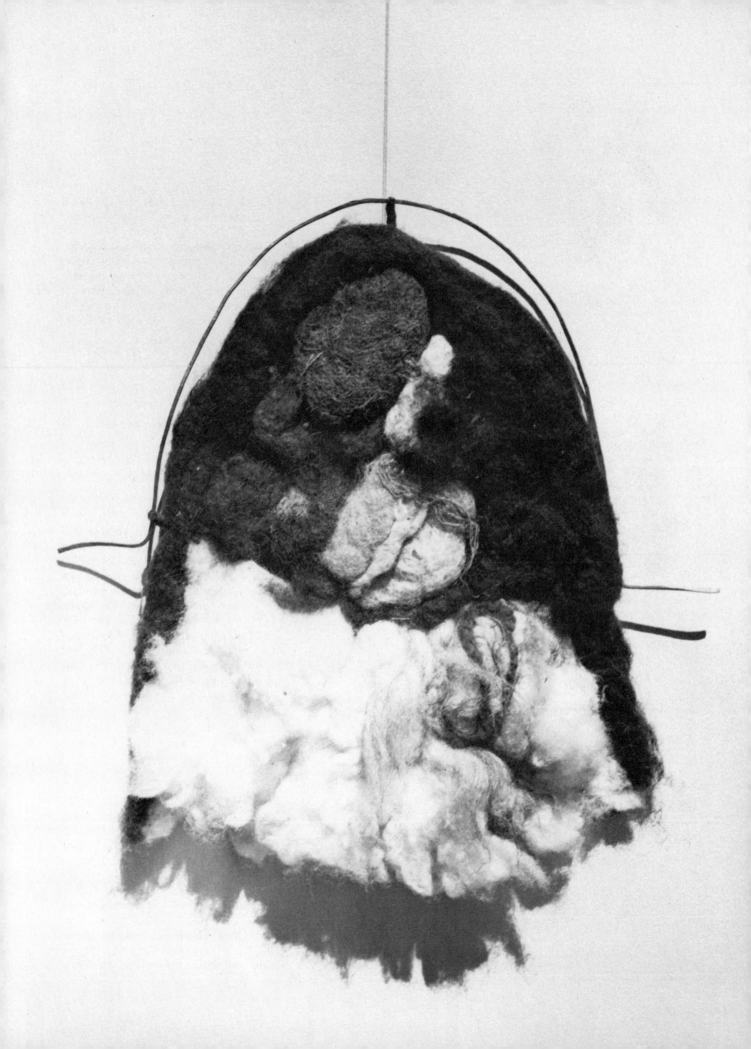

wool to excessive hot and cold temperatures. Any extreme temperature change causes the wool filaments to react or crimp, locking the scales together.

Pour boiling water over the basted wool (be sure to protect your hands with heavy rubber gloves). Remove the hot, wet wool and immediately submerge it in a cold water bath. Roll the basted wool tightly, using the muslin backing for support, and let it rest for a hour or so. There seems to be no specific amount of time for this rest; we only know that the pressure of rolling forces the filaments into closer contact.

Repeat the shocking process—a boiling water bath followed immediately with a cold water bath and pressure. The number of times you repeat the shocking and rolling will depend on how compressed you want the felt.

Variations. All forms of carded wool will felt, from the flat batts discussed here to sliver and roving. In the latter case, the fluffy rope compresses into a rather uneven, lumpy felt. Remember, too, that blends of wool and other materials—especially cotton—will felt. Animal hair such as rabbit and other fine, short-length furs may be added as is done in industry. In industry, however, the fur is carrotted first to allow the wool scales a rougher interlocking surface.

INDUSTRIAL FELTING

The felting steps just discussed are comparable to the industrial methods of making felt called hardening and fulling. The fiber batts are placed between metal platens that apply both heat and pressure. The platens jiggle slightly as these are applied This lightly felted piece is rolled and allowed to cool and drain. Fulling is accompished by systematically hammering, and thereby shrinking, the felt into the desired size. This shrinking may amount to as much as 50% and, incidentally, shrinking will occur in your work, too.

Each step thereafter is very much like those used for woven woolens and include scouring, dyeing, and finishing.

THE FUTURE OF FELTING

Few craftsmen have pursued felting to any esthetic end. Industry has limited its interest to producing products that capitalize on inexpensive manufacturing costs, such as gaskets and reinforcements for clothing. The bridge that needs to be crossed is the artist's knowing and using the basic nature of felt: its ability to absorb water and sound, to insulate against heat and cold, to polish and seal; to understand its limitations in terms of elasticity, tensile strength, and density. On the other hand, the wool industry and adjunct agencies could well look to the artist's imaginative uses of the process. All of the aforementioned qualities are ones that we encounter in our daily environments.

Felting is unique in its flexibility to achieve both hard and soft edges. No other textile technique offers you this option.

Wall Form by Carol Beadle, 9″ x 8″. The artist used felted wool, both natural and plant-dyed, in this diminutive wall piece. The forged metal frame serves as both a linear accent and as a support on which to stitch the felt. Photo by Candace Crockett.

Primitive Cotton "Factory." This photo, taken in Alabama, depicts cotton carding, loom weaving, two skein winders, and a spinning wheel. Photo courtesy of the Smithsonian Institution, Washington, D.C.

CHAPTER THREE

SPINNING

Spinning fibers into long, usable strands has been an important concern of mankind for thousands of years. Until the middle of the sixteenth century all fabrics were woven from threads that had passed through the fingers of the handspinner. Today's handspinner is not restricted by past standards that equated beauty and acceptability almost exclusively with fineness, uniformity, and strength. The contemporary handspinner is seldom concerned primarily with the production of yarn for fabrics, especially since machinery can do that job so successfully. Handspinners still can take pride in fine, strong threads, but at least as often spinners delight in the heavy, uneven, coarse yarn that can be achieved only by handspinning.

It is believed that spinning originated among people engaged in agriculture and that vegetable fibers were the first to be spun. At its simplest level, spinning needs no tools. Hold some fibers in one hand and twist them into a thread with the other hand. The work is slow and tedious, especially if any length is required, but amazing textiles have been made from yarn spun in this manner.

The next step was probably to wind the yarn around a stick so that the twist would remain, then to turn the stick to create the twist in the fibers. After that the stick was probably suspended and an object added for weight and momentum. The result was a hand spindle: a shaft and a whorl. Spinning is the simple process of drawing out fibers, twisting the fibers, and winding the yarn up. The distaff, which is also very old in origin and closely associated with spinning, developed no doubt as a means for holding the unspun material. It was tucked under the left arm or in the belt, and it allowed women to move around while spinning, so it be-

came possible to carry a water jug on the head, lead a horse, walk, and spin—all at the same time.

There is a special feeling among handspinners that comes partly from association with primitive spinners: the handspinners who throughout history have spun of necessity—to produce yarn to use in the production of practical fabrics. This feeling also comes from being one of a widespread and highly varied group of people who spin, and partly—largely —from the pleasure of producing by hand a strong, practical, beautiful material.

The equipment required for spinning is also minimal, and with just a little practice the spinner will be able to determine the kind of yarn needed, prepare the fiber, and spin up. The individual determines the extent of involvement, and while it takes relatively little instruction to learn to spin, there are those who have spent many years developing and refining their knowledge of the art.

SPINNING AS A WAY OF LIFE

Ross and Paula Simmons moved from the city to the country over 20 years ago. It took more than a year to locate two black sheep, since black sheep at that time were generally unwanted and unappreciated. Today, due to the popularity of handspinning, black fleece is in great demand. Paula Simmons began selling her handspun wool through a small craft shop, and by word-of-mouth advertising, gradually built up a mail-order business, which today keeps her and her husband busy the year round.

The Simmonses produce a high-quality product that cannot be maintained economically if mass produced. They begin with the sheep, breeding and selecting to produce the finest quality fleece. They shear their sheep by hand, slowly and care-

Shearing. Here Ross Simmons is shearing a black sheep with hand clippers. In commercial shearing, speed is all important. The sheep at the Yarn Farm, however, are shorn slowly and carefully to retain the full length of the natural fibers. Photo courtesy of Ross and Paula Simmons.

Anne Blinks with Her Black Sheep. The sheep shown here are a mixture of Corriedale and Lincoln, bred to produce heavy, lustrous black fleece. Their fleece grows quickly and they must be sheared twice a year. When photographed they were ready for their fall clipping. Photo by Candace Crockett.

fully in order to retain the full length of the natural fibers rather than as quickly as possible as more commercial establishments must. In commercial production, wool is washed mechanically and subjected to a carbonizing process to remove vegetable matter. In contrast, the Simmonses wash the fleece by hand with a household detergent that contains no bleach. The vegetable matter is picked out by hand. The natural resilience and character of the fiber are thus maintained.

Both Ross and Paula Simmons spin, much of it for special orders, but also for the functional products they weave and knit. Paula can control the weight of the yarn so closely as she spins it that several hanks 100 yards in length will not vary in weight by more than one or two grams. She produces, by sorting and combining, 40 different shades of yarn in natural colors as well as a number of colors using vegetable dyes.

The Simmonses feel that their intense involvement started when they began seeing their weaving, spinning, and sheep not as a way of making a living, but as a way of living—having to do with unity, independence, and the fulfillment of a creative urge. The following is an excerpt from a letter written by Paula Simmons in August, 1973:

"As for being a way of living, it has even been a way of relating to our neighbors. Normally, the craftsmen's way of life, their goals and their values, can set them apart, rather than making them part of the community. Here, we have our neighbors in the area raising dark sheep for us, they get the lambs for their freezer, we shear and get the wool. We spin so much wool per year, it is convenient to have a source of dark wool in addition to what we can raise.

"Being such a basic craft, spinning also encourages a basic kind of routine. No matter how busy we are, or how many orders ahead, we take time out to bake bread once a week. We 'clear the deck' of wool and yarn things, and get out the wheat germ and yeast and molasses and several kinds of flour. I measure, Ross mixes and kneads, and I take over to watch the raising, form the loaves, and time the baking.

"The vegetable garden does get neglected in the busiest time of the summer, but it still produces enough for eating fresh and freezing for winter, and sharing some of the unusual vegetables and herbs with a French restaurant. This may not appear to have much relation to yarn and wool and sheep, but it does. All the wasted hay on the barn floor, rich with sheep manure droppings, makes a priceless mulch which enriches our garden area year after year.

"We have no shop or studio open to the public (and no phone), but do our business by mail, selling direct to weavers and knitters, and supplying yarn to a few special shops, from California to Michigan. The yarn is 92¢ per ounce, and we have not raised the price in 18 years, although it is hard to hold the line now in the face of the current inflation. The cost of our winter supply of hay is exactly double what it was last year, and grain about twice the price also.

"I don't know what else to tell you, we enjoy our work together, although it does get hectic when we have so many orders ahead. We love the sheep, our business partners, and have them all named, of course."

Anne Blinks has been raising and breeding sheep for 14 years. Like the Simmonses, her interest is black sheep. For many years she has been interested in the study of textiles, primarily those of the Bronze and Iron Ages. She feels that to understand these textiles one must make them. She found that in many cases the weight of the yarn and the number of twists per inch, as well as the fiber character, were essential parts of the final piece. Her frustration at not being able to find or order the proper yarns led her to consider the source, and in 1959 she began to raise her own black sheep. After purchasing some sheep and fencing the pasture she quickly realized that a natural dark fleece and carefully controlled handspinning go together. This led her to another area of study which still, along with the black sheep and early textiles, consumes her interest. Her flock of "blackjacks" is mostly Corriedale, with some Lincoln. The lambs are coal black and remain so for two to four years, then

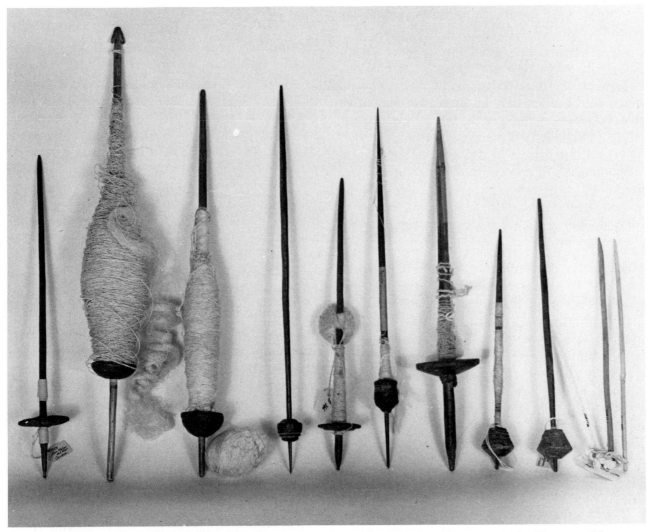

Indian Spindles from Mexico. On the right are two wooden needles with eyes. *Courtesy of the Museum of International Folk Art, Santa Fe, New Mexico. Photo by Candace Crockett.*

they gradually turn gray. Coming up with a black sheep of the right sort is not altogether easy. In 1972 she introduced a Lincoln ram to her Corriedale females. The two lambs "Flat" and "Sharp" in the foreground of the photograph were the result. She thought the Lincoln would increase luster and length (for worsted spinning for tapestry and rya rugs) but decided later that it was a mistake, since the lambs were too big for the ewes and had to be born by Caesarean section. The wool produced by those lambs is long and lustrous, but is too long for easy handling unless they are sheared twice a year.

Handspinning

Spinning is the process of twisting together and drawing out massed short fibers into a continuous strand. Fibers of short lengths, such as cotton and wool, as well as other fibers that have been broken into short lengths, can be drawn out and spun to produce yarn the length, size, strength, and texture desired.

The technique of spinning on the hand spindle is basically much the same with all fibers. Wool, because of its natural grease, is the easiest fiber to spin, and it is also generally the most readily available. Beginning spinners are usually advised to start off by spinning wool, and the instructions that follow call for the use of unwashed sheep's fleece.

Spinning is a marvelously rewarding activity. The rhythm of the movement and the feel of the woolen fibers can be totally absorbing; they can be enjoyed along with friendly conversation or interesting listening.

Making a Hand Spindle. A spindle is a simple tool consisting of a shaft and a weight, or whorl. The whorl gives weight, balance, and stability to the shaft as the spindle spins and the spun fibers are wrapped around the shaft. A good spindle can be bought from most weaving supply stores, or one may be made easily at home—without any special equipment—from common materials. Small, light spindles will spin thin, light yarns, and heavy spindles will spin heavier yarns. A spindle should always be comfortable to the touch, and an often-used spindle will almost inevitably have a special character and beauty of its own. The spindle used in the demonstration nearby has a tapered shaft 11" long, with a round whorl 3" in diameter. The wood is maple, and the entire spindle weighs 3 ounces.

Spinning with the Hand Spindle. This method is called "drop" spinning because the spindle hangs suspended as it spins. These instructions for spinning involve a series of steps that millions of spinners have used for millennia, for spinning up even more millions of miles of thread and yarn. Remember—especially if you feel a bit awkward with the fiber or the spindle—that each of those millions of spinners had to start at the very beginning, and that they, too, were taught by experience.

Attaching the Starting Cord. Cut a 3 foot length of wool yarn to use as a starting cord. Tie this firmly to the dowel or center shaft of the spindle above the spindle whorl. Turn the spindle clockwise (to the right) to wind up some of the starting cord, leaving about 20" of the thread unwound. Loop the starting cord around the shaft under the whorl, but do not tie a knot. Then loop the starting cord around the tip of the shaft at the spindle top. Suspend the balanced spindle by holding the end of the starting cord. You are now ready to begin spinning.

Adding the Fleece. Take a handful of greasy sheep's fleece and tease and loosen the fibers. Greasy fleece (still with its natural oil) is easier to spin and is best for the beginning spinner. Lay the starting cord between the left thumb and forefinger, with the teased fibers on top of the starting cord, and also between the left thumb and forefinger. Exert enough pressure with the left thumb to hold the fleece and cord together, with the spindle hanging downward. Using the right hand, spin the spindle clockwise. The wool fibers will twist around the starting cord, joining the two. This will give what is called a Z-twist to the yarn. Many left-handed spinners often use exactly the same approach, others reverse the process, still others devise their own variations.

Spinning. Spin the spindle again, slowly at first. As it turns relax your left thumb, and with your right hand draw the fibers out from the mass of teased fleece. The right hand controls the amount of fiber drawn out; the drawing distance depends on the length of the fibers. As the right hand relaxes, the spin will travel up the fibers to the left hand. Pressure from the left thumb prevents the spin from going up into the wool mass. Keep the spindle spinning clockwise or hold it still, but do not allow it to spin backwards, or "unspin."

Continue drawing the fibers out, allowing them to spin. As you need more wool, add a new teased mass by overlapping it with the previous fleece; it

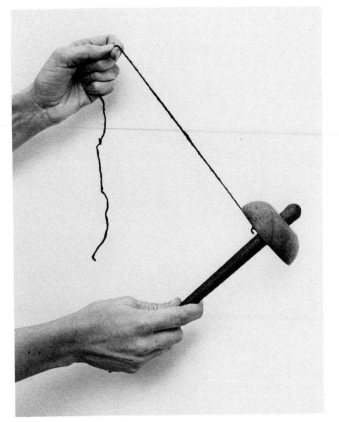

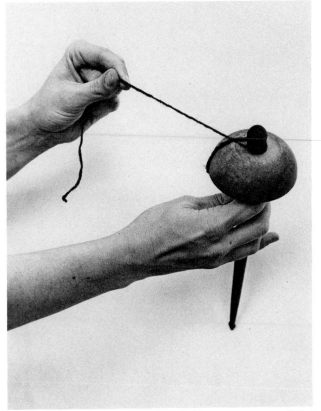

Spinning: Step 1. Tie the starting cord to the spindle shaft just above the whorl.

Step 2. From the knot, bring the starting cord around the spindle shaft just below the whorl.

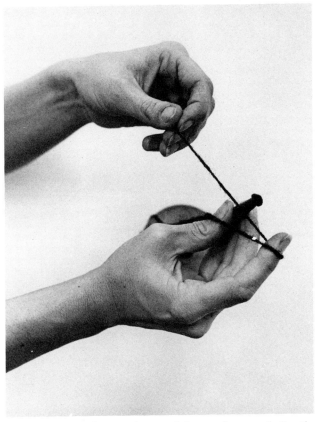

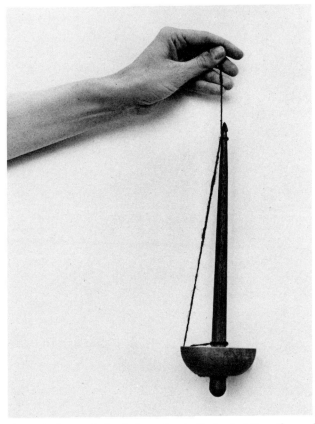

Step 3. Form the starting cord into a loop and slip the loop over the spindle tip.

Step 4. Suspend the balanced spindle by holding the end of the starting cord.

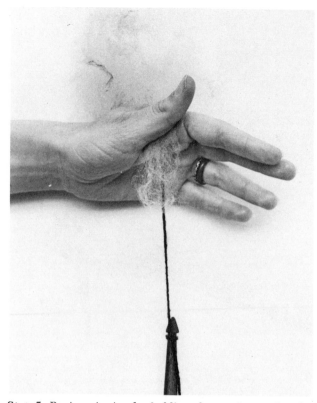

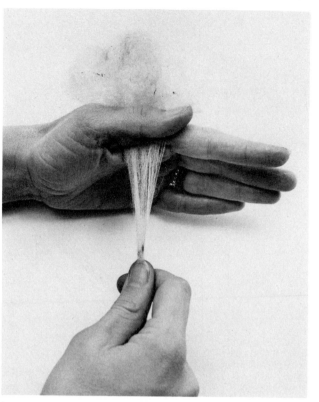

Step 5. Begin spinning by holding the starting cord and a small amount of teased fleece between the left thumb and forefinger, spinning the spindle clockwise with the right hand.

Step 6. As the spindle spins, draw out the fibers by pulling down with the right hand.

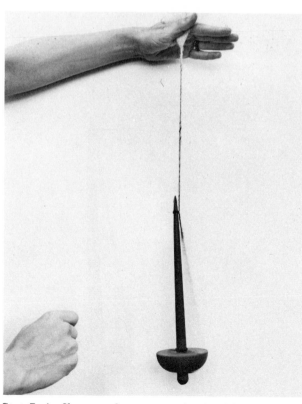

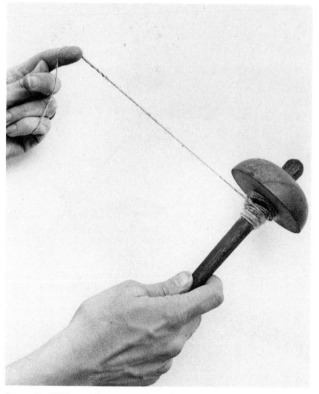

Step 7. As fibers are drawn out and twisted by the turning spindle, the length of spun yarn increases.

Step 8. When the yarn length increases so the spindle becomes difficult to work or reaches the floor, unloop the starting cord and wind the spun yarn around the spindle shaft above the whorl.

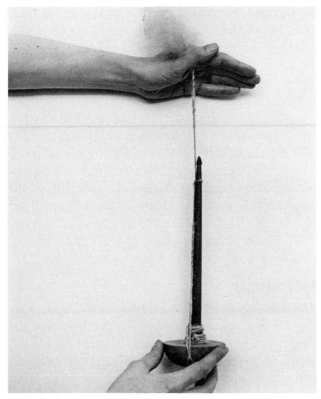

Step 9. Leave enough length of spun yarn so it can be wrapped around the shaft bottom and looped at the tip. Then continue spinning.

Step 10. As the process continues, wrap the spun yarn around the spindle shaft to form a cone.

Step 11. When the yarn on the spindle becomes too heavy or too bulky, wind it off into a ball or into a skein as shown.

Step 12. This photo shows the spun yarn and the spindle with the same starting cord ready for more spinning.

takes only a few fibers twisting together to allow for a join. A slight untwisting done with the right thumb and forefinger just before drawing the fibers out will prevent lumps and will allow the fibers to slide smoothly.

As the fibers spin up, the yarn gets longer, and eventually the spindle reaches the floor. When this happens, unloop the starting cord from the tip at the top of the shaft, and from the bottom end of the shaft, under the whorl. Wind the yarn onto the shaft of the spindle above the whorl by turning the spindle clockwise. Leave enough spun yarn free to loop around the spindle as you did in the beginning so that spinning may continue. Continue spinning, building up the spun yarn on the spindle into a cone shape.

Removing the Yarn. The spindle is full when it becomes too heavy or bulky to comfortably spin any longer. When this happens, the yarn is ready to be wound off into a ball, or over the back of a chair to make a skein. When wound into a skein the ends may be tied to one another, or wrapped around the skein and then tied on themselves.

Do not expect to be able to spin comfortably during your first attempts. Spinning undoubtedly comes more easily to some than to others, but it is a skill that will improve with experience.

Plied Yarns. Yarn can be spun in a clockwise direction resulting in a right-hand or Z-twist, or it can be spun in a counterclockwise direction resulting in a left-hand or S-twist. The kind of twist becomes important when several strands are twisted (or plied) together. Strands of yarn are frequently plied for strength. Yarns are usually plied in the opposite direction of the original twist, so if two individual strands are spun clockwise they are plied together in a counterclockwise motion. This is by no means a rule, and many interesting textures are created by combining different twist directions. Either the hand spindle or a spinning wheel can be used for plying. Whether using handspun or machine-spun yarn, plying different kinds and different weights of yarn can produce very interesting yarns.

Preparing Wool

The kind of yarn produced from wool depends on the breed of sheep that produces the wool, on the length and quality of the fibers, and on the way the fibers are prepared and arranged prior to spinning. Rough, funky yarns can be spun from locks or groups of fibers pulled directly from the shorn fleece, or the fibers can be prepared to produce a finer yarn. Each preparation step insures a finer, smoother, more controlled yarn (see Figure 2).

For centuries yarn was made without the benefit of fiber preparation, and many spinners still follow this practice. The industrial revolution brought a

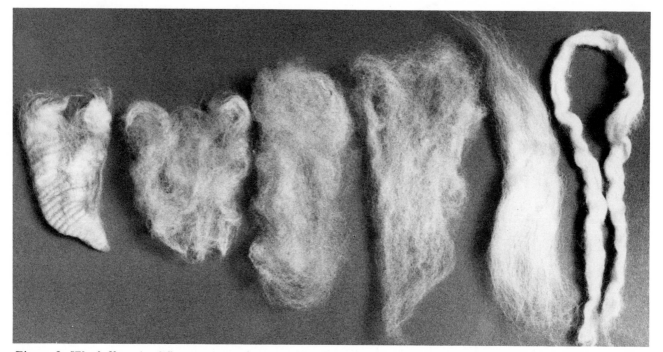

Figure 2. Wool fibers in different stages of preparation. Beginning on the left: a lock of fleece directly from the sheep, teased fibers, fibers carded with hand cards into a rolag, fibers carded on a hand carding machine, commercially scoured and carded fibers, and felted fibers. Photo by David Donoho.

need for fibers that could be spun easily, rapidly, and with great control to feed the voracious fly shuttle looms. Fiber preparation was a large part of the problem, and became highly developed. Many handspinners consider fiber preparation invaluable and necessary. The steps pertinent to the handspinner (any one of which can be omitted) are sorting, picking or teasing, scouring, oiling, and carding.

Sorting. The diameter and length of the fiber to be spun determine to a certain extent the appearance and function of the yarn. Every fleece has a variety of fibers. The more carefully these fibers are sorted, the more uniform the yarn. For instance, the belly wool on most sheep is very different from the wool on the shoulders.

Teasing or Picking. Teasing is a basic step in preparing wool and most other fibers for spinning. Teasing involves the gentle pulling apart of fibers so the mass of fibers becomes fluffy, airy, and more evenly distributed. During this teasing process matted areas should be pulled apart, burrs and vegetable matter picked out, and dirt and debris allowed to fall from the fleece. Once the fleece is properly teased, carding (or combing) will pull the fibers into a more parallel arrangement.

Scouring. Wool, more than any other fiber, needs washing. It can be washed at any stage—still on the sheep or already spun and woven. The oil in a sheep's fleece catches and holds dirt, so a thorough scouring (washing in soap until the water comes clean) of the teased wool before spinning will remove the grease and dirt. This washing makes the wool more difficult to spin, but insures clean yarn for the dyepot. Oil, either olive oil or specially prepared oil for spinning, can be added to washed fibers to make spinning easier.

Wash wool, whether unspun or spun, in the same way you would wash a wool sweater. Any sudden change in temperature—whether hot or cold —will cause the wool to mat, so such changes must be avoided. Wool fibers are covered by scales that form air pockets and give wool its warmth, lightness, and resiliency. Heat causes the scales to open, cold causes them to close. If either happens suddenly, matting occurs and the scales lock together. Harsh rubbing and twisting can also damage the scales and cause matting.

If a fleece is washed before teasing, the fleece will not come completely clean, but the natural character or look will be maintained. Teasing opens the locks and pulls the fibers apart, allowing the water and soap to penetrate. It is possible to wash the fleece in warm water without soap, so that most of the dirt is removed but the oil remains for easy spinning and a natural feel. Warm, soft water is best for washing wool. To scour the wool, a combination of either detergent or non-detergent soap and washing soda should be used. Work with large containers so the wool can float freely. Fill a large pan with warm soapy water and put in the wool. Press it up and down gently for a few minutes and then squeeze out the water. Do as many washings and rinses as are needed for the water to come clear. If the wool is dirty it can soak overnight. After washing, spread it out to dry.

Carding. Carding arranges the fibers in a more parallel order and can be done using hand cards or a small carding machine. Long fibers can be combed rather than carded.

Wool cards come in pairs and usually consist of two rectangular pieces of wood, each covered on one side with wire teeth that are bent slightly toward the handle. This covering is called the card clothing. Since ancient times hand cards have been made from thistles or prickly seed pods held in a wooden frame.

Carding with Hand Cards. Distribute a handful of teased wool evenly over the teeth of the card held in your left hand. Work the right-hand card toward the right, and the left-hand card to the left, so that the wool is carded between the teeth. Do not press the cards together; card the wool, not the cards.

After a few passes of the cards the fibers should be distributed throughout the wire teeth of both cards. At this point the wool on the right-hand card should be transferred back to the left-hand card. This transfer is important, and should be done with the reverse action shown in Step 3 of the demonstration nearby. Once back on the left-hand card the wool may be removed or carded again.

Remove the fibers simply by lifting them off, or by forming a roll of light, airy fleece. This roll—or rolag—is ready to spin. There is no standard for yarns, and finely spun yarns are not necessarily "better" than rough, lumpy yarns. Do remember that very carefully carded wool is easiest to spin, just as well-teased fleece is much easier to card. Different fibers, colors, and textures can also be carded together to produce blends.

Carding by Machine. The carding machine is much faster and less strenuous than the hand cards. Like

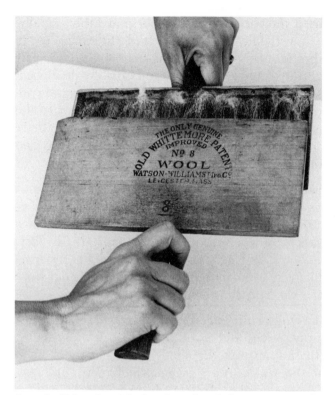

Carding: Step 1. Spread a small amount of teased fleece over the wire teeth of the left-hand card.

Step 2. Take the right-hand card and draw it across the left-hand card a number of times so the fleece is carded between the two sets of teeth. The cards are pulled in opposition, right to right, left to left. As they work, the fleece is distributed over both sets of teeth.

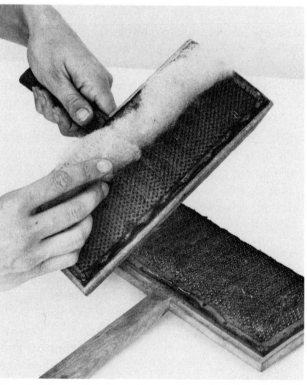

Step 3. Transfer the fleece from the right card to the left card. To do this, touch the top edge of the teeth on the right-hand card to the bottom edge of the teeth on the left-hand card. The fleece is transferred as the right card is drawn across the left card.

Step 4. The carded fleece is spread on the left card. Carding may now continue, or the fleece may be removed by rolling it off or by lifting and leaving it in the form of a rectangular sheet.

the hand cards, the machine is designed for wool, but can be used for many other fibers as well. Small amounts of fiber should be fed into the carder by placing them, fully teased, on the tray of the machine. As the crank is turned clockwise the fibers are drawn into the machine by the small roller and more fibers are added. The action between the small roller and larger roller cards the fibers in the same way as the hand carders. The carded fibers build up on the teeth around the large drum or roller, and the batt that is formed is removed by inserting a rod across the width and pulling up, so the fibers are separated, but not cut. If the handle is turned counterclockwise the carded wool can be peeled off easily. The carded wool can then be split up to form a long thin sliver ready for spinning. Especially long fibers are difficult to card, and might have to be combed like hair prior to spinning.

SELECTING YARNS FOR HANDSPINNING

The following will provide the general characteristics, advantages, and disadvantages of the main types of fibers suitable for handspinning: wool, flax, cotton, plant fibers, hair fibers, and silk.

Wool. There are many breeds and cross-breeds of sheep; some are bred for their fleece, others for their meat. The kind and quality of fleece can vary tremendously from one sheep to another. Some of the familiar breeds that usually produce good spinning wool are Cheviot, Columbia, Lincoln, Southdown, Corriedale, Romney, Suffolk, and Rough Fell. In selecting a fleece for handspinning look closely at the following characteristics: length of fiber, fineness or coarseness of fibers, greasiness, ease in separating fibers, color, and the amount of dirt and vegetable matter.

To do a thorough job of carding, the fibers should go through at least three cardings, with the wire carder teeth set progressively closer together each time. Many handspinners card just once, since to card three times requires having three sets of hand carders or three carding machines (or changing the card clothing for each step).

For easy spinning the fibers should be at least 3″ long. Very long fibers, more than 7″, are difficult to spin because they tangle, but are marvelous to use unspun in wall hangings and tapestries for their texture and body. The fineness of wool is graded on a count of 1 to 100. This is important in determining how the yarn is to be used—whether the spinner wants a coarse, rough yarn, or a soft, fluffy

yarn. A count from 30 to 45 is coarse, 45 to 60 is medium, and 60 to 80 is fine. The Merino breed of sheep is famous for its fine wool, and most breeds have some Merino blood in their background.

Very fine wool is difficult to work with and needs very careful fiber preparation. When a fleece is shorn there is a great deal of natural oil on the wool that makes it feel moist and alive—and greatly facilitates spinning. The oil literally glitters. If the fleece sits unused for too long after shearing, the oil dries and becomes powdery. Sometimes it coagulates, causing the fibers to stick together. This makes the fibers difficult to tease, and fleece in this condition should always be avoided. A good fleece should hold its shape, but it should also pull apart easily.

The color of a fleece is important for its final use. The color will always lighten if washed, but not all sheep are white and color can be important. Some sheep have yellow or brown casts to their fleece. The fleece from a black sheep can vary from light gray to black, often depending on the age of the sheep. The amount of dirt and vegetable matter in the fleece is an important consideration, since a great deal of time and soap can be spent washing wool; a dirty fleece can turn into a real chore. From 30 to 70% of the weight of a raw fleece is oil and vegetable matter. Since fleece is sold by the pound, a cheap dirty fleece is not necessarily less expensive than a higher-priced clean fleece. Unspun wool is sold by the pound and by the fleece. The source list on p. 189 has information on suppliers.

Flax. Linen yarn is spun from the long inner fibers of the flax plant. The quality of the yarn depends on how well the plant fibers are prepared. The steps are complex and take special equipment and experience. Flax prepared for spinning can be purchased at most large weaving supply shops.

The flax plant is a tall grainlike plant with a blue flower. It is harvested by pulling up the plant, root and all. Plants are then tied in bundles and set up in the field to dry. The seeds are removed by drawing the upper part of the plant through a comb—a process called "rippling." The fibers used for spinning are inside, so the covering and inner core must be removed without damaging these middle fibers. In a process called "retting," the stem is allowed to rot just enough so the bark and inner part of the stem will separate easily and leave just the usable fibers. "Scutching," a beating process, removes the last of the excess matter. In the final step, "hackling," the fibers are drawn through a coarse metal comb to separate the coarse and fine fibers. The last step results in two types of flax—line and tow. The long, straight, fine fibers that lie parallel compose the line flax. Tow is what remains after the hackling process (which produces the line) and is usually carded and spun into a rough coarse linen. Most flax that is available to the handspinner comes in a form called "top"—a long strip made for feeding into commercial spinning machines. This top is spun like wool and does not require a distaff. Preparing flax fiber for spinning is difficult, so most spinners buy flax that is ready to spin. The fibers are most easily spun when wet, so keep a bowl of water nearby to dip your fingers into.

Cotton. This plant produces a fluffy boll of light fibers and cotton seeds. The fibers can be spun with the seeds, or the cotton can be cleaned by removing seeds and dirt particles. This process is referred to as "ginning." The matted masses of fibers are pulled apart and arranged loosely in pads from which they can be drawn out in spinning. Cotton fibers are short, so the drawing distance during spinning is minimal, making it difficult to leave the spindle suspended. Resting the bottom tip of the spindle on a table or in a dish relieves the cotton of the spindle weight and prevents the yarn from breaking. Cotton can be carded to produce a roving for easier spinning. It can also be whipped or beaten with two sticks to fluff it up.

Other Plant Fibers. Hemp, jute, sisal, manilla, and ramie are plant fibers that are very suitable for spinning. They are usually inexpensive, and they all dye well. With the exception of ramie, they are usually coarse and fibrous, and are most easily spun when damp.

Hand-Operated Mechanical Carder. Teased fibers are fed in on the metal tray. As the crank turns, the fibers are caught on the drum and drawn out in parallel order. As more fibers are fed in they are built up into a "bat" on the large roller, then peeled off. Photo by David Donoho.

Hair Fibers of all kinds can be used for spinning, and hair from rabbits, dogs, cats, horses, and humans are especially suitable. Mohair (goat hair, usually the angora goat), camel's hair, llama, alpaca, vicuna, and other exotic hairs are good for spinning. Zoo keepers have been known to save special hair for spinners, and such places as barber shops and dog groomers should be investigated. Fibers that are at least 3″ long are most easily spun. Frequently these fibers are mixed with wool for body and ease in spinning. Oil can be added to give fibers adhering qualities.

Silk. Reeled from the cocoon of the silkworm, this fiber is generally a very fine continuous filament and therefore needs no spinning. However, there is often waste silk available in small quantities, and these short fibers can be spun nicely on the hand spindle or spinning wheel.

THE SPINNING WHEEL

The spinning wheel was probably invented in India during the early Middle Ages, probably between 500 and 1000 A.D. During this period the arts and crafts of India attained an unusually high standard of perfection. As is often the case, the spinning wheel came about over a considerable period of time, with many "inventors" in various geographical areas contributing to its development. During this time India was producing a fine cotton cloth of unrivaled quality that was in ever greater demand. As frequently happens, striving for increased production led to the introduction of more sophisticated mechanical processes. The spinning wheel is important in the history of the technical crafts as one of the first appliances where a continuous rotary motion was used for practical purposes. This wheel, the simplest of spinning wheels, is still in

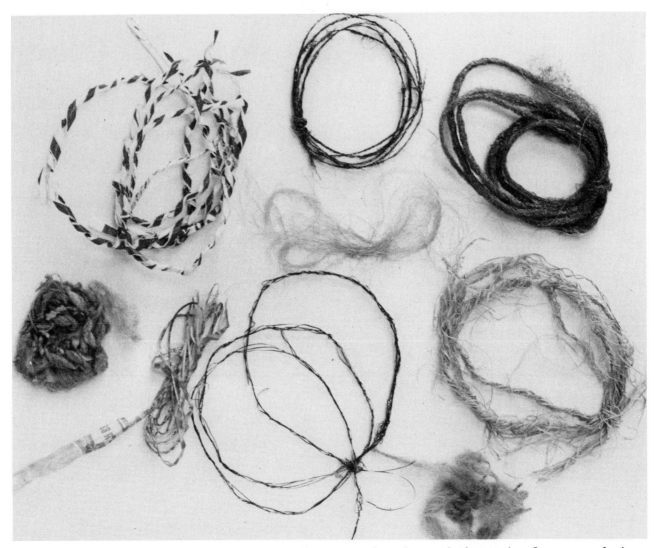

Fibers for Spinning. Some of the possibilities shown here are steel wool, corn husks, cat fur, fine copper shavings, corn silk, heavy copper shavings, Styrofoam, dryer lint, and plastic.

use today. The typical spindle on this kind of wheel is mounted so that the shaft sticks out, pointing toward the spinner and parallel to the ground. A large wheel off to the side has a drive band connecting it to what would normally be the whorl. It is similar to the one shown nearby. The right hand sets the large drive wheel in motion and causes the spindle shaft to turn. The left hand draws the fibers out from the shaft point, allowing the spin to come up the fibers until the arm cannot stretch any farther. Then everything stops and the yarn is held at right angles to the spindle and the drive wheel is turned in the opposite direction, allowing the thread to wind around the spindle. All spinning wheels without treadles and flyers are operated in this way.

The multiplying head is an adaptation of the simple spindle arrangement just described. A large drive wheel is connected by the drive band to a smaller wheel mounted on the spinning head. This smaller wheel is then connected by a second band to the spindle. This allows for greater speed.

The next technical developments in the spinning wheel occurred in Europe with the invention of the treadle drive and the fly assembly. The demand for faster production meant that the two processes of spinning, the spinning and subsequent winding, had to be unified. The foot treadle allowed the wheel to move by foot power, leaving the hands free. A flyer with hooks and a bobbin were mounted on the spindle shaft for continuous winding.

Most spinning wheels made today are of similar design with an eye through which the yarn passes first; a flyer which turns, twisting the yarn; and a bobbin onto which the spun yarn winds. Treadling with the foot causes the large wheel to turn, which causes the flyer to rotate, which spins the yarn and causes the bobbin to turn, which winds and holds the yarn. The hands control and feed the yarn as it spins through the eye. The action of the wheel causes the fibers to twist just as with the hand spindle, only everything happens at once and the motion is continuous. Hooks are distributed along the flyer so that the spun yarn can be built up evenly on the bobbin. A drive belt or band goes around the wheel, connecting it to the bobbin and flyer. Some wheels use a double drive band (a single band doubled), others use a single band. There is usually some method of adjusting the tension of the drive band so it can be tightened and loosened for perfect action. Spinning on a wheel proceeds much as it does on a spindle, but the wheel is much faster and all the motions happen simultaneously.

Each spinner must find what for him or her is the most comfortable and economical spinning position. Spinners have individual styles, and each individual style affects, however subtly, the kind of yarn produced.

Spinning Wheel. A castle-type spinning wheel from the Black Forest in Germany. The wheel is small and compact, measuring just 30" in height. Photo by David Donoho.

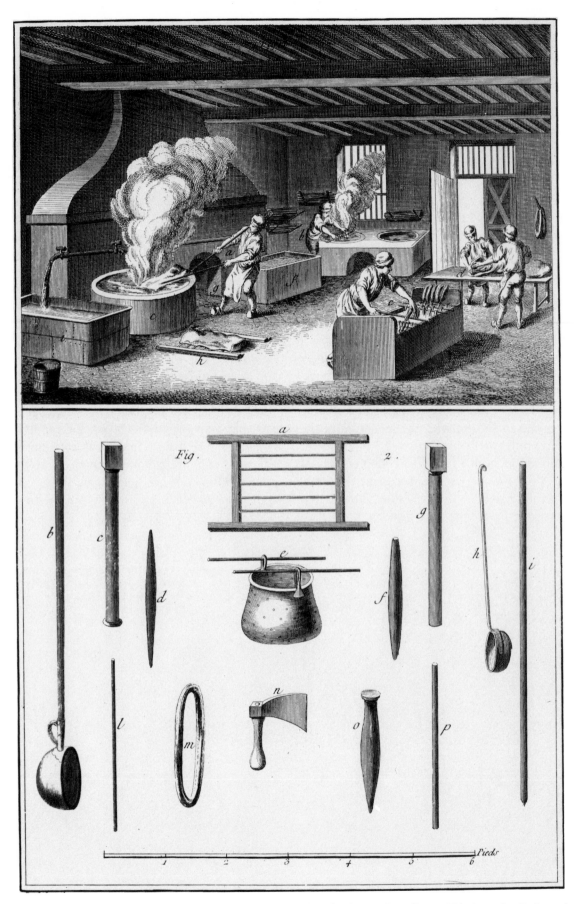

French Dye Workshop in 1772. The plate is from Diderot's **L'Encyclopedie, ou Dictionnaire Raisonné des Sciences, des Arts et des Métiers.** Photo courtesy of the Smithsonian Institution, Washington, D.C.

CHAPTER FOUR

DYEING

Color has always been an important part of man's life, as well as of textile production. Primitive man gathered feathers and scraped pigments from the earth to color his life. Color was not easily come by and remained at a premium until the late nineteenth century. Today, with the development of synthetic dyes, color is everywhere and is readily available in many forms. It is easy, therefore, to think of the color problem as solved, but color still remains elusive. The challenge for today's craftsman lies in the production of specific colors as well as subtle variations and ranges of color. These results can only be obtained through home dyeing.

Natural dyeing involves the use of plants and in some cases insects to produce color. For many craftsmen natural dyeing is closely associated with handspinning and natural fibers. Colors, especially in combination, must always be carefully selected and watched. Many weavers choose natural dyes to color their fibers because of their relation to antiquity and their closeness to nature and mankind. Natural dyes give subtle, rich, warm colors that are unique. They have a mystery and a life that continues to fascinate and satisfy. Synthetic dyes, derived from coal tar and other synthetic substances, are available in every dime store and grocery store. They are generally more easily prepared, more readily available, and more consistently dependable. These manufactured dyes are also less expensive and require less time and energy than natural dyes. They do not give you the opportunity to tromp through the woods and learn about nature, but they can give a wide variety of colors and color ranges that are highly satisfying. Synthetic dyes are easily mixed and used. Rich, deep colors can be obtained by overdyeing—the application of

one dye over another. The home dyer is often surprised and delighted with unexpected results, or with the results of "accidents."

This chapter, which is meant only as an introduction to the art of dyeing, presents both a brief history of dyeing and information on both natural and synthetic dyestuffs. The books listed in the Bibliography on p. 185 will provide far more information for the reader who wishes to study the subject seriously.

THE HISTORY OF DYEING

The making of color, or dyeing, is basic to all people. From the beginning man has used available sources for obtaining color. The simplest and most primitive use of color is the application of natural products without any preparation—leaves, flowers, fruits, feathers, wood, shells, and hair. The next step was the use of pigment colors, mainly minerals and earths, that usually gave whites, blacks, and reds. These pigments were crushed into a powder and rubbed onto the surface to be dyed. Such dyes, which are not necessarily fast to water or wear, are characteristic of "primitive" cultures all over the world. The use of mordants to fix colors brings the process within the category of real dyeing. Heating the dye bath was also a major step forward.

In the history of natural dyeing there are three kinds of dyes: direct, vat, and mordant. Direct dyes are substances that are soluble in water and dye directly. Very few direct dyes are fast to light and washing. Some plants used in direct dyeing contain a substance that naturally acts as a mordant. This makes them mordant dyes applied by direct dyeing. In vat dyeing, dyes that are soluble in alkaline liquids are transformed into compounds;

these are then fixed on the fiber by oxidation or exposure to air. Chief among these dyes is the indigo plant.

In mordant or adjective dyeing, the mordants act on the fiber to form an indissoluble compound with the dye. Mordant is the French word "to bite." In natural dyeing mordants are metallic salts that have an affinity for both fibers and dyestuffs. They improve the color fastness of certain dyes. Mordants are found as natural deposits in the earth in many parts of the world, and most natural dyes are mordant dyes.

The earliest kind of mordant dyeing was the use of mud and clay containing iron. Alum, in the form of plant and mineral substances, has also been widely used as a mordant, but it is generally found only in highly "civilized" cultures. Peruvian and Egyptian pieces thousands of years old still have bright, clear colors—good evidence of a high level of sophistication. The first mordant dyeing was probably done in China before 3000 B.C., and records indicate that it goes back to 2500 B.C. in India. The first western dyers were the Swiss Lake dwellers (about 2000 B.C.). Dyeing was highly developed in Persia as well at an early time. It was probably brought by Phoenician traders to Egypt, then spread to Greece and Italy and throughout Europe.

We know that dyes were carried over the ancient trade routes between China and the Mediterranean, finding their way to the great trade markets of Baghdad, Damascus, Cairo, and eventually Venice. From the seventh century forward the Chinese obtained many of their dyes from India and Persia, and the colors became similar to those of Europe. In the highly developed cultures of the ancient world, dyeing was raised to the level of a precise and exacting art. Dyeing and dyestuffs were very important to the economy; dye centers and houses grew, expanded, and specialized, handling great quantities of dyestuffs. In many cases dyeing was a state monopoly, with rigid standards and tight controls. It is interesting that throughout the history of dyeing, obtaining and making dye was very serious business; it was often connected with all sorts of taboos, rituals, and superstitions. Dyeing fabrics in any quantity was hard, unpleasant work, and the dyer himself seldom enjoyed a high social status.

Tyrian Purple was the most sought after and costly dye of the ancient world. It was obtained from a mollusk found in various parts of the Mediterranean. The most important center for Tyrian purple dyeing in the ancient world grew up along what is now the northern coastal border of Israel. Huge quantities of these mollusks were required to obtain a small amount of dye. The dye, which gives a fast brilliant purple, quickly became highly desired, expensive, and traded over a large area. The industry thrived until 638 A.D., when it was destroyed by conquering armies; by that time, however, other sources had been developed for purple. Evidence indicates that purple or murex dyeing was also done in ancient Peru and ancient Aztec civilizations of Mexico, and that it was in use until the eighteenth century in those areas.

Madder is a root plant native to Asia Minor, and along with cochineal and indigo is very popular today among natural dyers. Madder was important as a dye early in the history of India and later was widely used throughout Europe. Dyeing with madder, which produces a color called turkey red on cotton, was a secret in the Orient until about 1750. Madder was eventually grown on a large scale in Italy, France, and Holland. It was eventually brought to America by the English and Dutch.

"The whole process was, according to one dyer, the most complicated application of mordant in the whole art of dyeing, requiring in addition to madder, an oil, galls, alum, dung and—in one recipe—the intestinal liquor of a ruminating animal and the blood of oxen or sheep."

from *Natural Dyes in the United States* by R. Adrosko

Kermes and Cochineal are scarlet dyes derived from insects. They both belong to a species of the shield louse and produce similar colors. Kermes was used in Europe and the Orient in ancient and medieval times to dye wool, silk, cotton, leather, and as a non-poisonous food dye. The first recorded use of kermes was in 1727 B.C., and it was a very highly prized and sought-after dye. When Rome conquered Spain, half the tribute was paid in kermes. With the discovery of America, cochineal replaced kermes as the principal source of scarlet dye.

The Woad Plant and Indigo. Woad was used as the primary source of blue dye throughout ancient Europe; the indigo plant was the primary source in Asia. Woad and indigo both contain indogin and are chemically similar. They are both vat dyes requiring oxidation. In Europe, the growing and preparation of woad for dyeing was such an important economic factor that many towns grew and developed around it. England, from the thirteenth to the sixteenth centuries, was the center of commercial woad production. So although the indigo plant, ten times more potent, was known in Europe from about the Christian period, the emphasis was on woad. The use of indigo was forbidden by law in many places, and under Henry IV the use of indigo was a capital offense. In spite of every obstacle, indigo eventually broke the woad trade to become the most popular of all dyes. Indigo, perhaps because of its special preparation—no mordant and affinity for many different fibers—is still very popular as a natural dye. Many shades of blue are possible with indigo, and the preparation of the vat will influence the blue shades produced.

Dyeing was highly developed throughout Europe by the late Middle Ages. It was frequently tightly controlled by law, and actual dyeing was usually done by experts in large complexes. Beginning around the thirteenth century, France had a large and efficient textile industry, and it was from here that a dye chemistry based on scientific principles emerged and spread.

In 1856, William Henry Perkin, working in England, took the first step in developing the synthetic dye industry, which very shortly forced nearly all natural dyestuffs into limited use. Perkin accidently discovered a lavender dye (aniline purple) artificially produced from a constituent of coal tar. This discovery attracted wide attention throughout France, England, Germany, and Switzerland, and led to the development of many dyes using analine as a base. Eventually alizarin (the primary component of madder) was synthesized and synthetic indigo was produced. All these discoveries and changes took place between 1856 and 1900. A large part of the effort in developing synthetic dyes went into making dyes that were quick, easy to use, safe, dependable, and that could be applied to silk, cotton, and wool. Within a few years the natural dye industry was wiped out. Later the problem became as it is today—not how to apply new dyes to old fibers, but to find ranges of satisfactory dyes for new fibers. The dyes are as important as the fiber, because it is their color that makes the majority of textiles most immediately attractive to buyers. With the development of synthetic dyes, the commercial process and the "art" of dyeing were no longer the same.

Since the industrial revolution there have been many movements to counteract the hard wall of industry. These movements are usually led by sensitive craftsmen in search of a better, more interesting, and more intimate product; fortunately, these movements continue. William Morris (1834–1896), the prime leader of the crafts movement in England, saw the artist and craftsman as one. Unable to obtain the clear, permanent colors he desired for his textiles, he turned to experimenting with ancient dyes and methods. He established a special dye house and worked with many natural dyes, particularly indigo, in the production of his goods.

In this country there has been a strong movement among the Navajo rug weavers of the southwest to use vegetable dyes as a reflection of their environment and past, and so the product will be more truly Indian. There has also been a strong movement continuing from the twenties in the southern highlands of the Appalachian mountains to preserve the crafts, including natural dyeing, which had remained unchanged—by-passed and forgotten by the efficient industrial world. Attempts have been made to record the knowledge which was passed on by word of mouth, usually from parent to child. One such record follows in the words of a mountain woman—Mrs. Sally Gayheart of Knott County, Kentucky:

"Indigo Dye. To two gallons of warm water add one pint lye from wood ashes. Mix one pint of madder with one pint wheat bran, and a little water—enough to wet it. Put this in the bottom of the kettle with a white plate over it. Put the indigo in a thick cloth in the two gallons of water and when it is soft rub out the dye. Then put in the blue yeast saved from the last dyeing. Keep it warm—just milk warm—for four or five days without bothering it. At night draw hot ashes plumb around your jar, and in the daytime keep it setting by the hearth just lukewarm all the time.
"For a dark blue let the yarn lay in several hours. Take it out and air it and put it back. Be sure to wet the goods before you put it in. Rench it in cold water when you take it out. If you want a light blue, dip it over and over till you have the right color.
"Red. Have the yarn clean, washed with soap and renched well. Bile it in alum water a small while. Take it out and throw out the alum water. Then make a thick flour starch and put in the madder and put the yarn in and bile it till it makes a good color. Hang it out to dry: Take one pound of madder to every three yards of goods, or four pounds of yarn."

from *A Book of Hand-woven Coverlets*
by Eliza C. Hall

GENERAL DYEING INFORMATION

Natural and synthetic dyeing can easily be done today in the home, school, or outdoors. One can approach either kind of dyeing in an exacting way or casually and spontaneously. The equipment needed for dyeing is found in most kitchens and should include:

1. A large stainless steel or enamel pan for mordanting and dyeing. Cast iron and copper pans are sometimes used in natural dyeing, but they act as a mordant and influence the dye.

2. Pans, buckets, or tubs of any material, including plastic, for rinsing and wetting yarns.

3. Stirring rods of glass or stainless steel are recommended since the dye will not penetrate them, but most dyers use large wooden spoons.

4. A thermometer measuring temperatures as low as 100°F. is convenient, but is necessary for only a few dyes.

5. A scale that weighs pounds is needed for weighing yarn to be dyed, as well as the natural dyestuffs. A scale that weighs ounces and parts of an ounce is needed for natural dyeing. Most synthetic dyes are already measured in packages or are measured by the teaspoon-full.

6. Rubber gloves will help protect the hands.

7. A strainer or colander is needed to strain the dye when cooking plants to produce a dyebath.

8. A heat source is necessary for most dyeing.

9. Quantities of water, preferably soft, are needed for dyeing.

The testing and documenting of dyes and their effects are important to the serious craftsman. There is a simple dye test for color fastness to direct sunlight that can be performed at home. Take samples of each dyed yarn and place them outside in the direct sunlight. Cover part of each sample so that only half is exposed to the sun. Check each day to see if, or how much, the color fades. If no fading occurs after five days then consider the dye a good one. Remember, all dyes will fade eventually, and dyes within a particular dye group are not always equal. After dyeing, yarns should be rinsed until the rinse water comes clear. Dyes that continue to bleed are generally undesirable. For later reference each dyebath can be fully documented with dyed samples and the following information:

1. The dye material—the brand name or the plant material.

2. The date the dye material was collected and the location.

3. The mordant used and whether it was applied before, during, or after dyeing.

4. If the dyebath was used more than once.

5. The weight of the yarn and the weight or measurement of the dyestuff.

6. The length of time spent in the dyebath.

7. If it is important, the temperature of the dyebath should be recorded.

8. The date dyeing occurred.

Dyeing can be done at any stage of fiber preparation, but the orientation of this chapter is on the dyeing of fibers already spun into yarn. Spun wool yarn is used in the general directions for dyeing that follow. It is important to know that wool is susceptible to matting when exposed to sudden temperature changes. The temperature of wool must be changed slowly so that the wool is not shocked. Material to be mordanted and dyed should always be clean or the dye will not penetrate properly. In dyeing and mordanting, skeins (yarn wound to produce a loosely bound grouping) of wetted yarn are submersed in the bath and frequently stirred so all the yarn is dyed evenly.

Special Effects. Yarn can be treated in other ways to produce special dye effects. One way, frequently referred to as dip-dyeing, is to group strands of yarn and dip only part of the strands into the dyebath. Other parts of the yarn can be dipped into different dyebaths to produce a number of different colors, one bleeding into the next along the length of the strands. Previously spun yarns can be bound in sections to form a resist, so when the yarn is dyed the dye is unable to penetrate the bound areas. This process is usually referred to as ikat or tiedyeing. Yarns can be prepared this way to produce special designs in a woven textile. The designs are the result of carefully dyeing the yarns before weaving rather than being of the woven structure. If the warp or vertical threads are dyed in this manner the weaving is a warp ikat. As the warp threads are placed on the loom before weaving they are shifted and arranged to put the color variations in just the right places. If the weft or horizontal threads are dyed in this manner and then woven the weaving is a weft ikat. As weaving progresses the weft thread is brought across and adjusted to put the color in the right position. This makes an uneven selvedge edge which can, if properly controlled, add to the beauty of the fabric. The photo-

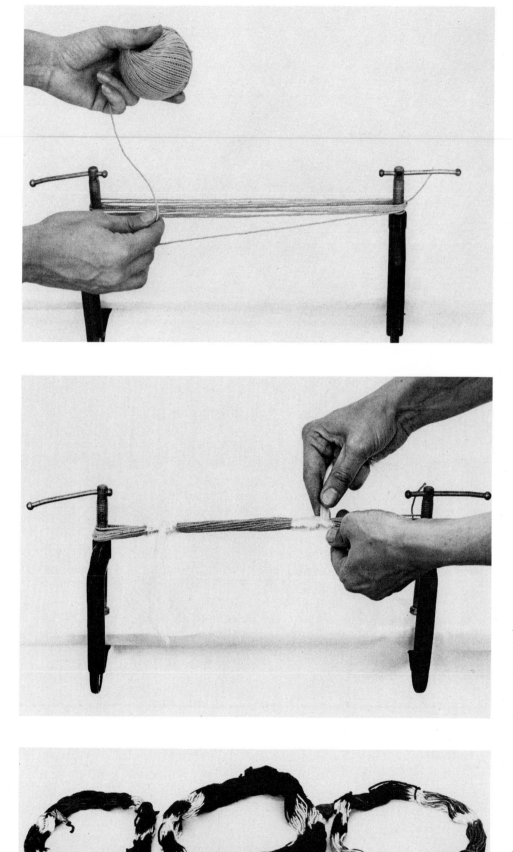

Tie-Dyeing: Step 1. To tie-dye skeins of yarns, first wrap the yarns between two anchor points so they are under tension.

Step 2. Bind the taut strands to form resist areas. Wide strips of plastic were used here, but any material that binds tightly may be used. After the yarn is slipped from the anchor points it is ready for the dyebath. Tight binding will prevent the dye from penetrating.

Step 3. Remove the bindings after the skeins have been dyed. The tie-dye process can be repeated many times on one skein, or on any grouping of threads.

Warp Ikat Sumba Cloth. The designs and patterns in this Indonesian cloth were created by tying and dyeing the warp before it was placed on the loom. The weft thread does not show. Photo courtesy of the Anneberg Gallery, San Francisco, California.

graphs nearby show how to bind or tie-dye yarn for a weft ikat.

It is also possible to dye fibers before carding (arranging the fibers in parallel order in preparation for spinning) and before spinning so they can be arranged or blended during the carding or spinning process to produce special color effects. Different kinds of fibers will take the same dye differently, and they can be mixed in the same bath and later spun together to produce new color combinations and ranges.

Natural Dyeing

This discussion of natural dyeing deals primarily with wool fibers, which have an affinity for natural dyes. If you are interested in dyeing other materials with natural dyes it is suggested that you consult the Bibliography, *Hopi Dyes* by Colton and *Vegetable Dyeing* by Lesch in particular. Also, do not hesitate to experiment.

Natural dyeing involves the use of plant material or insects to produce a dyebath. Many craftsmen use plants that are readily available in their own immediate environment. Many dyers will also pick up different plants as they travel, or get them from friends to experiment with. Others choose to use the natural dyes (primarily indigo, cochineal, and madder) in powder form.

Various kinds of flowers, barks, leaves, husks, lichens, and gall nuts will give dyes. Almost every plant material will give some color, usually in the yellow, orange, gray, or brown range. Experiment with plants that you have available to find those that will produce the best colors. You can perform a simple test by taking a handful of the potential dye material, putting it along with some water in a small enamel or stainless steel pan with a few strands of yarn, and cooking it for awhile. If a reasonable color appears then try some mordanted samples to see if it is worth pursuing. Some of the all-time dye favorites are onion skins (yellow and red skins), poplar leaves, willow leaves, peach leaves, oak gall nuts, Scotch broom blossoms, marigolds, all parts of the eucalyptus tree, golden rod, privet, lichens, and black walnut hulls. The best approach is to experiment. Leaves from a peach tree gathered one day can produce a bright yellow on alum mordanted wool. Leaves from the same branch gathered four days later can give a dark brown color to the same wool.

Mordants are an indispensable part of natural dyeing and can be purchased from any chemical supply house. They aid in making the colors fast to light and washing, and usually influence the shade of the dye. Mordanting can be done before, during, or after dyeing. The clearest, brightest colors usually come from mordanting the yarn before dyeing in a separate dye bath. There are many different kinds of mordants, but the ones usually used by today's dyers are tin, alum, chrome, and iron. Mordants should be weighed accurately in accordance with the recipes that follow (all are for mordanting one pound of wool). Cream of tartar (potassium bitartrate) is frequently used with mordants to keep colors bright and clear. Recipes for mordants using one pound of wool are listed below:

Alum (potassium aluminum sulfate):
3 ounces alum
1 ounce cream of tartar (potassium bitartrate)

Chrome (potassium or sodium dichromate):
½ ounce chrome

Tin (stannous chloride crystals):
¼ ounce tin
½ ounce cream of tartar

Iron (ferrous sulfate):
½ ounce iron
½ ounce cream of tartar

Cochineal. Cochineal is a tiny parasitic insect that is ground up and used to dye various shades of red in the scarlet range. It is frequently overdyed with blue to produce purple, and is sometimes combined with madder to produce wider varieties of red. Cochineal, already ground into a fine powder, can be purchased from natural dye suppliers. For best results cover the cochineal to be used with cold water and allow it to soak for 12 hours before preparing the dyebath. Just before dyeing, add the cream of tartar and boil the solution for 10 minutes. Add water to keep the solution in a liquid state. After boiling, add the solution directly to the dyebath, mix thoroughly, and add the wetted yarn. Bring the dyebath to a simmer and cook for one hour. The recipe that follows is by no means absolute; every natural dyer seems to have a different version.

Per pound of wool, use 2 ounces cochineal and 2 ounces cream of tartar. Tin mordant produces light scarlet; alum mordant, dark scarlet; chrome mordant, purple scarlet; iron mordant, black scarlet.

Madder. Like cochineal, madder is a natural dye that has been used for centuries to produce red

Mordanting Wool: Step 1. Prepare the yarn by winding it into one or more loose skeins. All surfaces should be exposed for mordanting, and each skein should be loosely bound in a number of places to prevent tangling. It is a good idea to label each skein for later identification with masking tape and a waterproof marker. All skeins that will go into one pot should be looped onto a loose cord for ease in handling.

Step 2. Weigh the yarn while it is dry to accurately calculate the amount of chemicals needed.

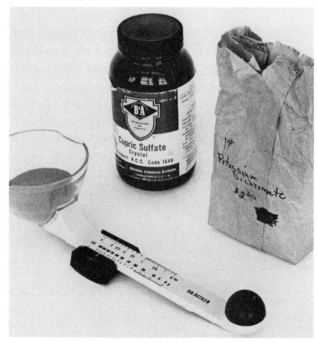

Step 4. Measure or weigh the proper amount of chemical according to the recipe. Careful measurement is especially important in mordanting.

Step 5. Fill a large enamel or stainless steel pan with enough water to allow the yarn to float freely. Chemicals should always be added, dissolved, and stirred before the yarn is introduced.

Step 3. *After weighing, yarn should be wetted in preparation for mordanting. Wool can be submerged in lukewarm water for 10 to 20 minutes. This wetting or boiling will allow the mordant to penetrate quickly and evenly.*

Step 6. *Squeeze the excess water from the wetted yarn and place it gently into the prepared bath. Heat the bath, slowly bringing it to a boil so as not to shock the fibers. Wool should be kept just below the boiling point and should simmer for a full hour. Frequent stirring is important for even mordanting. Allow the wool to cool in the mordant bath or shift it directly to the hot dyebath.*

dyes. Madder (a root native to Asia Minor) is closely associated with earth reds in the orange and terra-cotta range. The temperature of the dyebath strongly affects the color produced. If the dyebath is allowed to boil, the dye will turn brown. The root particles should be ground as fine as possible for maximum dye production. The dye material should be soaked overnight in preparation for dyeing, and then poured directly into the dyebath. Good results come from using 4 ounces of madder and keeping the dyebath between 160° and 180°F. The shades of red-orange produced by the different mordants are difficult to describe, but tin is the brightest and most orange, while iron and chrome are dark.

Indigo. Indigo is used as a direct or vat dye requiring no mordant. It is the most mysterious and dramatic of all the natural dyes. Indigo, in proper solution, takes to many different kinds of fibers, and the dye procedure seems almost magical. In its normal state indigo will not adhere as a dye to fibers. It must be dissolved in water by sulfuric acid, hydrosulfite and lye, or urine in order to penetrate the fibers. The vat produced by urine and hydrosulfite is clear, with a bluish-green scum sometimes appearing on the liquid surface. The wetted yarn is added to the solution and does not take on any color until it is removed from the dye for airing. The oxygen in the air causes the indigo to turn blue, as if by magic. Repeated dippings and airings darken and set the dye. The recipe for direct indigo dyeing with sulfuric acid, which follows, is taken from a book by Edward Worst, who speaks of it as being used by the Norwegians. Because of the acid, the utmost caution and care must be used in preparing and dyeing with his formula.

Dyeing with Olium. Approximately ½ cup of olium is used per pound of wool to produce a dark blue (less olium will produce lighter shades). First pour the measured olium into some cold water, stir, and then pour the solution into the lukewarm dyebath (enough water to cover the yarn). Mix thoroughly, add the wetted yarn, and bring the dyebath to a simmer, stirring constantly, and simmer for 30 minutes. Let the yarn cool in the dyepot, and then neutralize the acid by rinsing the yarn in a chalk bath (1 tablespoon chalk to 1 gallon water).

The Preparation of Olium. Mix 15 grams (½ ounce, or 1 tablespoon plus 1 heaping teaspoon) of powdered indigo with 125 grams (¼ cup) of sulfuric acid (100% strong) in a glass jar which has a well-

Vegetable Dyebath: Step 1. After gathering the plant material, break, chop, tear, or crush it into small pieces. Most flowers and leaves may be used just as they are when removed from stalks or branches. Chop woody material and crush hulls and galls. The photograph shows eucalyptus leaves, brazil wood, onion skins, and marigolds ready for the pot. The plant material should be put into a large enamel or stainless steel pan, covered with water, and boiled.

Step 2. Strain the dye liquid obtained from boiling and discard the plant matter. The dyebath is now ready for the mordanted yarn. If it appears that the bath will be too crowded, add water.

Step 3. Squeeze out excess liquid from the yarn and shift the skeins from the mordant pot directly to the dyebath. Bring the bath to a high simmer (slowly for wool) and cook for ½ to 2 hours depending on the color shade desired. Frequent stirring is important for even dyeing. Allow the yarn to cool in the bath, then rinse it until the water comes clear. A light washing with soap should follow all dyeing.

fitting cover. Stir the mixture until it is smooth, either with a glass rod or a wooden stick. Metal should not be used. Close the bottle and allow the mixture to stand at least 24 hours befort using. The olium can be kept in an airtight bottle for some time without losing its potency. It is a highly concentrated acid solution and will burn both skin and clothes on contact. Varying amounts of this solution are used for dyeing different shades of blue.

Synthetic Dyeing

Synthetic dyeing at home usually involves purchasing manufactured dyestuffs, and then preparing and dyeing the textiles according to the specific directions of the manufacturer. There are many brands of dyes on the market, and in many cases the same dyes are packaged under different brand names. The four most common types of synthetic dyes for home dyeing, and the methods for using them, will be discussed in this section: fiber reactive or procion dyes, direct dyes, acid dyes, and household or all-purpose dyes. A more complete discussion of dyes and home dyeing can be found in *Contemporary Batik and Tie-Dye* by Meilach (see the Bibliography on p. 185).

Fiber Reactive or Procion Dyes are cold-water dyes for viscose rayon, silk, linen, cotton, and other plant fibers. Some of the brand names and distributors of procion dyes are Dylon, Fabdec, Putnam, and Color Fast. Fiber reactive dyes have excellent penetration quality; they actually form a bond in the fiber, and they are generally very fast to light and washing. It is very important that directions be followed, and that the material or yarn be in the bath from start to finish. The short method for dyeing 1 pound of material or yarn with procion dyes is given here. Any fiber reactive (procion) dye can be used with this recipe.

Use ¼ to 5 teaspoons of dyestuff, depending on the color shade desired. First mix the dyestuff in cold water, then dissolve the paste in a little hot water. Mix this solution into enough lukewarm water to cover the yarn to be dyed. Add common uniodized salt to the dyebath (about 6 to 9 tablespoons depending on the desired color intensity). More or less salt is added depending on the amount of dye. Now place the yarn in the dyebath for from 6 to 10 minutes and stir it constantly. In a

separate container dissolve 2 tablespoons of washing soda (also called sal soda) in warm water, and remove the yarn from the dyebath. Add the soda solution to the dyebath, stir, and put in the yarn for another 15 to 20 minutes stirring it occasionally. This will fix the dye, and procion dyes will not take without the washing soda. Then remove the yarn and rinse it in cool water. Allow the yarn to dry slowly, so the dye will set properly, then wash it in warm soapy water. Some manufacturers include soda in the package as part of the dye, or in a separate package to be added to the dyebath. Read the instructions on each dye package. Deeper colors can be obtained by adding more dye, salt, or leaving the fabric in the bath longer. Procion dyes can be used for wool, but the dyebath must simmer, and white vinegar (¼ cup to 1 gallon of water) must be used in place of the washing soda.

Direct, Acid, and Household Dyes. Similar procedures are required for direct, acid, and household dyes. With these the dye does not actually bind in the fiber, but surrounds and coats it and is fixed by the addition of salt. These dyes work best at high temperatures, and the dyebath should simmer or boil during dyeing. Direct dyes are for viscose rayon, cotton, linen, and other plant fibers. Acid dyes are for wool. Household dyes or all-purpose dyes are designed for cotton, linen, silk, wool, acetate, nylon, rayon, and other plant and hair fibers. Household, or all-purpose dyes, are often available in grocery and dime stores (some familiar brand names are Tintex, Rit, Union, and Cushing's Perfection). These dyes are usually purchased in packages that contain enough dye for 1 pound of yarn. How much dye you use will vary depending on the shade desired. Common salt is added to direct and household dyes (if it is not already in the dye) to exhaust and "fix" the dyes (about 4 tablespoons per pound of yarn). In acid dyeing, white vinegar is used rather than salt in the proportion of ¼ cup vinegar to 1 gallon water. In all three of these dye classes the yarn is added to the dyebath after the dye and salt or white vinegar are introduced. The dyebath should simmer or boil for from 20 to 60 minutes, depending on the dye shade required (remember that colors always look darker when wet). After dyeing the yarn is rinsed or washed until the water comes clear.

The Brassempouy Lady (Les Landes), c. 36,000 B.C. This ivory head is only 1″ high. Photo courtesy of the Reunion des Musées Nationaux, Paris, France.

CHAPTER FIVE

SINGLE-ELEMENT CONSTRUCTION

The art of netting is so ancient that no date can be found for its invention. Our oldest record is found in a small ivory sculpture called *The Brassempouy Lady*, dated around 36,000 B.C. It is the oldest known representation of a human being and shows her hair held in place by a net. We can assume several things from this ancient record. Knotted netting must have existed before this date and, while practical use was a major factor in its making, it was also decorative. A certain amount of forming is implied by the diminishing lags between the knots, especially around the crown.

Net, network, or netting is only one of several techniques that come under the heading of single-element construction. In this chapter we will be discussing those which use only one continuous working element as well as those that use a continuous working element in conjunction with a second, unpaired element. Paired and multiple elements will be discussed in following chapters.

DEFINITIONS

As indicated by the Brassempouy Lady, a great number of single-element constructions have a timeless history. Its use and popularity have risen and fallen with the historical times and, most certainly, with the introduction of industrial adaptations and substitutes. The techniques with no pre-date in time include simple looping, knotted netting, and variations within each. Other single-element constructions with starting points in our time system include crocheting and knitting. Net, as we are using the term, refers to an open-structured quality, for example, fisherman's net. The construction of net or network may use many techniques—not just those included here, but some covered in other chapters as well.

COMMON CHARACTERISTICS

All the techniques included in this chapter have several characteristics in common. First, they are all worked with a continuous element. Even if the material you choose has a natural or artificial length, it can be joined with another identical length, thus making it continuous.

Second, all have a certain amount of stretch to the body of work. There is a property of "openness" and "closedness" in each technique. This may be why they are referred to as nets—in some references implying a double meaning. This stretch occurs in both flat and circular work and in both lateral and vertical directions.

Third, construction in all but crochet and knitting does not depend on interlooping. In other words, if a break occurs in the body of the work, the break is contained or isolated and the work will not unravel.

Another interesting point is that many of these techniques interchange in their application at different points in history. Here we are primarily concerned with structure. An example of this interchange is the simple looping and cross-knit stitch discussed later. These have been and may be applied as stitchery to a separate web, which makes the work a surface embellishment.

Conversely, the open network may become the base web with embellishments added to it. An example of this is the simili-velour stitch. Historically, specific forms of lace fall into this group.

There was a decline in interest in this craft

among industrial nations in the early 1800's, as machinery began to imitate or duplicate much of this continuous element work. At the same time, there was an increase in interest in interlooping techniques such as crochet. Due partly to its portability, crochet also offered more individual expression than the mass-produced counterpanes.

PERU AS A CULTURAL REFERENCE

While all single-element construction is timeless, occurring throughout various cultures, we are indebted to some areas more than others for the records we have, and Peru is a major contributor. In our time, we are most indebted to Dr. Junius Bird of the American Museum of Natural History.

"To me the record in Peru is intriguing because it presents a long record of development, at least 4,500 years, that we know about. 4,500 years ago certain things were well developed, well established at that time; and that to me is evidence that 4,500 years ago was not the beginning dateline for it,

that there was a tradition prior to that.

"I know that they were capable of good spinning and the creation of fine cordage, well prepared fibers, good quality spinning, and then doubling and tripling to make excellent lines 6,000 years ago. Now, between that 6,000 year level there was something ahead of that, and between that and the 4,500 year level there is a gap in our knowledge, (something) we don't know about. And nowhere else in the world do we have such a record relative to textiles as (Peru). . . . What we see in Peru will help us to build up and understand and better record what we developed in Europe, the Near East, and everywhere else."

To compare these Peruvian weavers with other cultures, according to Dr. Bird their importance lies in "the range of the accomplishment rather than the high level in any particular one. You can sight high levels in all these things but it is the total range of accomplishments achieved (that is notable)."

Peruvian Trim (detail). *Polychrome wools loop stitched on foundation cords. This fragment of cross-knit border trim is approximately 10 feet in length. The charming duck's heads are spaced at 1¼" intervals along the edge. The lower portion of the strand is sewn onto a lightweight, loomed cotton fabric. Collection of Kenneth Shores. Photo by Marcia Chamberlain.*

As in history, let's start with the most simple of single-element techniques and then go on to those that developed later. In sequence these would be single looping, cross-knit looping, the overhand knot, knotted fish net, the simili-velour stitch, lark's head net, crocheting, and knitting.

LOOPING

In Peruvian textiles there are two looping techniques that are used for small sculptural edgings, especially on the Paracus textiles. Some are quite humble, as illustrated in the edging of ducks shown here. Dr. Bird says, "The very finest, the most elaborate of these I know of is the famous piece in the Brooklyn Museum in New York. This apparently is an altar cloth and it has the most complex, three-dimensional edging that you can conceive of, the succession of mythological people and others, and you can spend weeks just following that border around, admiring the various things and trying to interpret them."

Both the altar cloth and duck design edging include two techniques—simple looping and cross-knit looping—worked on a foundation cord and referred to as a "Venice stitch." It is not included here as it is a simple adaptation of the two primary techniques, adding only body to the work.

Simple Looping. All looping takes place on a foundation row. Start with a single slip knot at the end of your working strand. Hold this in one hand between the thumb and forefinger. Pass the working strand through the loop, pulling it down over the top of the loop you have just made. Pull closed and repeat for the desired length.

Working without a foundation cord will make a self-edge and be as flexible or stretchy as the textile body. If you use a foundation cord, it must remain in the starting row or, if using a dowel, be replaced with a second element. Otherwise, the row of loops will unlock.

When you reach the end of your foundation row, start looping in reverse. To reverse for the second row, bring your working element around the end in a figure S before starting the first stitch in the row. This half loop will keep the fabric at a constant width. Do not make this loop if you want to decrease; if you want to increase, make this loop and add a second one at the end of this row before turning for the third. In simple looping, the working element passes through the bottom lag, or U, that is formed as the loop is made. Always be sure that the working element is pulled over the loop

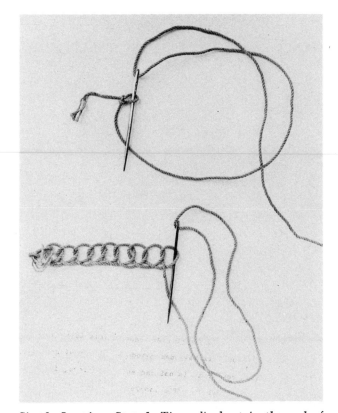

Simple Looping: Step 1. Tie a slip knot in the end of your working strand. Start the foundation row by stitching downward through the slip knot. Notice that the needle exits over the top of the working strand loop. Pull closed, holding on to the starting slip knot. The lower example shows the foundation row of loops as it has progressed.

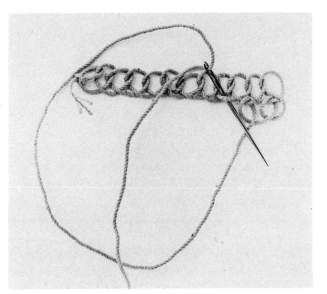

Step 2. When you reach the end of your foundation row, bring your working strand around the end in a figure S, as shown on the right. Otherwise you will have decreased the number of loops in your third row and therefore decreased the width of the fabric. The loops in successive rows are made by passing the needle through the lower triangular opening as shown by the position of the needle. Repeat the figure S at the end of each row. The rows are worked left-to-right, then right-to-left.

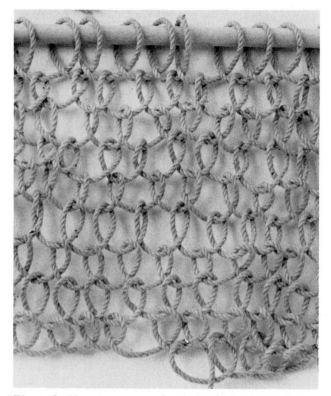

Figure 3. *Here is an example of simple looping as it was done in Peruvian textiles. There is some degree of elasticity in this type of work. There are, however, examples of simple looping where a second transverse strand is worked with each row of looping. Using the second strand reduces the stretchy quality of simple looping and is usually referred to as the "Venice stitch."*

just formed. This gives a rather loose, net-like structure, stable but not heavy or sturdy. The faces are similar as you can see in Figure 3.

Cross-Knit Looping. Cross-knit looping is a variation of simple looping. The first step is identical to that of simple looping.

To make the subsequent rows in cross-knit, pass the working element through the X formed by the loops in the previous row. You are picking up two strands instead of only one as in simple looping. Cross-knit looping gives a denser fabric and the faces are dissimilar—see Figure 4.

Both of these instructions are for flat surface work. To make a dimensional form, work in one direction and do not do the reverse looping. Work continuously into either the U or the X without adding the compensating S unless you want to increase.

A variation on simple looping is sometimes called loop and twist. This makes an even more open body of work and is obtained by giving an added twist to the working element before pulling it closed.

There are several examples shown here which illustrate open and closed looping and combinations of both. The element is usually worked with a blunt tapestry needle. However, the sculpture by Ruth Asawa shown nearby best illustrates that concern should be for the statement. Here, the tools, the material, and the form are synthesized in their purest form.

KNOTTED NETTING

A slip knot is a sheet bend that has not pulled the element on which it is tied into its body. If the sheet bend engages this second element, it will be secure. The slip knot of the sheet bend mentioned above will not slip because the working element, when pulled closed, will engage the knot. The sheet bend may be used with either intent in maintaining the open quality of netting. Another name for this knot is the overhand knot.

When you tie the overhand knot, you do so to pre-determine the length of the suspension loop, or the distance between each knot. While the term "netting" denotes an open quality in the work, the knots may be drawn very close together. The body of the work will be very dense and bulky if this is done. The faces are dissimilar. Here are two ways to do knotted netting:

Overhand Knotted Net. Tie a slip knot at the end of your working element. Place it on a temporary holding cord or dowel, either straight or circular. Loosely cast loops around the holding cord, back to front in spiral fashion. When the desired width is reached, start tying the overhand (sheet bend) knot as shown into the lower lag, proceeding from right to left. (Refer to Chapter 6 for further instructions on a sheet bend.) Work left to right for the third row. Alternate directions as each row is completed if you are doing flat work. Work in a spiral for circular nets, not changing direction. The knot demonstrated in the picture nearby is being tied at the end of the third row.

Sewn lark's heads may be cast onto the holding cord, allowing a lag between each knot. When the temporary cord is removed, an edging of larger loops will occur. A square knot, as shown in Figure 5, can also be used in place of the overhand or sheet bend.

Using a Netting Shuttle. The knotted net just described can be made to any dimension and usually uses a needle in working the element. Other nets, fishing nets for example, use a shuttle. This

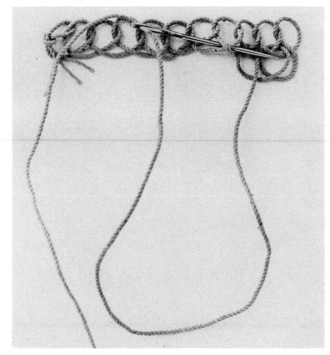

Cross-Knit Loop Stitching. The foundation row for this loop stitch is the same as Step 1 of simple looping. Again, make an S stitch at the end of each row. It serves the same function as in simple looping—to avoid decreasing. In the loop stitch, the needle works an X in each loop. It picks up two strands in the previous loop as opposed to simple looping which picks up only one (the only variation between them). Again, you work left-to-right, then right-to-left.

Figure 4. This form of cross-knit has a disymmetric face and is done with a loop stitch. A more complex, dense, and less supple fabric results.

makes it possible to carry a longer working element and reduces the number of splices in your work. To use the netting shuttle, load it by passing the cord around the flexible tongue in the center of the shuttle, down and around the body of the shuttle, returning to make the next loop around the tongue from the reverse side. Note the alternate loops around the tongue in the first demonstration photo of knotted netting.

Knotted Netting. Tie a loop with a bowline knot at the end of the working element. The bowline knot will not slip if you keep the tension constant. Drop the loop onto a hook that is secure enough to hold a constant pull while you work. To start, center the bowline in the left center of the loop. Hold this with your thumb and forefinger, at the same time pulling the loop taut with your little finger.

Pass the shuttle through the loop, back to front. Stop the flow of the working element with your little finger at whatever distance you want the lag. Still holding the bowline between your fingers, cast

a loop upward, left to right. Pass the shuttle under the two lines on your right and through the loop you just made with the working element. Close the knot by pulling downward and slightly to your right with the shuttle. *Do not release your thumb and forefinger until the knot is closed.* This is very important. It is the constant tautness of both the knotting element and the pendant loop that makes this a secure knot.

Make a chain of loops. After each knot, remove the chain from the hook and turn it so the last knot lays to your left. This places it in the same relationship as it was when you made the first loop. The chain will lengthen away from the hook.

Once the chain is the desired length, remove it from the hook and lay it flat on a working surface. Traditional fish netting is made 1½ times the desired size.

Pass a hanging rod through each mesh and secure temporarily to a wall or table. This rod should thread through the loops consistently with the element passing back to front as shown here. The working element should feed from the lower left-

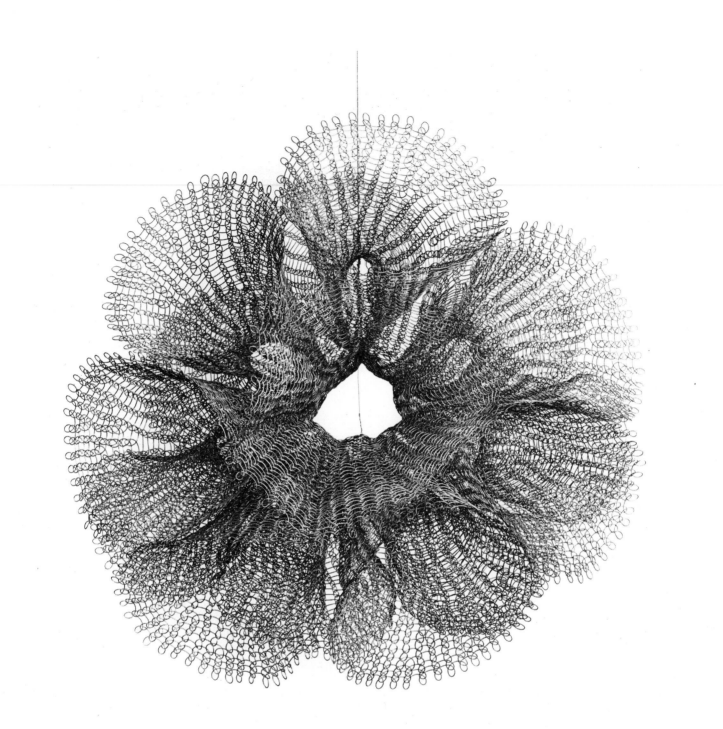

Public Anemone #1 (Left) by Edwin Geer. Rayon velour, 8½″ x 14″. Working in a material reminiscent of the natural sea form, the artist has cross-knit a colorful and eccentric sculpture. A number of stitches were used and adapted throughout to develop a variety of surfaces. Photo by David Donoho.

Sculpture (Above) by Ruth Asawa, 1964. Copper wire, 21″ x 21″. In this intricate piece the artist has translated a cross-knit stitch into her own wire media. The form flows from convex to concave over a lacelike surface, thus emphasizing both repetition and fluidity. Photo by Laurence Cuneo.

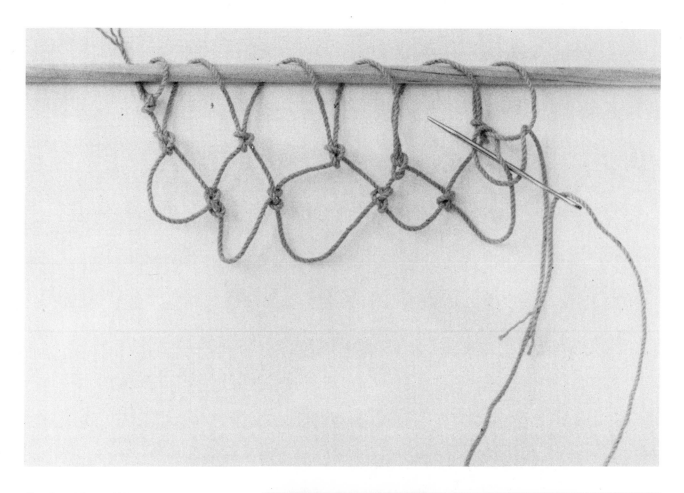

Overhand Knot (Above). First a slip knot is tied in the working strand and placed on a temporary dowel. You could also use a permanent cord or loop, either straight or circular. Each loop varies in size and is controlled by an overhand knot. These knots are unstable, however, and will slip through the body of the work unless placed very close together. To make the knot, loop part of the working strand through a previously tied mesh and pick up the back strand as illustrated here by the placement of the needle.

Figure 5. While the most frequently used knot in Peruvian netting was the overhand knot, fine examples of square-knotting have also been found. Using the square knot produces a disymmetric fabric as shown here.

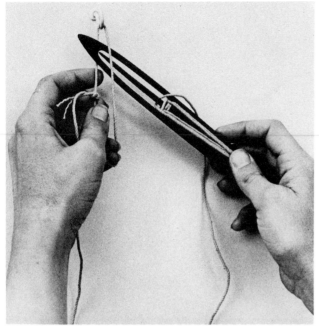

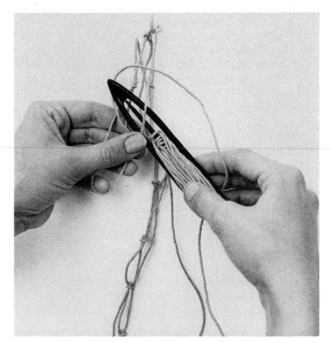

Knotted Netting: Step 1. Make a loop by tying a bowline in the free end of your cord. Secure this loop to something sturdy to provide a constant tension. Stretch the loop with the knot placed to your left as shown. As you place this knot and tie the next, you automatically determine the symmetry or asymmetry of the mesh. The mesh must be kept taut; here it is held open by using the little finger.

Step 2. Make a chain of mesh the length of the net desired, remembering that each time you complete a knot the chain is turned so the last knot completed lays on your left. To tie the knot, pass the shuttle up through the loop, stopping the flow of cord with your little finger. Grasp the previous loop and working cord with your thumb as shown. Then cast a loop across to the left and return, passing the shuttle under the two mesh cords and through this loop. Close tightly by pulling downward and slightly to your right. Do not release your thumb and forefinger until the knot is tied.

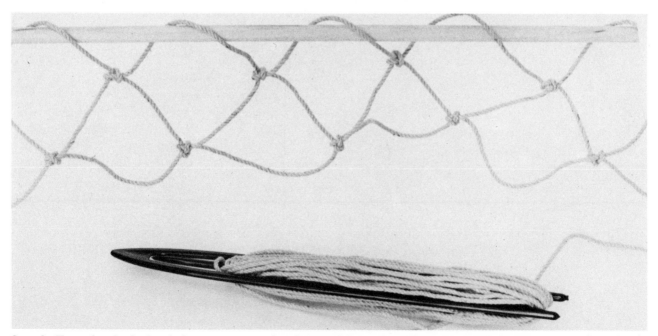

Step 3. To make the body of the net, remove the chain and lay it flat. The net is made by tying on to the side of the chain. Pass a hanging rod through each of the mesh (all mesh should pass around the rod in the same direction) and secure either to a wall or table. The working cord should feed from the lower left-hand knot. To make the second row repeat Step 2, passing the shuttle through the mesh to the right of the knot. Work the third row right-to-left by changing the shuttle to the left hand. Each row alternates working left-to-right, right-to-left when making a flat net. Circular nets can be worked continuously in the same direction.

Step 4. Increasing or decreasing the mesh is an option you may want to use. An added knot, as shown here, is formed on the previous row of knots, making two mesh loops where you would ordinarily have only one. To decrease, reverse this procedure by skipping one loop in the previous row. Increasing or decreasing not only makes the form larger or smaller when kept at a stable width, it also makes the pattern more open or dense.

Mexican Fishing Net and Tools (Below). Nets and their tools are found wherever fishermen work. On long piers in San Diego, Naples, or Taipei, on the banks of lakes or seas, net of many sizes can still be found at rest. Courtesy of the Museum of International Folk Art, Santa Fe, New Mexico. Photo by Candace Crockett.

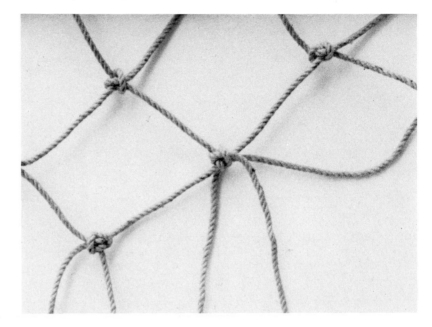

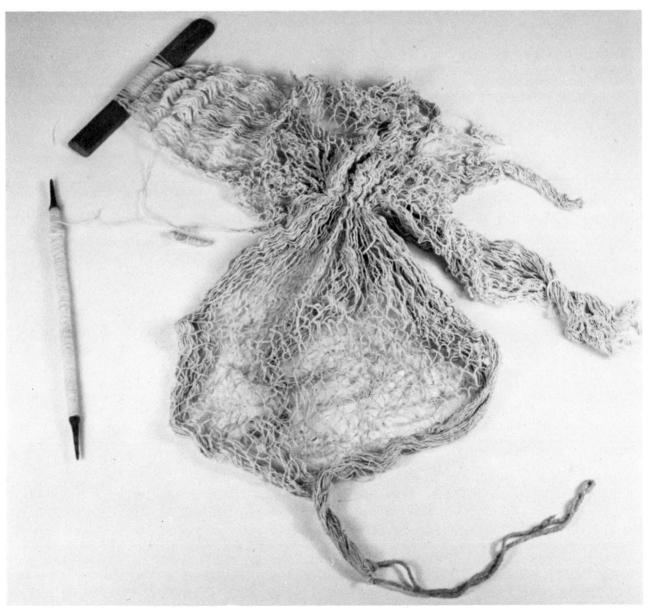

hand knot. Repeat the knotting as previously described. The size of the lag between each knot is up to you, each time controlled by the little finger as the knot is tied.

In flat work, each row is worked alternately, left to right, right to left, changing the shuttle from one hand to the other for each row. Circular nets are worked continuously in the same direction.

To increase the number of lags between knots and thus increase either the size or density of the netting, tie a knot both in the lag and at a previously tied knot. This will double the number of lags in the subsequent row.

To decrease, tie the knot in select lags, skipping whatever number you choose. This will either decrease the physical size or let it develop an even more open quality.

The network we have been exploring is made with a continuous element and usually is open, loose, airy, and lightweight. Some network introduces a second or third element in its construction. For example, when simple looping or cross-knit looping introduces a second strand, they then become the Venice stitch in Peruvian textiles.

USING AN ADDITIONAL ELEMENT

Let's explore two other types of Peruvian netting using second elements: the simili-velour and the lark's head net. Each uses the lark's head knot as a base. The lark's head is illustrated again in Chapter 6 as you would tie it in macramé.

In the simili-velour and lark's head net the knot is tied with a continuous element, progressing one to the next, forming the body of the work.

Sewn Lark's Heads. Measure the width you want on a knot-bearing element and tie a single overhand knot at this point. Working vertically with the knot at the top and the end at the bottom, pass the working element over the face of the knot bearer, right to left. Stitch under the knot bearer exiting over the top of the loop just formed.

Reversing the above will give you the other half of the lark's head. When the knot is completed, there will be two mirrored loops on the bearer element joined by a lag.

Continue these two steps down the bearer cord until the end. Be sure that all lags are uniform and on the same face.

Simili-Velour Net is dense with a slightly stretchy body. One face is enhanced by a second loop or cut pile. The intrinsic structure of the base net dictates

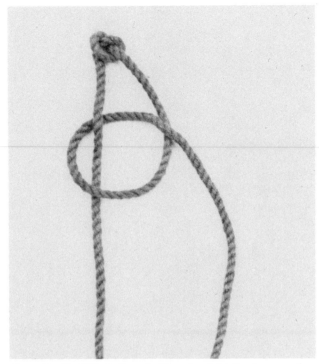

Sewn Lark's Head: Step 1. Tie a knot in the base cord or knot bearer at the width you want. The body of the work is usually flexible but this cord is not, so be sure to allow enough length. Work vertically, down the cord away from the knot. The cord can be held in your hand or laid on a flat surface. Pass the knotting cord over the face of the knot bearer; stitch under the knot bearer returning over the top of your working strand.

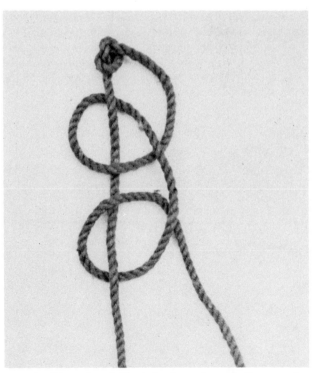

Step 2. The other half of the knot is made by reversing Step 1. You pass the knotting cord under the knot bearer, over the face of the knot bearer, and under your working strand. Pull tight to complete the lark's head.

Simili-Velour Stitch: Step 1. Stitch a series of lark's head knots on a bearer cord the desired width. By reversing your line of knots, you will place the bearer cord on your left, the working cord and the line of lark's heads on your right. Notice the alternating lags in the lark's heads. One loops over itself, the next loops behind. It is important to have this alternating correct. The second row of lark's heads is worked in the manner shown by the needle's placement. Sew both parts of the knot through the same loop, and always pass the needle behind the loop of the previous row.

Step 2. After you have completed two rows of lark's heads, you are ready to introduce a second strand that will create the fabric face. This strand is stitched with a second needle through the cross loop not used when building the second row of lark's heads. Pass the needle between the inner loop of each overlapping lark's head. Return between the next comparable inner loop and under the same cord you crossed to begin. The photograph shows the reverse face and the inner loops through which the cord passes.

Figure 6. This is a sample of the face of simili-velour. Notice how all surface strands lay in one direction. While the looped foundation has a degree of elasticity, the bearer cord does not.

that the pile fall in one direction. Increasing the knotting occurrence of the second element will decrease this directional pile and make a more dense, less flexible work. An example of one face worked in simili-velour stitch is shown in Figure 6.

To begin, stitch a series of lark's head knots on the bearer cord as described above. After the first row, reverse the line of knots so the working element again is at the top and to your right. On a correctly knotted series the loops are connected with a lag that alternates first on one face and then on the other. Work the second row of lark's heads down the line of knots as you did on the bearer cord in the first row.

Use the lag that is on the reverse face to make the knot. When this row is complete, check to see if you have knotted each into the correct lag. One way to do this is to check the appearance of the lags from one row to the next. They will have an alternating scalloped effect.

The next step can be done as you work the base net or added after it is complete. If you add the second element as you work, begin after completing the second lark's head row. The second element threads its way parallel in each alternating lark's head and in each alternating row.

Pass the needle between the inner loops of each overlapping lark's head. Return between the next comparable inner loop and exit under the same lag you crossed at the beginning. In so doing, you will duplicate or parallel the lag portion in the previous lark's head. This strand may be left in an exaggerated loop or cut to form a pile.

The Lark's Head Net when worked traditionally is very stable, probably because there is more than one lag tightly joining each separate unit. The historical example we have of this is also worked symmetrically, evenly dividing the number of knots to each unit. There is no reason why this pattern must be followed, however. The only thing to keep in mind is the scale between the foundation circle and the working element forming the knots if the foundation is to be fully covered. Figure 7 illustrates the di-symmetrical face in this net as it is worked traditionally. The directions that follow are for a similar net.

Select either a ready-made ring or make one by wrapping foundation material several times around your finger. How large the ring is depends on a number of your decisions—the major one being how covered you want this ring to be in the finished work. You can estimate the size of the ring with

relationship to the working element by wrapping 20 times around the ring. If you use a foundation cord instead of ready-made rings, wrap this cord at least twice around your finger, always allowing a slight overlap at the cut ends.

With the working element, make a lark's head on the first ring in the same manner as you did for the simili-velour. Here the ring acts as the bearer cord. If you use a ring you made, tie this first knot where the ends overlap. After the first knot, lay the work on a flat surface so the working element is on the left and the tail end is on the right as you look at it. Join a second ring by repeating the first step. Pull these together so the circles are contiguous.

With the two rings drawn together, add a third. As you add these rings, note that the last lark's head tied splits. One lag leads to one circle and the other lag to a different circle. Tie three complete lark's heads on one circle before splitting the last in adding a new circle.

The net forms as you work successive circles, usually in sets of four. If you introduce different-size rings, this may change. In using equal-size rings, a diamond shaped space evolves between the circles as the net is assembled.

Several colors may be used in tying this net. To change the working element and to assure a finished look, sew the ends under the lark's head and keep the rings parallel.

OTHER HISTORICAL EXAMPLES

So far the techniques shown have had their roots in Peruvian history. It must be noted that other cultures on other continents evolved similar techniques. To paraphrase Dr. Bird, it is the high level of accomplishment and the extensive variety of material available to us that commands our attention in Peruvian textiles.

Scandinavia, for example, is an area where we find early evidence of single-element construction. The best preserved example of vantsom, or knotless-netting, is a glove found in Vastergotland.

To do this technique, it is best to work with a firm, smooth material. The work is very dense, firm and, in historical examples such as gloves or over-stockings, waterproof. Like the Peruvian single-element constructions, it is worked in a series of stitched loops. And again, if an element breaks it will not run, which may account for it being classified as a net technique rather than a knit.

The working tool is a flat needle with a large eye about 4″ long. You must be able to get a firm

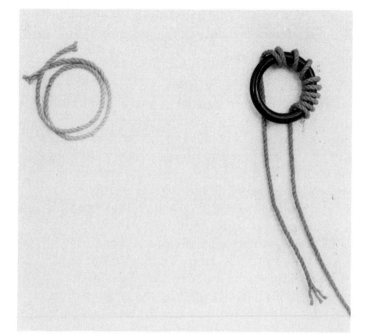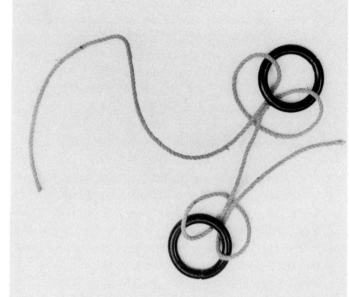

Lark's Head Net: Step 1. Select a ring or make a circle of cords. The size depends on the relative size of the material you are using (refer to the text for ways to estimate this). The metal rings used here are too large for a closely formed net. They were selected so the knots could be opened out for analysis.

Step 2. Using a tapestry needle, make a lark's head in the same manner as described earlier in this chapter. The only difference is that your bearer cord (ring) is round instead of straight. After one knot is tied on the first circle, lay this on a flat surface so the working cord is on the left as you look at it, the tail (non-working end) on the right. Have a second circle ready and repeat Step 1. In doing finished work, pull the circles close together.

grip on it as you work. In the Scandinavian example, single-ply yarns are used that are tripled in the needle. This gives a loop at the end for splicing a new element without tying a knot.

Vantsom Knotless Net. First tie a slip knot at the end of your working element. Hold this knot between your thumb and forefinger with the loop to your right and the working element to your left, hanging over the back of your thumb. Thread through the loop and pull, making a loop around your thumb.

Repeat this process, threading through the first loop, under the thumb loop, and under the working element. Pull, allowing the first thumb loop to slip to the front of the thumb, leaving one loop on the back of your thumb and two on the front.

Repeat again, threading through both the first loops, under the thumb loop, and under the working element. Pull, allowing top thumb loop to slip to the front of the thumb. You now have three loops behind the thumb and one around the thumb.

Thread through all three loops, under the thumb loop and behind the working element. Pull, letting go of the old thumb loop, retaining the new loop

as before. You now have four loops behind the thumb.

Thread through three loops, leaving the fourth. Pass under the thumb loop and the working element. This completes the basic stitch. Continue looping and stitching until the desired length is reached.

When this length is reached, turn the plait to the right. Stitch into the loops that lie to the right, being very careful not to pull the loops loose. Continue working the three loops behind the thumb, under the thumb loop, and the working element.

Knitting and Crocheting

The oldest remnant of true knitting dates back to 250 A.D. and was found near Palestine. Literary references are numerous before this date, but this is our earliest primary evidence of the existence of the technique. Other earlier techniques have the surface appearance of knitting—empacted countertwining or the forementioned vantsom knotless netting, for example.

In 1589 an Englishman, Rev. William Lee, invented a flat bed machine for knitting hosiery cloth. This increased knitting production tenfold.

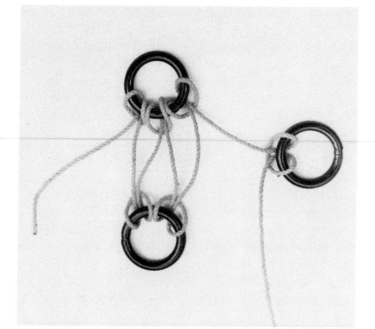
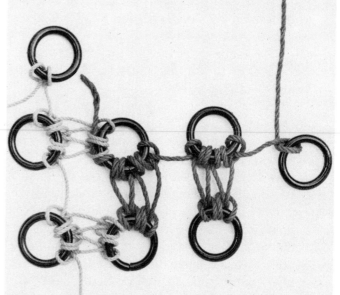

Step 3. Here we have introduced a third ring. The ring at the top is ring 1. It has been joined to the second ring by a series of lark's heads: three on ring 1, two on ring 2. The third lark's head on ring 1 divides to join with the third ring on the right. To proceed, add two more lark's heads to ring 3 before introducing a fourth ring.

Step 4. Several incomplete areas are shown here to illustrate phases the net will go through. The completed netting will have alternate round and diagonal open spaces. The foundation of the diamond takes place when the third lark's head divides (shown at the lower left). We have used two colors to illustrate how end strands are sewn back into a circle for a finished look. Note the darker strand on the center circle.

Figure 7. This shows a completed lark's head net.

Almost two centuries later, the first circular knitting machine was developed, and in 1775 Crane of England invented a tricot machine for warp knitting. All single-element constructions were weft techniques up to this time and, when done by hand, knitting still is.

One other invention should be noted as having an impact on the textile industry in general and the knitting industry in particular. In 1801, Joseph Marie Jacquard, a Frenchman, created the first Jacquard head. The head differs from the loom in that we can put any type loom underneath the Jacquard head and harness and the head will accept a program, or designated pattern. It was the first computer of man. The cards are large, usually about 3″x18″; there are smaller French cards that measure 1″x11″. These cards, as well as plastic tapes, work on a pneumatic suction system.

Today industrial knits have claimed a large part of the textile industry. Jack Lenor Larsen, a United States leader in the design and production of art fabrics, has been making stretch fabrics to be used in upholsteries since the late 1950's. One of his current interests is for both the apparel and home fashions industries to become monolithic. He cites as an example the success of the hosiery industry in engineering inexpensive form-fitting garments.

Mr. Larsen speculates: "Think that if there was an upholstered chair covering that you could slip on and off, wash, etc., just as you can the pantyhose or a sweater. . . . It would appeal to the theatrics of living, the seasonal change, without the great expense we have now. . . ."

Not just the apparel and home fashion industries have been affected by the increased industrialization in knitting. In medicine, for example, knitted vascular prostheses have been in use for a number of years and they are experimenting with a knit artificial heart. In space travel, a small, gold-plated knit gasket solved the structural defect that caused the Apollo 13 tragedy. In communications, a knit antenna circles the world in space.

Similarities. There are a number of parallels between crochet and knitting besides the obvious one of working with a continuous element. While each is a looping process, there are a number of structural differences both in the working and the surface results.

In crochet and knitting, each stitch is completed but not secured before the next one has been worked through it. Second, pulling the active element will tighten the stitch. Each and all of you will do this differently, and it is the only primary characteristic over which you have any essential control. The third characteristic knitting and crochet have in common is that any edge becomes a finished edge as you work. Crochet requires at least one stitch to secure the final edge and knitting a row of closing stitches. All other edges are self-edged. Fourth, they are both stretchy in character.

Tools and Materials. Common nomenclature identifies crochet as being made with a hook and knitting being made with needles. In each case, size and material vary and, in the case of knitting needles, they are made straight, circular, and single or double pointed. Actually, there are examples of knitting needles with hooks on the end, and one of the simplest braids shown in Chapter 7, called finger knotting and similar in structure to crochet, uses no hook at all.

Both knitting and crochet tools—hooks and needles—have identifying systems associated with size. Some are identified with numbers and some with letters, and not all manufacturers follow the same system.

For any typical-size work, there are many crochet hooks and knitting needles on the market. However, once you choose to work with large-scale elements, you may have to make the tools yourself. Crochet in large scale is best worked with the hands, primarily using a single crochet stitch. Knitting, on the other hand, has interesting challenges. Most familiar to those who already knit is knitting done with broomsticks.

In either crocheting or knitting, using a large hook or needles with fine or very pliable material tends to make the body of work soft and flimsy, lacking stability. Any pattern development will be lost in the openness of the oversized loops. Small crochet hooks used with larger, bulky material will develop a dense, stiff, and heavy body. Any pattern will be lost with this combination, too.

Mary Walker Phillips, one of today's most prominent artists using knitting, points out two basic considerations in selecting your needles—or making them—for knitting. First, they should be smooth. Nothing will slow you down more nor be more irritating than having a tool that is not in prime condition. In knitting, this means needles that will slip easily across each other as well as in and out of the working elements. Second, be sure the needle has a long, gradual point. A good pencil sharpener may be used as a temporary measure, but for the long haul, work it down to a smooth point.

The selection or style of knitting needles is up to you, but should be chosen in relation to the job to be done. The circular needle will serve best for general all-around use. It offers you an option of working either flat or round. Straight needles, unless double pointed and used in more than pairs, will not work a circular form.

A final word from Mary, "You'd better learn to be a good ripper. I probably spend as much time undoing as doing when I knit. It is, I think, the only way to perfect an original piece."

Interlooping Shorthand. There are symbols, or a shorthand system, for identifying the placement of the hook or needles, the placement of the linear element, and the number of movements needed to form a stitch. These symbols, while of no special use when you are experimenting with the technique, are very useful as a shorthand for reference at a later time. All crochet and knitting patterns are written in these symbols. It is the one universal thing about these techniques: each of you will have a different interpretation of a given pattern, even though each of you will be reading the same written text. Notice the duplication in a number of the symbols.

Crochet	**Knit**
ch = chain	k = knit
sc = single crochet	p = purl
ss = slip stitch	sl = slip stitch
st, sts = stitch(es)	st, sts = stitch(es)
yoh = yarn over hook	yo = yarn over
	tog = together
dc = double crochet	psso = pass slip stitch over next stitch
hdc = half-double crochet	
tr = triple crochet	dp = double-pointed needles
inc = increase	inc = increase
dec = decrease	dec = decrease
* = repeat from	* = repeat from

For British Readers: the names of the basic crochet stitches used in this book differ slightly from those used in standard British patterns. The key below provides the necessary equivalents.

Stitch Given Here	**British Equivalent**
Single crochet	Double crochet
Double crochet	Treble crochet
Half-double crochet	Half-treble crochet
Treble crochet	Double treble crochet

In knitting and crochet, each stitch is interlooped into a parallel stitch in the next row. The relative size will increase in each subsequent row if you increase the number of stitches as with all single element constructions. In decreasing, the converse is true.

Knitting. To begin knitting, you "cast on" a row of loops that serves as a foundation for further interlooping. Do not cast on too tightly. This first "cast on" row along with your second row is referred to as the selvage.

Casting On. Measure a distance from the end of the working element that allows between ½″ and 1″ for every stitch you plan to cast on. Tie a slip knot at this point and place the loop on one of the needles. Pull the knot closed.

Hold the needle with the loop in one hand. Thread the free element and working element together between the ring finger and middle finger of your other hand. Spread these elements with your thumb and forefinger. The working element is over the forefinger; the free element over your thumb. In working, your hands should be close enough together to be able to touch.

Pull the free element out to form a loop using your thumb. Put the knitting needle through this loop. Pick up the working element and draw it through the loop and onto the needle. Pull closed. You now have two loops on the needle. Repeat these three steps for the needed number of stitches.

Knitting and Purling. Knitting is the act of (1) inserting a first needle through a loop that is held on a second needle, (2) casting the working element around the point of the inserted needle, and (3) drawing this loop back, thus transferring a new loop into the first needle. You have several choices in doing this:

1. You may place the working needle through the loop and under the second needle with the working element at the back. This is K (knit).

2. You may place the working needle through the loop, under the second needle with the working element at the front. This is P (purl).

3. You may cast the working element over the working needle and draw the loop from back to front. This is K (knit).

4. You may cast the working element over the working needle and draw the loop from front to back. This is P (purl).

Figure 8. *You could say you are doing a different knitting stitch each time your working strand is cast differently from the previous stitch. The two primary stitches in knitting are the knit stitch and the purl stitch. The top of this picture shows one face of the knit stitch; the bottom section shows one face of the purl stitch. In each, every row is the same stitch. Alternating rows of knit and purl stitches is called "stockinette stitch."*

5. You may insert the working needle into the front side of the loop. This will make the K or P more stretchy.

6. You may insert the working needle into the back side of the loop. This will reduce the stretchiness in P or K.

You usually work with the active needle in the hand that is dominant, with the needle holding the body of work in the subordinant hand. In other words, all of the work will be in your left hand when you begin a row if you are right-handed. As the row transfers with the new loops, so will the work. Again switch the work to the subordinant hand when you begin the next row.

All knitting stitches are combinations of the choices listed above. Combinations with the most common names are: the *Garter Stitch* where every row is knit with choices 1 and 3 in sequence, and the *Stockinette Stitch* with alternate rows of K and P, 1 and 3 alternating in one row and 2 and 4 in sequence for one row. These two stitches are shown in Figure 8.

The best way to become acquainted with the multitude of variations in knitting is to knit some samplers. Begin by making your choices from the above methods, combining if you wish. For example: if you cast on an even number of stitches and decide to K4, P4 in the same row and repeat this for several rows, you will have a pattern called *Ribbing*. You can develop ribbing in any combination of K-P in the same row providing the multiples match the number of cast on stitches. This may be either an even or uneven number. This is a rib pattern and, if repeated a number of rows before changing to a different pattern, can be written K4, P4, repeat from * (the number of times).

When you begin your experiments, make notes on the different patterns you create using the shorthand symbols. A pattern may not be discernible at first. Remember that in the beginning, someone like you said to him/herself, "What can I do with two pointed sticks and a long string that will hold together? How can I put some order into what I make? How can I make it my own and make it beautiful, too?"

Crocheting. Crochet has a unique quality, because every other row worked is the face of the stitch and alternate rows show the back of the stitch. There are two ways of altering this characteristic if you want the face to be similar in flat work. Either work a row of smaller loops (SC) on the return

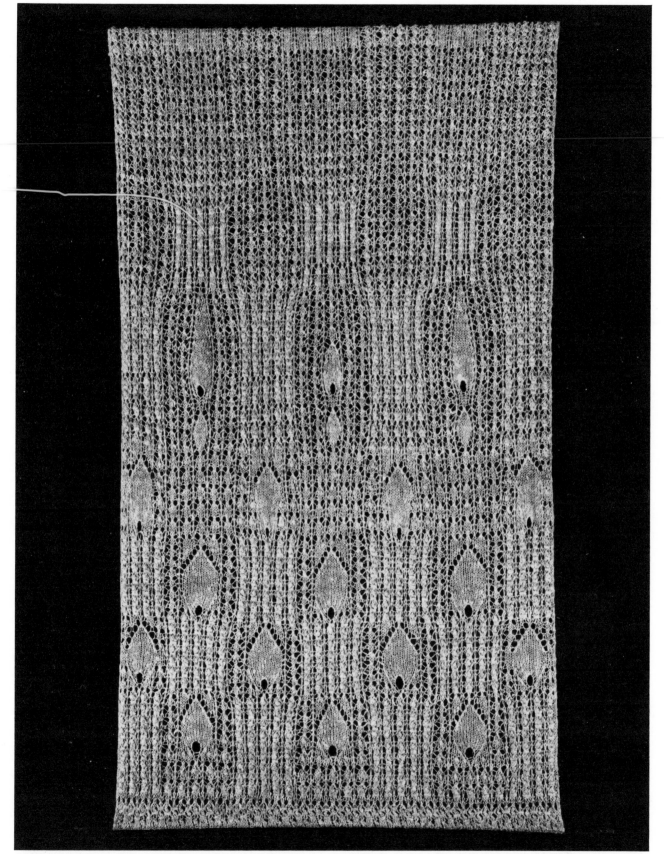

Wall Hanging by Mary Walker Phillips. Natural linen and synthetics, 63″ x 42″. More than any other contemporary craftsman, this artist has successfully pursued knitting as an artistic expression. She mainly relies on selecting stitches that will exploit the interstices in counterplay against the solidity of the stitches themselves. Photo by Ferdinand Boesch.

Lambrequin (detail), 24″ deep. Lambrequins originated in medieval times to cover the upper openings of windows or doors. This nineteenth century crochet adaptation (then a popular handcraft) resulted from the expanding amount of leisure time due to industrialization. Courtesy of the Brooklyn Museum, New York.

row or turn at the end of each round and work the rest in the opposite direction.

Circular crochet is only practical when there is no break in the contour. This is another variation from knitting where form may flow into one section from another by adding needle sets. Only forms that have no interruptions in the circular contour are successful with circular crochet. A second characteristic of crochet, not found in knitting, is the interlocking of loops both vertically and horizontally. Knitting interloops only vertically.

There are only five basic stitches in crochet. Whatever name they go by, all the other stitches are variations on these basic stitches. It is possible to simplify these even further. By analyzing the position of either the hook or the yarn, you will realize that the variants are even fewer.

The working yarn passes over the crochet hook from back to front in all crochet (YOH). The loops of yarn made with the hook are worked into the back side of the fabric's chain. There are no variables in this unless specifically directed in a given pattern. There are only two variations in crochet. First, how many YOH take place and second, how many of these are pulled through loops as they are pulled by the hook.

We are concerned here with five major crochet designations. They are: chain, simple crochet, half-double crochet, double crochet, and treble crochet. You will find stitches with other names, but they are combinations of these five basic ones with specific variations.

The foundation of all crochet is the chain, sometimes called the "Tambour stitch." The first row of any stitch is worked into the upper strands of the chain row.

Chain. Tie a slip knot near the end of your working element. Hold this between your thumb and forefinger. Slip the crochet hook through the loop and tighten. Just as with knitting, you should not work crochet too tightly. Pass the hook under and over the working element, then draw the loop through the loop on the hook. This will put a new

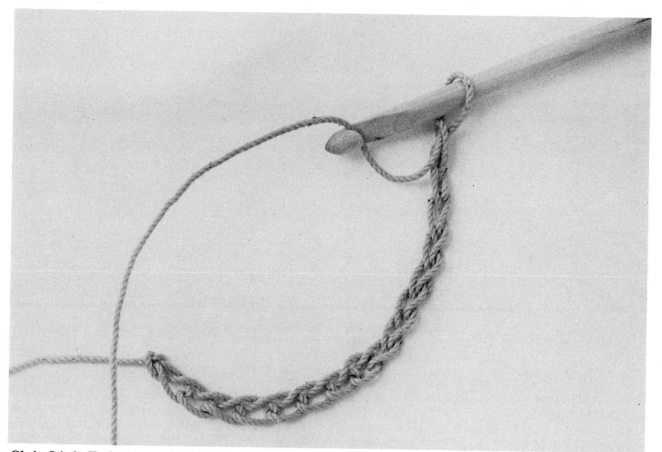

Chain Stitch. To begin, tie a slip knot near the end of your working strand. Hold this knot at the base with your thumb and forefinger. Insert the crochet hook through the loop of the knot and under the working strand that is looped over the forefinger. Slip the strand through the knot and tighten the stitch on the hook. The working strand is looped over the forefinger, in front of the next finger, in back of your ring finger, and around the little finger to control tension.

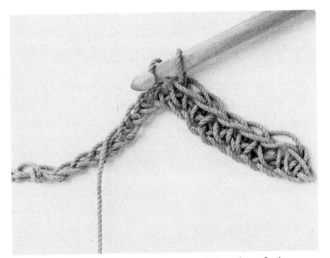

Single Crochet: Step 1. Working with a foundation row of chain stitches, leave the last chain on the hook. The hook is inserted front to back through a chain stitch. It goes under the working strand and is pulled back leaving two stitches on the hook. Note: on the first row of single crochet you begin on the second chain stitch. You begin on the first chain stitch on all subsequent rows.

Step 2. Pass the hook under the working strand on your forefinger and pull through both stitches. This leaves one stitch on your hook. Repeat until a row has been worked. Chain one stitch before starting the next row. Here we show the strand before it is pulled through the loops.

Half-Double Crochet: Step 1. In the half-double stitch you pass the hook under and over the working strand before inserting it into the chain. Skip two stitches in the chain and insert the hook under both upper strands of the third. Pass the hook under and over the strand on your forefinger and draw it through the stitch. Pass the hook under and over the strand on your forefinger and draw it through the three loops on the hook.

Step 2. This shows the hook ready to pull the strand through the last three loops. You will complete the stitch with one loop left on the hook. A double crochet stitch is made the same way except you insert the hook into the fourth stitch from the hook. Your working strand will be drawn through two loops after each pass.

loop on the hook; the other will drop into the chain. Repeat until the desired chain length is reached.

Single Crochet. Working with a foundation chain, leave the last stitch on the hook. Insert the hook, front to back, into the second stitch from the hook. Pass the hook under and over the working element and draw back the loop. There will be two loops on the hook.

Insert the hook under the working element and pull through both loops, leaving one loop on the hook. Begin in the first stitch of the previous row on all of the following rows of single crochet.

Half-Double Crochet. Working with a foundation chain, leave the last loop on the hook. Pass the hook under and over the working element. Insert the hook, front to back, into the third stitch from the hook, skipping the first two. Pass the hook under and over the working element. Draw the loop back through the chain. There will be three loops on the hook.

Pass the hook under and over the working element and pull it through the three loops leaving one on the hook.

Double Crochet. Pass the hook under and over the working element, through the fourth stitch from the hook in the chain. Pass the hook under and over the working element and draw it through the stitch. Pass the hook under and over the working element again and draw through the first two loops on the hook. Repeat, drawing the working element through the last two loops, leaving one on the hook.

Treble Crochet. With the hook in the last loop on the foundation chain, pass the hook under and over the working element twice, insert the hook into the fifth stitch. Work successive loops back as in the previous directions for double crochet.

Crochet is one of the few single-element constructions that has not been industrialized. The closest industry has come is in the use of the Cidega machine, used to make openwork knits. It is an interesting historical phenomenon that the home artist made crochet so popular in the nineteenth century as an answer to the industrialization of lace, and that industry has yet to find an answer back.

North African Caps. *These contemporary black and white caps are worked in single crochet. Each cap has six sections, making it possible to fold it flat for carrying. Collection of Candace Crockett. Photo by David Donoho.*

Costume by Bonnie Britton. As a technique, crochet is very like the looping used in making mail for armor. Both the elaborate design and the crochet stitches contribute to the medieval feeling in this two-piece, contemporary costume. Photo by David Donoho.

Wall Piece (Right) by Bonnie Britton. Natural jute twine, buttons, 27″ x 18″. In this crocheted hanging the artist reiterates her current interest in heraldry and Teutonic form. Photo by David Donoho.

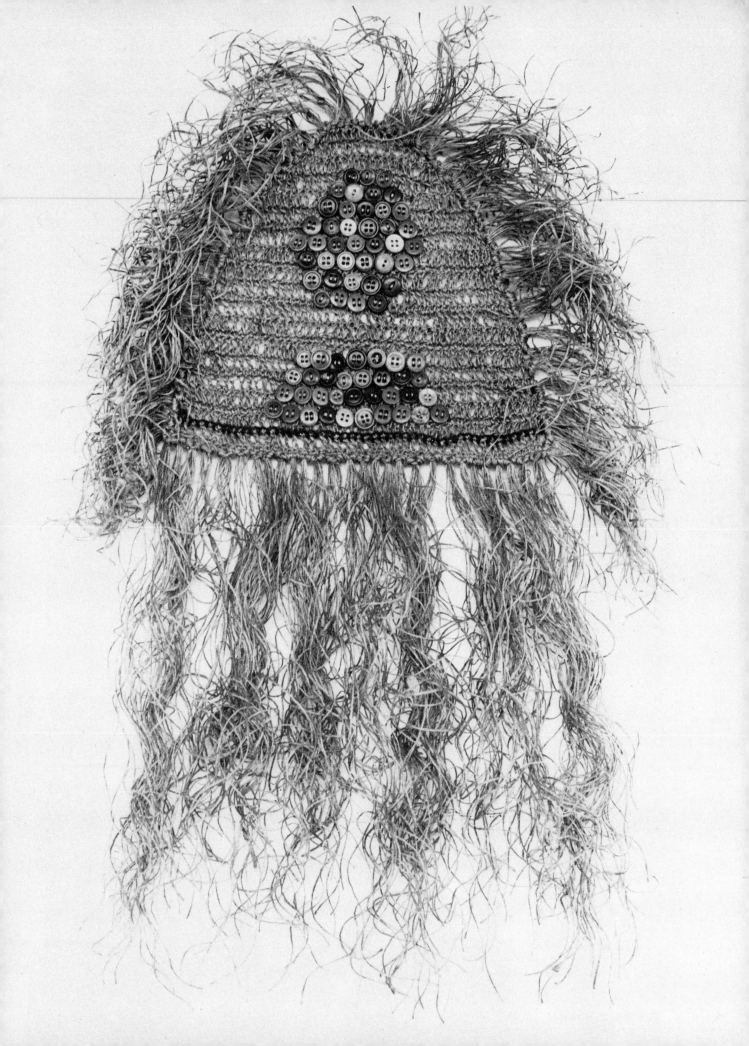

Card-Woven Hanging by Candace Crockett.
Wool, 120″ x 40″. This tapestry combines
a card-woven center with a loom-woven
backing. Natural fleece has been knotted
into the backing of each side panel.
Photo by David Donoho.

Bedspread (detail), American, late
nineteenth century. This crocheted
detail displays all the virtuosity,
innovation, and concern for dimensional
form sought by today's artists.
Collection of Candace Crockett.
Photo by David Donoho.

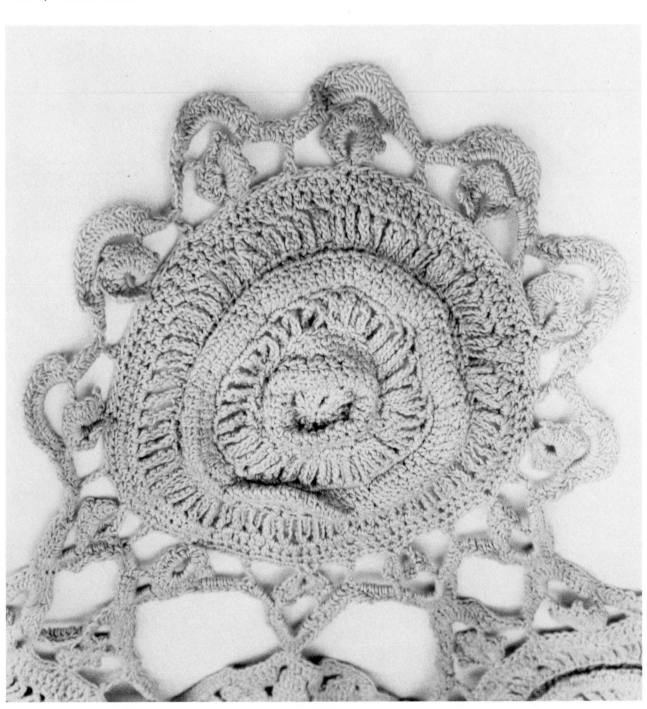

Landscape by Robert Freimark.
Tapestry made in the
Art Protis technique, 24″ x 48″.

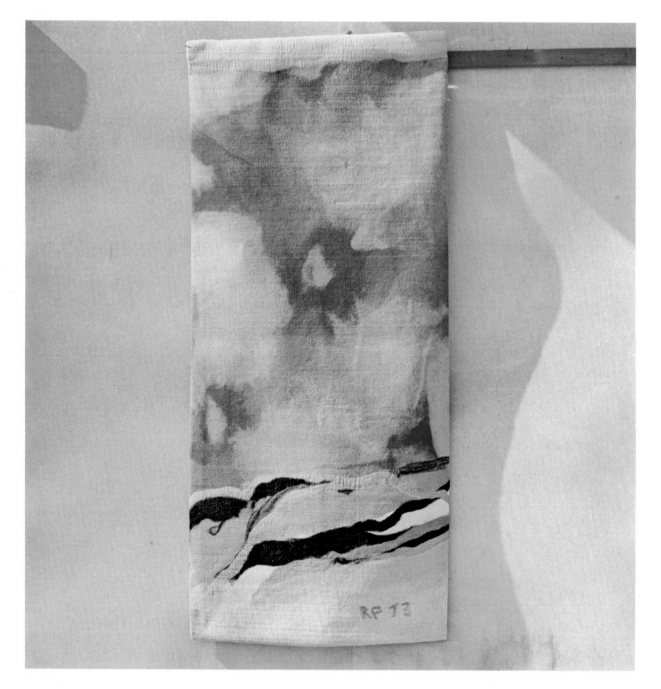

All Seeing Eye Mandala by Robert Freimark, 1973.
Ceiling tapestry done in the Art Protis technique, 53″ x 55½″.
Collection of Dr. Vladislav Stastny, Brno, Czechoslovakia.

A stack of Freimark tapestries await
processing in the textile machine at Art Protis.
The top work is **Border,** 1973.

Rocking Chair by Carol Shaw.
Crocheted wool yarn.
A Volkswagen hood serves
as the armature
for this rocking chair.
The detail below shows
both its whimsical and
sculptural qualities.
Collection of Kendrick
and Marilyn Kellogg.
Photos courtesy of the artist.

Croatian Woman's Jacket. This detail shows a decorative and traditional use of wool felt. After the wool was dyed and felted, small pieces were cut and stitched in one or several layers to the already tailored jacket. Collection of the Museum of International Folk Art, Santa Fe, New Mexico. Photo by Candace Crockett.

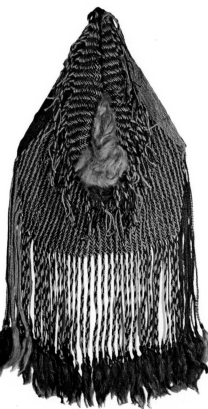

Hanging by Bonnie Britton. Jute, indigo and commercial orange dyes, approximately 6 x 3 feet. Using a classic Hopi wedding sash technique, the artist went a step further by cutting and opening out the circular band after the braiding was complete. Photo by Candace Crockett.

Basket by Joan Austin. Wool yarn. This unusually shaped basket was worked in the simple twining technique. Photo courtesy of the artist.

Basket by Lora Kopp. Wicker and raffia. Weft twining has been used for this small wall unit. A portion of the warp has been returned to the body of the form; other parts have been left to end unfinished. Photo by Marcia Chamberlain.

August 1970, Del Mar, California by Christine Oatman. Cave, ocean, linen thread. This selection
of photos from a series of 30 records a conceptual weaving. Photos by Karen Schroeter.

Nigerian Coiled Mat. Approximately 13″ in diameter.
The strong geometric design of this mat
is a result of the method of construction.
Collection of the Museum of International Folk Art,
Santa Fe, New Mexico. Photo by Candace Crockett.

Red Forest II by Claire Zeisler. Jute, 9 x 38 feet.
One of a series that the artist feels demonstrates
"the nature of yarn." Repetitive in form,
each wrapped coil invites the viewer both
visually and tactually to know yarn. The sculpture
was first shown at the UCLA Deliberate Entanglements
Exhibition in 1971. Photo by Richard Gross.

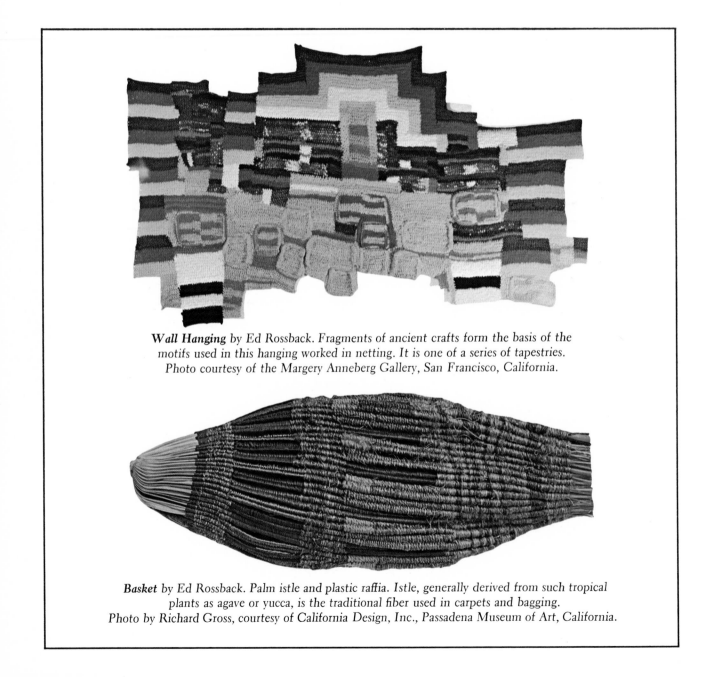

Wall Hanging by Ed Rossback. Fragments of ancient crafts form the basis of the
motifs used in this hanging worked in netting. It is one of a series of tapestries.
Photo courtesy of the Margery Anneberg Gallery, San Francisco, California.

Basket by Ed Rossback. Palm istle and plastic raffia. Istle, generally derived from such tropical
plants as agave or yucca, is the traditional fiber used in carpets and bagging.
Photo by Richard Gross, courtesy of California Design, Inc., Passadena Museum of Art, California.

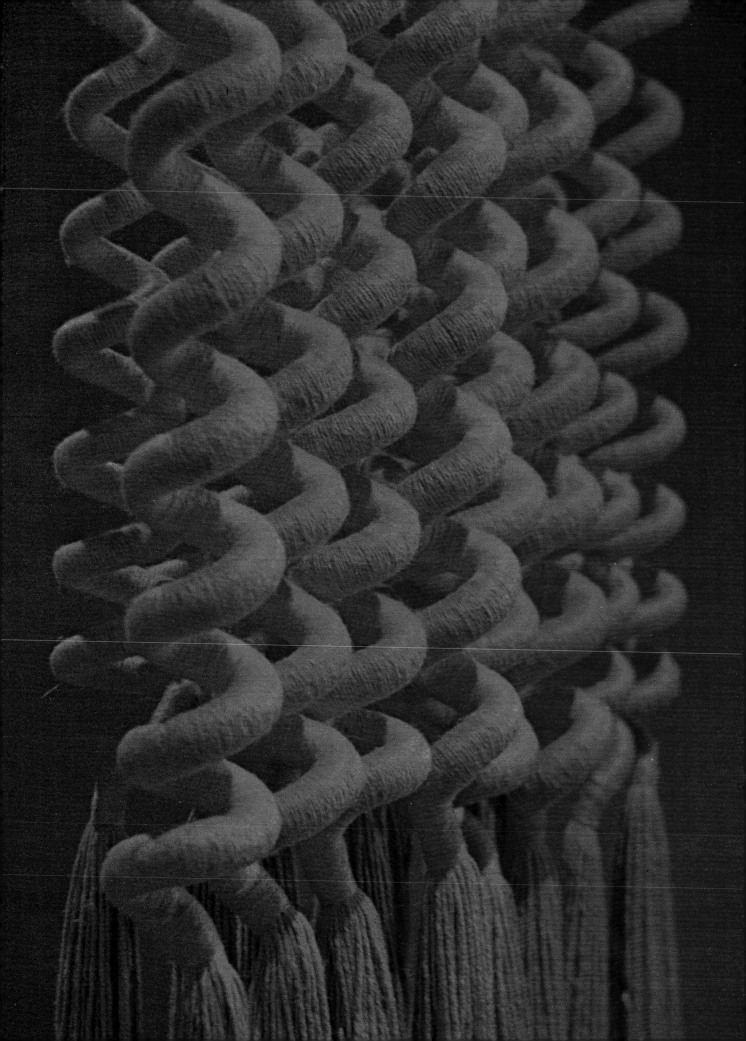

Skeins of Homespun Yarn.
Poplar, onion skin, and marigold dyes.
These yarns reflect the rich spectrum possible
when using common plant materials as dyes.
The sample cards show one of the ways to
codify both plant materials and mordants.
Photo by David Donoho.

Santa Fe by Gerhardt Knodel.
Silk, synthetics, and wire, 7 x 7 feet.
Here is a sensitive resolution
to mixing new synthetic materials
with the richness of natural silk.
Batiked silk strips are wrapped
on an ethafoam core
with nylon monofilament before
being strung to copper wire.
A detail is shown below.
Photos courtesy of the artist.

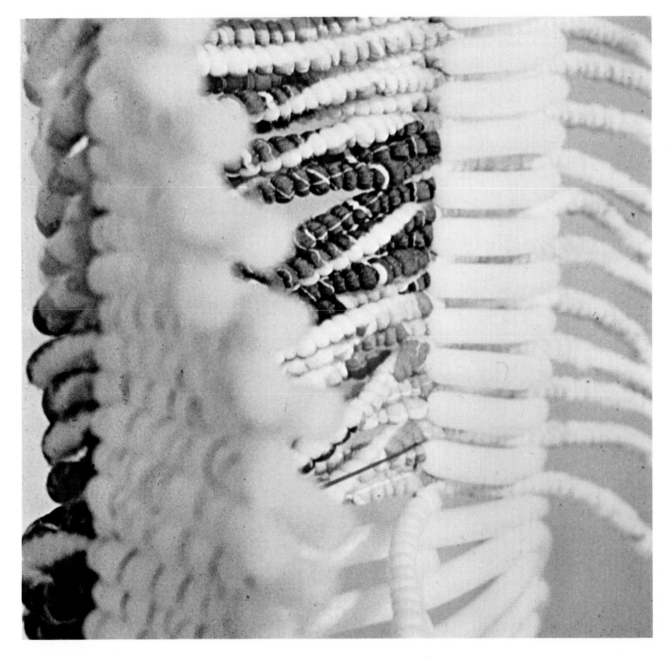

Fur Bag by Joan Austin. Mohair, fur, and gold metallic thread, 5½" x 14". This diminutive twined bag shows all the design qualities associated with much larger pieces. Photo courtesy of the artist.

Card-Woven Panel by Sandra White. Wool, 55" x 8". This detail shows the possibilities of achieving a diminishing and expanding edge by dropping warp cards. The dropped warp later becomes part of the edge, face, or end fringe. Photo by Candace Crockett.

Twined Basket by Carol Shaw. Linen, metallic thread, and shells, 5" in diameter. Photo courtesy of the artist.

Basket by Lynda Sexauer. Handspun wool and silk thread, each section 4" x 3". This two-piece basket holds coils wrapped in exotic colors. Photo by Candace Crockett.

Kurdish Bride's Sock. Finely-spun, multi-dyed cotton, approximately 11" x 4". Collection of the Museum of International Folk Art, Santa Fe, New Mexico. Photo by Candace Crockett.

Five White Elements
by Françoise Grossen.
Cotton, 9 x 5 feet.
This large-scale macramé
tapestry shows the subtle
and innumerable variations
possible in repetition.
Outsized scale is typical
of the artist's work, and this
piece is smaller than most.
A detail is shown below.
Photos by Richard Gross.

CHAPTER SIX

KNOTTING

Knotting is a process whereby one or more elements, usually cords, are locked together by loops to form a structure. Knotting is so old and widespread that there are no records of its beginnings. In one form or another it is native to all cultures and basic to man. Knotting is a function of everyday life and, at its simplest, forms a process that we go through without notice or thought. Volumes and encyclopedias have been written about the hundreds of existing knots that serve one purpose or another—whether to hang a man or to tie a shoelace.

Knotting has evolved through the ages in both practical and decorative directions. Decorative knots have frequently developed out of practical knots. Many people, especially sailors, take pride in their ability to tie a great number of knots. Even practical, useful knots have a beauty that makes them "decorative." For every knot there are many variations, having different names in different areas and among different kinds of people.

Historically, knotting is closely associated with the sea and sailors. Sailors, particularly in the nineteenth century, depended on ropes and developed a strong and broad familiarity with knots of all kinds. Many knots owe their origin and their name to the sailors of the square-rigged ships. The sailors at sea from an early age without books, radio, or television had both rope and time, and they made great contributions to knotting.

"The interest of seamen in their knots was widespread and intense, and often decidedly competitive. Complicated knots were explained under pledge of secrecy; often a knowledge of one knot was bartered for another. I have heard of a sailor who carried an un-finished blackjack in his ditty bag for several voyages until at last he found a ship mate who could teach him the knot he wished to finish off with. A sailor was judged by his chest beckets and his bag lanyards. A superlative knot tier, in the middle of the nineteenth century, stood in the estimation of the Forecastle about where the Artist of the Cavern Walls stood in the Cro-Magnon days."
from *The Ashley Book of Knots* by Clifford W. Ashley

The word "macramé," credited with an Arabic origin, has today been identified with sculptural knotting. In Arabic, its meaning is closely associated with fringe; knotting in this context was thought of as a decorative way of working the fringes of a woven fabric, which gave the necessary elements to work with (the end warp threads). Later, primarily in the nineteenth century, macramé came to designate ornamental knotwork in general. Today, with weaving and fibers being constantly reinterpreted in new art forms, the definition of macramé has been extended to include any fabric structure composed of a set of elements interworked by knotting. The photographs in this chapter of knotted sculptures are meant to be seen as an indication of what is possible, and as examples of knotting as an art form. But knotting, whatever the method or result, can be a satisfactory activity for all ages and all kinds of people. The two basic knots, the square knot and the double half-hitch, are easily mastered and pleasingly versatile.

MATERIALS

Many different kinds and weights of material, from fine metal wire to heavy rope, can be used for knotting. The only prerequisite is that the fibrous "stuff" be flexible enough to form into loops, which can then be locked into place by other loops. The traditional material, used by many sailors past and present, is the white cotton seine twine available from any hardware store. Produced in different weights and plies, seine twine is a smooth, functional cord, with a hard or tight twist. It is very satisfactory to work with, it holds well, and it shows the knots clearly.

Some kinds of materials are more easily worked than others. Very slippery materials can be a problem, since the strands will not hold well and the knots continually come loose. Particularly stiff materials will be hard on the hands and will not pull tight, while extremely soft materials will not show the knot structure very well and will sag. Generally speaking, a smooth, hard-twist fiber of medium weight is the easiest and most successful knotting material. Satisfactory cords for macramé include cotton, linen, jute, and synthetic fibers.

The knotter always has the option of leaving a knot loose or pulling it tight, and frequently this decision is determined or suggested by the bulk or nature of the material as well as by the intended use and design. A knotted structure can be open and airy, or heavy and dense. Knotting can be easily worked flat or three-dimensionally. In learning how to make a knot it is best to work with a medium-weight, hard-twist cord. The samplers in the instructions here, with the exception of two that were worked in a heavier weight nylon cord, were knotted in two colors of a medium-weight seine twine. Working with two colors can be very helpful—it allows you to see how the loops intertwine to form the knot. In many of the knotting samplers the cords are arranged (by means of a lark's head knot) on a holding cord. This is only one of the many possible ways of holding and arranging pairs of cords.

In knotting with unfamiliar materials the best approach is to make a sampler, trying various knots to get the feel of the material and to see how the knots look and react. This is also the only way to determine the length of cord needed for a specific project, as different knots with different materials will require different lengths of cord. Adding cords and dealing with unwanted ends in a finished piece can be a problem. Careful planning and measuring before cutting are necessary. Frequently the cut lengths will be three to five times longer than the final piece. For ease in knotting, the long ends can be individually wound into a loop and held with rubber bands.

In most knotting some means of support is helpful and is often necessary. Many knotters work with a soft board (Celotex or cork board) and use T-pins to hold the knots and cords in place. A grid drawn on the board can be helpful in keeping the knotted piece from becoming misshapen as the knotting progresses. Larger pieces can be attached to a bar or armature. Dimensional pieces can be worked around either a temporary or permanent armature, or suspended from the ceiling.

THE BASIC KNOTS

This chapter offers a few knots, with step-by-step instructions, that will be of interest to the person working with fibers as a means of artistic expression. With the exception of the first two knots described, both used for joining yarn ends, the knots are particularly useful in forming dimensional or sculptural tapestries and in combination with other non-loom art forms. The step-by-step instructions show and explain a number of individual knots in their simplest form. Expanding the minimal groupings dealt with in the instructions to form a larger fabric is simply a matter of adding more cords; the cords are knotted in groups on one row and then on the next row the groups are broken and paired in a different order so the strands are interlocked.

Weaver's Knot. The weaver's knot is very old; found wherever there are weavers, but seldom elsewhere. Like the weaver's square knot it is very useful in joining ends. The weaver's knot cannot be tied when the two ends are under tension, but once tied, tension can be applied, and the knot will remain tied and will not slip. It is frequently used to join broken warp threads and to join the yarn ends during continuous warping. The knot is shown as it appears before and after tightening.

To begin the knot, form a loop with cord 1 so that the apex of the loop is on the right. Take the end of the second cord (coming from the right) under the loop apex, over the bottom part of the loop, under the loop, over the top part of the loop, and under cord 2.

Weaver's Square Knot. This knot is similar in structure to a square knot, but is worked differently. Like the weaver's knot, it is useful for joining ends. It is quick and easy to tie and it holds under tension. The knot will come loose if one of the ends is pulled.

Begin the knot by looping cord 1. Bring the end of cord 2 under the loop apex and over cord 1 to

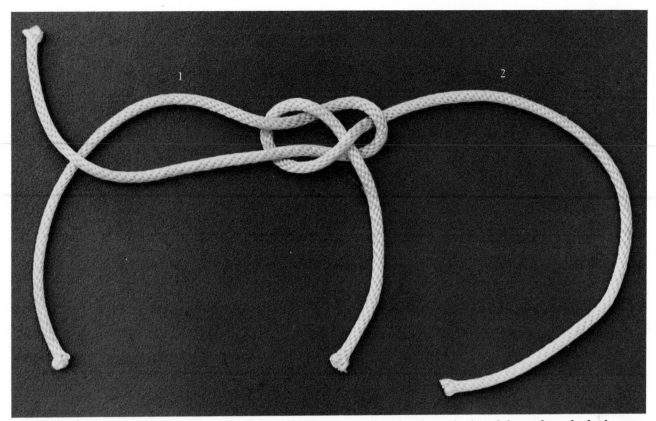

Weaver's Knot: Step 1. To make the knot, form a loop with cord 1. Take the end of cord 2 up through the loop to the left, down under the two parts of cord 1, over the top section of cord 1, under 2, and over the bottom section of 1.

Step 2. Pull the knot tight.

the right. Then take cord 2 to the left under two parts of cord 1 that form the loop, then to the right over the first part of cord 1, and down under the loop apex.

Ghiordes (yor-dēz) Knot. The ghiordes knot is the main knot used in weaving pile rugs and is frequently used for adding fringe in all weaving-related techniques. The photograph shows the knot, a simple loop, done with one strand between two warp threads. The knot must be pulled tight and held in place by means of weaving or knotting. Frequently the loop is composed of many strands.

To tie the knot in its simplest form, loop one strand (cord 1) around two holding strands (cords 2 and 3). Beginning on the left take the end of cord 1 to the right over cord 2, then above to the left under cord 2, over cords 2 and 3 to the right,

then down under cord 3 to the left, and back over cord 3 to the right.

The textured pile areas in loom-woven tapestries are often made up of rows of ghiordes knots held in place by rows of tabby weave. The ghiordes knot allows fibers to be securely attached, while also allowing them to maintain their natural flow and character, creating a dense surface texture.

Lark's Head Knot. The lark's head knot is frequently used as a means of mounting paired sets of cords on another cord or element, usually in preparation for working. It is also a good knot for adding and arranging paired threads, whether for knotting, fringe, or other non-loom fiber techniques. The lark's head is always knotted around something: bar, warp thread, weft thread, or holding cord.

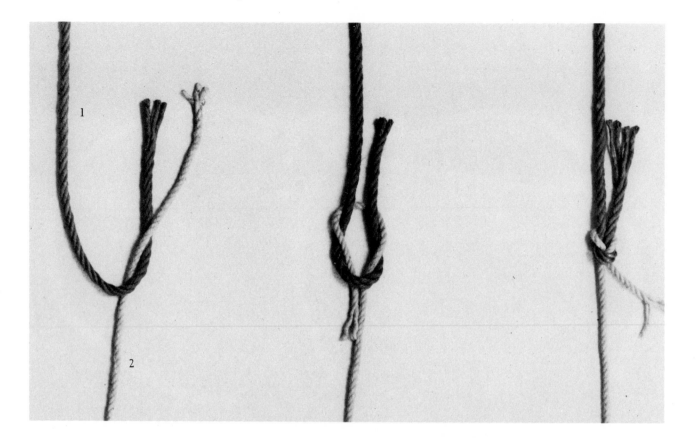

Weaver's Square Knot (Above). Begin the knot by looping cord 1. Bring the end of 2 up through the loop and over to the right. Take cord 2 to the left under the two sections of cord 1, then back down through the loop. Pull the knot tight.

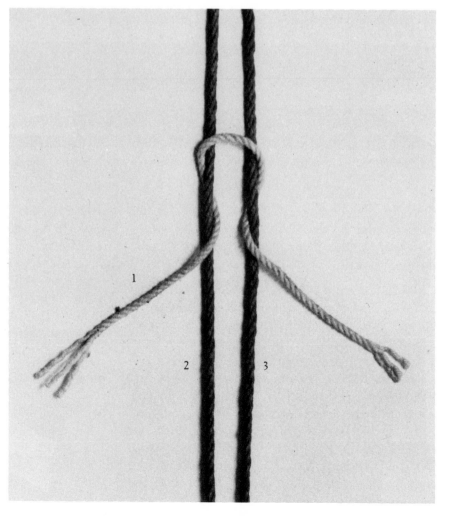

Ghiordes (yor-dez) Knot. Beginning on the left, take cord 1 to the right over cord 2, to the left under 2, over 2 and 3 to the right, then under 3 to the left and back over 3 to the right.

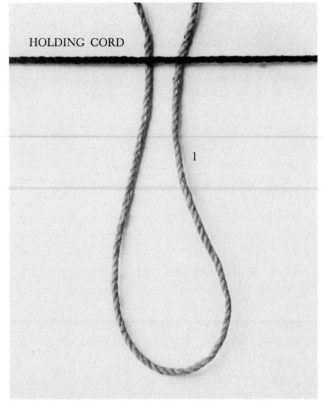

Lark's Head Knot: Step 1. The holding cord is passive. Loop cord 1 in half and bring the loop down under the holding cord.

Step 2. Bring the ends of cord 1 down over the holding cord and under cord 1 at the loop apex.

Step 3. Pull the ends of cord 1 to tighten the knot.

Figure 9. The lark's head knot can be done continuously around a core to form a decorative knot.

To make the lark's head, one cord is doubled to make a pair of cords. Loop the cord to be knotted (cord 1) in half and bring the loop down under the holding cord. Then bring the two ends of cord 1 down over the holding cord and under the loop. Pull the two ends of cord 1 and slip the loop up to tighten the knot. If a number of strands are desired as vertical elements, many pairs can be arranged on the same holding cord. Although it frequently acts as a practical beginning, the lark's head knot is also used as a decorative interlinking knot. In Figure 9, lark's head knots are knotted vertically around two central cords. One cord on each side works alternately, producing directional loops. A whole series of vertical elements could be interlinked by using many cords and alternating central cores.

Half Knot. The half knot worked around a central core is frequently found in decorative rope work. It forms the first half of the square knot and when worked in a series forms a spiraling braid. To begin a half knot arrange two cords on a holding cord using the lark's head knot to make four working cords. Cords 1 and 4 will knot around cords 2 and 3, which remain passive. Take cord 1 over cords 2 and 3 and under cord 4. Now take cord 4 to the left under cords 2 and 3, up between cords 1 and 2, and over cord 1. Pull the ends of cords 1 and 4 to tighten the knot around cords 2 and 3. Continue the braid by repeating the knot. As knotting continues the braid will spiral counterclockwise. If the movements of cords 1 and 4 are reversed the braid will spiral the opposite direction. If cords 1 and 4 are different colors, horizontal bars of alternating color will appear on the braid surface.

Square Knot. Like the half knot, the square knot also involves four cords with the two outer cords knotting around the two inner passive cords. The square knot shown here is a decorative knot sometimes referred to as a Solomon Knot. To make the square knot, arrange two cords on a holding cord (using the lark's head knot) so there are four working cords. The first part of the square knot is the half knot: take cord 1 over cords 2 and 3 and under cord 4, then bring cord 4 under cords 2 and 3 and up between cords 1 and 2 and over cord 1.

Begin the second part of the square knot by bringing cord 1 (now on the left) over cords 2 and 3 and under cord 4. Now take cord 4 to the right under cords 2 and 3, and up between cords 3 and 1, and over cord 1. Pull cords 2 and 3 to tighten

and adjust the knot around the passive cords. At the completion of the knot, cords 1 and 4 are back in their original positions. Continue square knotting in the same manner to form a flat braid. If cord 1 is black and cord 4 white the knot will form to make the top surface predominantly white. The right and left sides of the square knots have a different appearance because of the way the cords go over and under. This can be reversed by beginning the knot with the right-hand cord and reversing the movements; begin by taking cord 4 over cords 3 and 2 and under cord 1.

The square knot is frequently used in this manner to construct a wide, knotted fabric. The fabric is worked in groups of four cords; the knotting cords alternate from one row to the next so that on the first row cords 1 and 4 square knot around cords 2 and 3, and on the second row cords 3 and 6 square knot around cords 4 and 5. In this way active and passive cords continually interchange to form a fabric.

Half-Hitch and Double Half-Hitch. The double half-hitch, sometimes called the clove hitch, is the knot most frequently used in contemporary fiber sculpture. It can be worked vertically, horizontally, and diagonally. The knot is always worked around something (usually another cord) that acts as a holding cord or stuffing. The double half-hitch is a form of wrapping or binding, and the half-hitch is the basic part of the knot. A double half-hitch is composed of two half-hitches worked with the same cord. To make a half-hitch, take the end of cord 1 to the right over cords 2, 3, and 4, then around and under cords 4, 3, and 2, bringing the end up between cords 1 and 2 and over cord 1. Tighten cord 1 so it encircles and binds the other three cords.

For the double half-hitch, simply make the described movement twice. If the knot is repeated over and over again with the same cord it will spiral around the cord it is binding. Figure 10 shows a series of double half-hitches worked alternately by cords 1 and 4 in vertical progression around cords 2 and 3. The knots are left loose to show the loop structure. If all the knots were pulled tight and worked close together, they would form a tight, dense binding encasing the central core. This arrangement of double half-hitches produces a flat braid. If cords 1 and 4 are different colors they will show in alternating pairs in the braid.

The next series of photographs illustrates how the double half-hitch is worked horizontally using

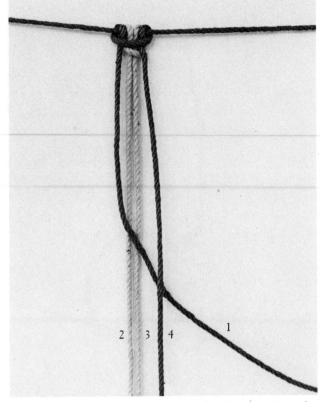

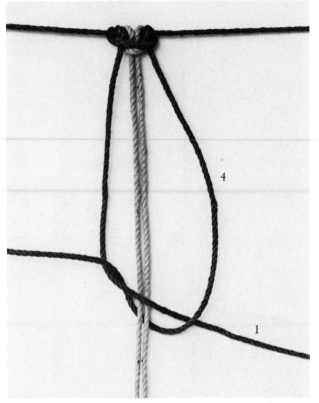

Half Knot: Step 1. Arrange two cords of contrasting color on a holding cord, using the lark's head knot. There are now four numbered cords. Take cord 1 over 2 and 3 and under 4.

Step 2. Take cord 4 to the left under 2 and 3, up between 1 and 2, and over cord 1.

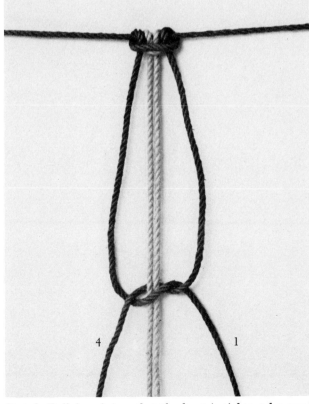

Step 3. Pull 1 and 4 so that the knot is tightened around cords 2 and 3.

Step 4. Continue to form half knots and they will spiral around the inner cords.

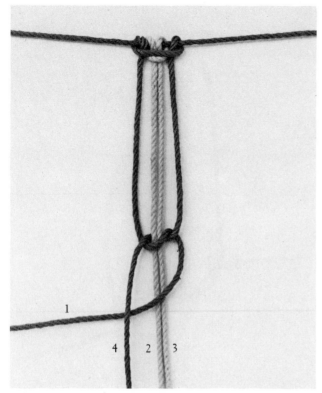

Square Knot: Step 1. The first part of the square knot is one half knot (repeat Steps 1, 2, and 3 of the half knot). Begin the second part of the square knot by bringing cord 1 over cords 2 and 3 and under cord 4.

Step 2. Take cord 4 to the right under cords 2 and 3, and up through the right-hand loop.

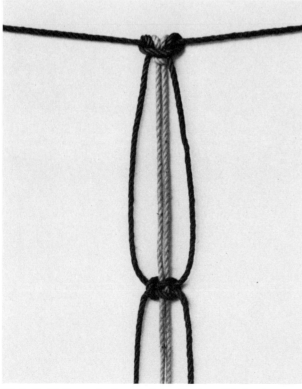

Step 3. Pull cords 1 and 4 to tighten the knot around cords 2 and 3.

Step 4. Continue to square knot by repeating Steps 1–3.

Half-Hitch: Step 1. Arrange the cords as for the half knot. Take cord 1 to the right, over cords 2, 3, and 4, then around to the left under 4, 3, and 2, then over itself and down.

Step 2. Pull cord 1 to tighten the knot.

Figure 10. Two half-hitches worked with the same cord to make a pair form a double half-hitch. The photograph shows a series of double half-hitches worked from both sides, knotting around the same central core.

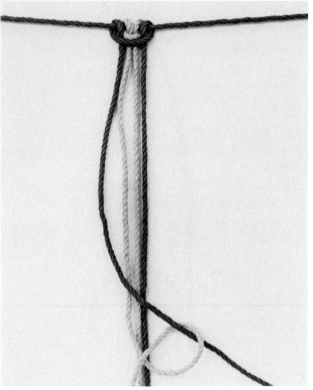

Double Half-Hitch: Step 1. This series illustrates the half-hitch worked horizontally in pairs. Cord 1, which will become a holding cord, goes across the top of 2, 3, and 4 to the right.

Step 2. Cord 2 half-hitches around cord 1 by going over the top and back under to the left.

Step 3. Step 2 is repeated with the same cord so there is a double half-hitch.

Step 4. The knot is pulled tight by pulling cord 2. Now double half-hitch cord 3 around cord 1 just as with cord 2. Then double half-hitch cord 4. There will be a row of horizontal double half-hitches.

four cords. Cord 1 becomes a holding cord: the passive element or core around which the other cords will, one at a time, make a double half-hitch. Draw cord 1 over the top of the other cords. Make a half-hitch around cord 1 with cord 2 by going over the top and under to the left. This knot is repeated with the same cord so that there is a double half-hitch. Continue knotting to make a row of horizontal double half-hitches by double half-hitching cord 3 around cord 1, and then double half-hitching cord 4 around cord 1. The passive element, which in this case is cord 1, can be angled or curved to direct the double half-hitches.

Chinese Crown Knot. The Chinese crown knot is a tight, square-shaped knot worked with two elements. If two different colors are used the color will alternate as small boxes within the knot. The Chinese crown knot is a flat knot which is particularly interesting if many strands make up each of the two elements. This produces an arrangement of alternating groups of horizontals and verticals. In the demonstration, the knot is worked with two elements, each composed of two strands. Push cord 1 into place, so there is a bulge at the top that goes to the right, and then a second bulge that goes to the left. Thread cord 2 through the bulges made by cord 1. To do this take cord 2 under A, over B and C, and back under C, B, and A, so the end comes up between cords 1 and 2. Then take the end of cord 2 to the left over A and B and under C. Tighten the knot by pulling cords 1 and 2. Cord 1 in the finished knot appears horizontally and cord 2 vertically in alternate order. Notice that cords 1 and 2 have reversed positions, and if the knot is repeated the color position will be just the opposite of the arrangement in the preceding knot.

Josephine Knot. The Josephine knot is a decorative knot with flowing lines. Like the Chinese crown knot it is flat, and the pattern shows best when a number of strands are worked as one. The knot is worked with two elements. In the photographs each element is composed of two strands.

Begin the knot by looping cord 1 to the right, bringing the end back and under itself. Now bring cord 2 to the left by going over the loop formed by cord 1 and under cord 1 below the loop. Loop cord 2 and weave it to the right by taking the end over cord 1 above the loop, then under the first part of the loop (A), over cord 2, and under the second part of the loop (B). The Josephine knot is pulled into a snug, flat knot by pulling cords 1 and 2 and working the loops into place. Figure 11 shows two ways of working a series of Josephine knots. Four strands of waxed linen make up each element. When the knot is repeated in a series, the two elements can function in the same positions over and over. There is a tendency in A for the entire band to spiral. The alternating elements in B counteract this tendency, and the band lies flat.

Monkey's Fist. This is a dimensional knot producing a tight, round ball. The size is controlled by the thickness of the cord, how many loops are made, and by the size of the object or stuffing that the knot is worked around. It need not be worked around an object, but to make it tight and compact some kind of round solid form should form the center. The knot is worked with one element. The ends can be tucked inside or left free. The monkey's fist is sometimes worked as an ending knot to give weight and solidity to fringes and ends. To make a monkey's fist, take the cord and form a series of loops. The loops can be controlled by winding them to the right around two fingers, going over the top and around to the bottom (the demonstration shows four complete loops). Then take the end on the right behind the loops toward the left. The end that went under the loops toward the left now goes completely around the loops at the center (four times) with the last circle ending by going through the top of the original loops toward the left. The same end now goes around and through the bottom and top of the original loops. (In the demonstration it loops once, but to balance the knot it should circle three more times.) The loops are made as three separate groupings. Each series may be made up of any number of loops, but if each group has the same number of loops the knot will be symmetrical. The completed knot shows the loops pulled to form a ball. The last looping was done once, the first two four times each.

Crown Knot. The crown knot is a useful foundation knot. It is used in preparation for a back splice, where the ends are woven or worked back into the cord. It is also used as a basis or foundation for other knots. Three elements are used for the crown knot demonstrated, but the same kind of knot can be done with more elements. To make the crown knot take cord 1 to the right under cord 2 and over cord 3. Then take cord 3 over cord 2 to the left and through the loop formed by cord 1.

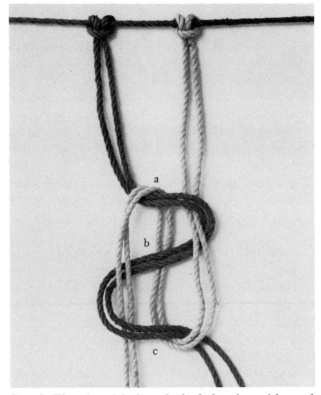

Chinese Crown Knot: Step 1. Arrange two cords of contrasting color on a holding cord. The knot is worked with two elements. Push cord 1 into position as shown with a bulge to the right and one to the left.

Step 2. Thread cord 2 through the bulges formed by cord 1: under a and over b and c, then back up under c, b, and under a so the end comes up between 1 and 2. Then take cord 2 to the left over a and b and under c.

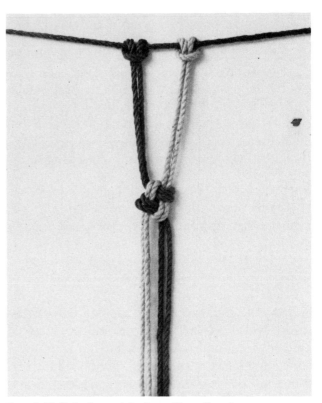

Step 3. Pull the knot tight by pulling all ends.

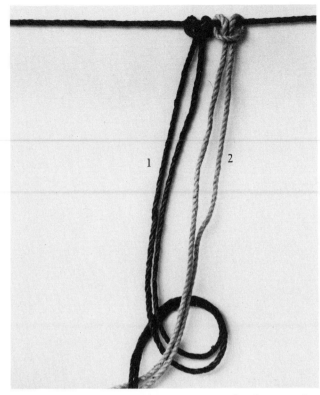

Josephine Knot: Step 1. Arrange two cords of contrasting color on a holding cord. The knot is worked with two elements. Loop cord 1 to the right, bringing the end back and under itself as illustrated. Bring cord 2 over the loop and under cord 1 to the left below the loop.

Step 2. Loop cord 2 back over 1, under a, over 2 and under b.

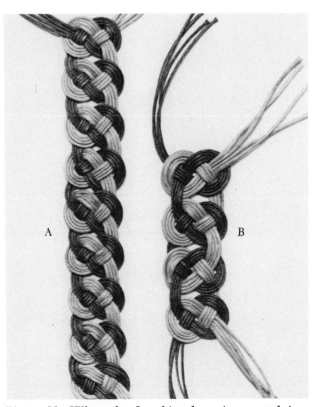

Step 3. Pull all ends to make the knot tight and flat.

Figure 11. When the Josephine knot is repeated in a series, the cords can function in the same positions over and over as in A, or they can alternate positions as in B.

Monkey's Fist: Step 1. The knot is made using one element. Take the cord and form a series of loops (four complete loops are shown). The loops can be controlled by winding them to the right around two fingers, going over the top and around to the bottom four times. Then take the end on the right behind the loops toward the left as shown.

Step 2. The end that went under toward the left now goes completely around the loops at the center four times, with the last circle ending by going through the top of the original loops toward the left.

Step 3. The same end goes around and through the bottom and top of the original loops. The knot can end here, or Step 3 can be repeated three times to form a balanced knot.

Step 4. Pull the knot tight by working all the loops into a tight ball.

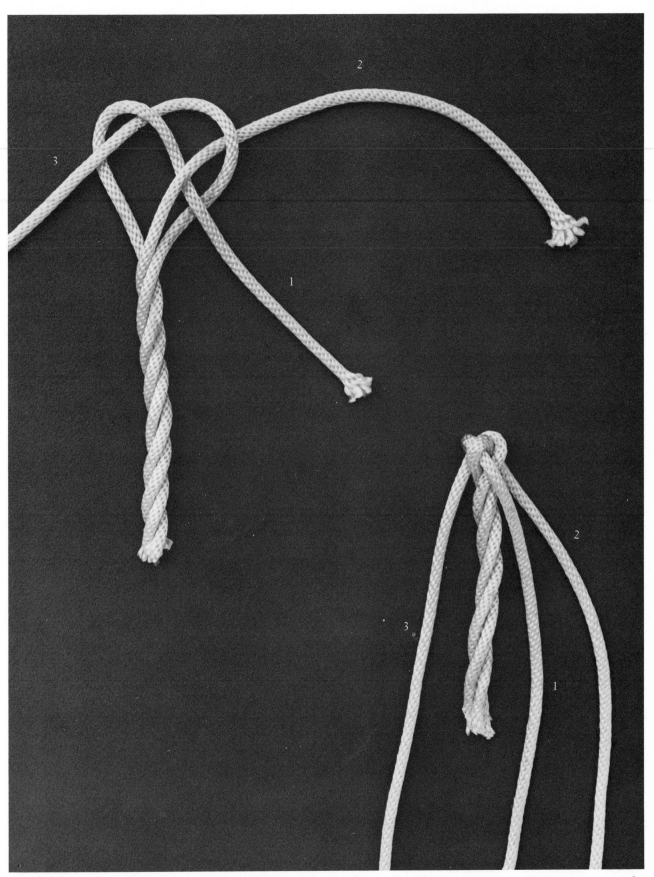

Crown Knot. Three elements are used for this knot, but the same kind of knot can be done with four or more cords. Cord 1 goes to the right under 2 and over 3. Cord 3 then goes over 2 to the left and through the loop formed by 1, going first under then over. Pull the three cords to tighten the knot.

FINGER KNOTTING

This knot is done around the forefinger and second finger, with one element continually looping around and over to form a tight square braid. The same knotted braid can also be worked on a two-pronged fork, referred to in different parts of the world as a chain fork, a hay fork, a lucet, and a snoddgoffel. The knotting can be rough on the fingers if a coarse cord is used. The flexibility of the fingers is very helpful in the knotting process, since the tension on individual parts of the loops must be constantly adjusted to pull the knots tight. One cord or element is used for this knot. The first end of the cord remains dormant and is held between the thumb and palm of the hand. Wind the cord around the forefinger by bringing it first between the forefinger and the second finger. Then take the cord behind the second finger and back to the palm side of the hand. Now take the cord under and around the forefinger, drawing it to the right. Take the bottom loop on the left side of the forefinger over the top loop and pull the loops to tighten and adjust the knot. Now take the cord back between the forefinger and the second finger, and around the second finger to the palm side of the hand, and then draw it to the left. Now take the bottom loop on the right side of the second finger, over the top loop on the same finger, and again pull the loops so that the knot tightens. Continue looping and shifting the previous loop over, first on one finger, and then on the next.

Finger Knotting with One Loop. Finger knotting with one loop is very easily worked using the thumb and forefinger. The loops are worked on the forefinger, and the thumb is used for tension. This form of finger knotting produces a triangular braid. The knotting process and the resulting braid is shown in Figure 12 without the use of fingers. Begin by tying a slip knot in the center of a cord. To do this, loop the cord so that both sides are equal and number them 1 and 2. Bring cord 1 over cord 2 so the loop at the top is maintained. Take cord 1 around behind the loop, then over 1 to the right, and immediately under 1 so cords 1 and 2 dangle parallel in their original positions. Now begin the knotting sequence by taking cord 1 to the right behind cord 2. Form cord 1 into a loop and insert it into the original loop. Pull the original loop tight by pulling cord 2 and adjust the new loop by pulling cord 1. Repeat the step using cord 2. Continue knotting using alternate strands to form the triangular braid.

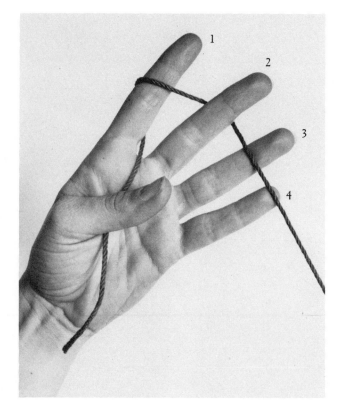

Finger Knotting: Step 1. One cord or element is used for this knot. The first end of the cord remains dormant and is held between the thumb and palm of the hand. Wind the cord around finger 1 by first bringing it between fingers 1 and 2. Then take the cord behind finger 2 and over fingers 3 and 4.

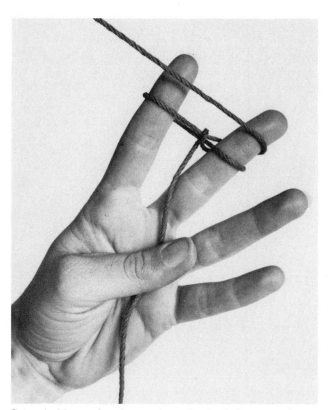

Step 4. Now take the cord to the back between fingers 1 and 2 and around finger 2. Pull the cord to the left.

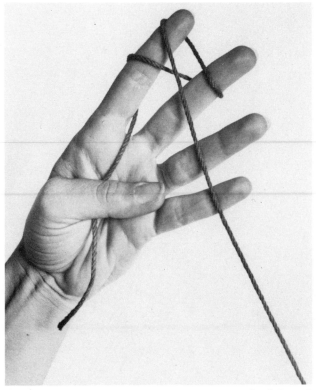

Step 2. The cord now goes over finger 2 to the left and under finger 1 and is brought to the palm side of the hand and drawn to the right.

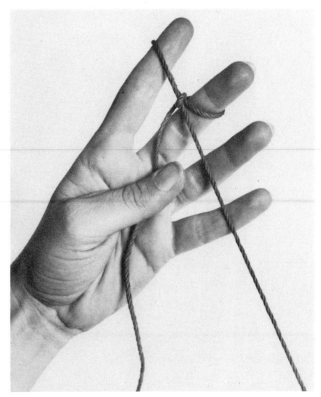

Step 3. Take the bottom loop on the left side of finger 1 over the top loop and pull to tighten.

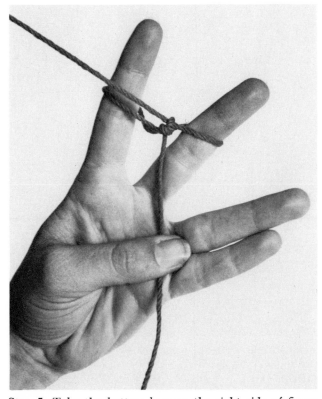

Step 5. Take the bottom loop on the right side of finger 2 over the top loop on the same finger and pull to tighten.

Step 6. Continue repeating Steps 2 through 5 to form a series of knots making a square braid.

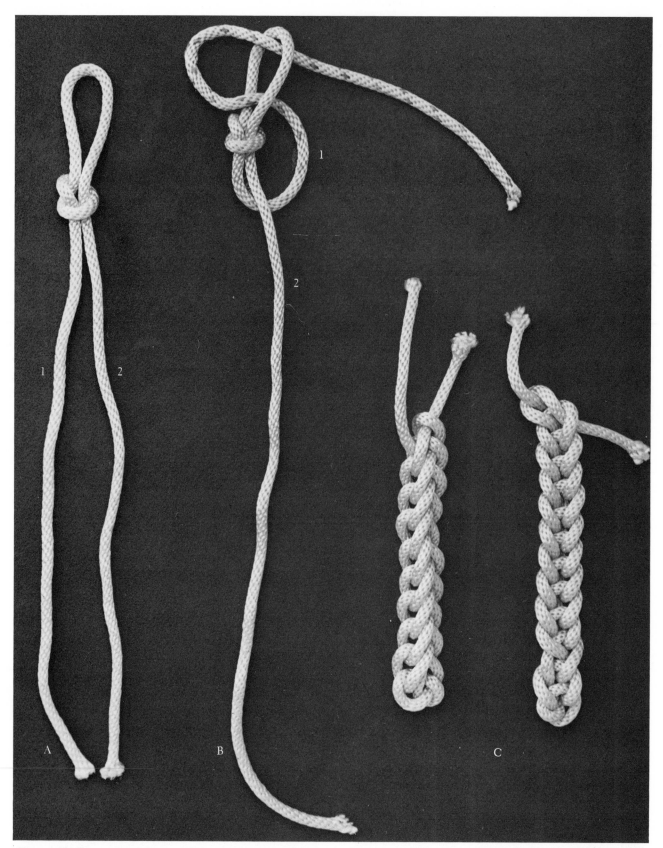

Figure 12. Finger knotting includes a variation using just one loop. Begin by tying a slip knot in the center of the cord (A). To do this, loop the cord so that both sides are equal and number them 1 and 2. Bring cord 1 over cord 2 so that the loop at the top is maintained. Take cord 1 around behind the loop then over 1 to the right and immediately under 1 so that 1 and 2 dangle parallel in their original positions. Take cord 1 to the right behind cord 2 (B). Form 1 into a loop and insert it into the original loop. Pull the original loop tight by pulling cord 2. Then adjust the second loop by pulling 1. Repeat the step using cord 2. Continue knotting using alternate strands to form a triangular braid.

Whaler's Whisk (Above). Sisal, 8″ high. This recently-woven traditional whisk uses a knot based on the crown knot. Black cord wraps around the neck to hold the fibers tight. Courtesy of the Museum Shop, San Francisco, California. Photo by David Donoho.

Les Noces by Gabriele Schmidt. Seine twine, 86″ x 42″ x 8″. This piece is mainly worked in double half-hitches with some half knots and reversed lark's heads.

Dearly Beloved We Are Gathered Together (Left) by Robert J. Mills, 1973. Polypropylene fibers, 84″ high. This fiber sculpture uses a mixture of wrapping and knotted half-hitches. Photo by Sharyn Amii Mills.

Knotted Basket (Above) by Ferne Jacobs. Natural linen and wool, 6¾″ x 5½″. This basket with an egg form uses horizontal half-hitches. Courtesy of the Museum of Contemporary Crafts, New York. Photo by Bob Hanson.

Chinese Braid by Mary Anderson, 40″ x 15″. As the braid progresses, strands gradually move from one side to the other. Photo by Gary McNair.

CHAPTER SEVEN

BRAIDING AND PLAITING

The words braiding and plaiting have so often been used to describe identical techniques that they have become synonymous; they are used interchangeably in this text. "Braid" is also frequently used to mean narrow band, therefore a row of knots or a narrow weaving is legitimately called a braid. In braiding, cords or single elements interlace obliquely to form a structure. The elements of a braid work over and under in much the same way as warp and weft threads, except that in braiding the warp and weft threads are not differentiated (warp threads cross over and become temporary weft threads). The braided structure is distinguished by oblique crossings of the cords and a distinctly diagonal trend. Simply speaking, braiding is a process of taking each element under or over other elements that cross its path, usually in a systematic way. There is no looping, wrapping, or knotting, but a diagonal under-over progression that does not employ a separate weft thread.

The three-strand braid is very widely known because of its constant use. An understanding of the three-strand braid will help you to work braids that require four or more elements. Variations of the three-strand braid can be worked simply by increasing the number of elements, and by altering the order of the over-under sequences. The concept of braiding will become clearer as the chapter describes braids that require many elements. The first group of braids described relate very closely to the three-strand braid. The second group are woven braids, which are flat and often used as sashes. They closely resemble weaving, as the strands move across in an over-under progression. They are braided, however, not woven, since the

warp and weft threads interchange and move on the diagonal.

Sprang netting, frequently referred to as plaiting or twining, is also considered a braid technique. In its simplest form, each element interlinks obliquely with the adjoining element. The cords are worked back and forth by fingers and dowels, and no weft is involved. In the more complicated forms of sprang, elements move diagonally from one edge to the other, a distinct characteristic of braiding.

Frame braiding is similar to sprang in that it is usually worked with the aid of sticks on a continuous warp. It is worked from alternate sides and the strands interlace, but do not interlink, moving diagonally in a twill progression from one side to the other. Twisted braiding is a process in which cords in paired groups are laid across one another so that a twisted or linked fabric is constructed. Twisted braiding is similar in structure to bobbin lace. In bobbin lace, the long cords or elements are wrapped around bobbins that act as weights and make the threads easier to handle. The bobbins are moved over and under, usually in pairs, to form an interlinking structure. There are many kinds and types of braiding but the ones discussed and shown here are representative.

MATERIALS

Any material that is flexible can be braided, and cord or yarn is all that is required to do most of the braids described. With the exception of the frame braiding employing the Hopi wedding sash technique, all the demonstrations in this chapter were worked in a medium-weight plied cotton seine twine, usually in red and yellow. Fingers are the

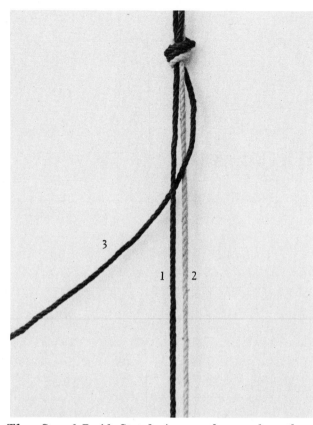

Three-Strand Braid: Step 1. Arrange three cords so there is a dark cord on each side and a light cord in the center. Take cord 3 over 2 and under 1.

Step 2. Bring cord 2 over 1 and under 3.

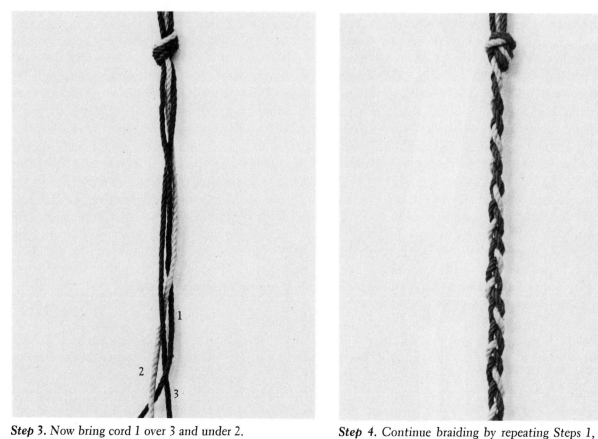

Step 3. Now bring cord 1 over 3 and under 2.

Step 4. Continue braiding by repeating Steps 1, 2, and 3.

main tools used in braiding, but sometimes bobbins (turned wood cylinders, dowels, or nuts and bolts) are used to wind strands onto and to add weight. A Celotex board and T-pins are useful in holding cords and ends. A frame with adjustable tension and dowels is used for sprang and loom braiding, and instructions for building one are given later in the chapter.

Three-Strand Braid. The three-strand braid is a simple braid, but a close examination of how it works will allow you to see the basic formula of braiding in a minimal structure. Look at a simple three-strand braid and note carefully how the strands are woven across in an over-under progression. Even simple braids can be combined in various ways to make attractive wall hangings. The materials used can also make a difference in the final effect of your work.

Begin by arranging three cords so there is a dark cord on each side and a light cord in the center. Take cord 3 over cord 2 and under cord 1. Cord 2 is now on the left. Take it over cord 1 and under cord 3, leaving cord 1 on the left. Take it over cord 3 and under cord 1. The cords are now back in their original positions and the sequence is repeated to continue the braid. Each step is exactly the same movement, the cord on the right goes over one, then under one to the left.

The same braid can be made by reversing the movement; take the left cord over one and under one to the right. Another way to make the same braid is to take the far left cord over one to the right and then the far right cord over one to the left. The braid is continued by alternating from one side to the other. Even in the simplest braids there are many ways to arrive at the same structure.

Four-Strand Braid. The four-strand braid is a very useful and attractive round braid, frequently used for fringes and straps of all kinds. Mixed colors tend to give it a symmetrical, controlled appearance. The size of the braid is increased by using many cords as one element.

To begin, arrange four cords so there are two dark cords in the center and a light cord on each side. Take cord 4 under cords 3 and 2 and then back over cord 2 to the right. Now take cord 1 under cords 2 and 4 and back over cord 4 to the left. Two movements have been completed, the first with cord 4 on the left, the second with cord 1 on the right. Braiding continues by alternating between these two movements. In the next movement, take

the cord on the right under two cords and back over one cord to the right. The next movement takes the cord on the left under two and back over one to the left.

The original color arrangement of the four cords affects the final appearance. In Figure 13 the color arrangement of braid A is dark, light, light, dark, and in braid B the color arrangement is light, light, dark, dark. It is possible to rearrange the colors on a partially completed braid to change the surface appearance.

Six-Strand Round Braid. The six-strand round braid is worked in a manner very similar to the four-strand round braid. You simply add one step in each movement in order to deal with the increased number of cords. Begin the sampler by arranging six cords so there are three light cords on the left and three dark cords on the right. Take cord 1 under four cords (2, 3, 4, 5) to the right, then back to the left over one cord (5) and under one cord (4). For the second movement, take cord 6 to the left under four cords (5, 4, 1, and 3) back over one cord (3) and under one cord (1). Continue braiding by alternating between these two movements. Step 3 shows the braid after six movements. The two movements are the same, but reversed. First the cord on one side goes under four and comes back over one and under one, then the movement is repeated by the cord on the other side. Figure 14 show two examples of the same braid with different color arrangements. Braid A began with alternating light and dark cords. Braid B began with three light cords on the left and three dark cords on the right. The appearance of the six-strand round braid is similar to the four-strand round braid, except there are six sides rather than four. The size of the braid can be increased by using heavier cords or by treating many cords as one element.

Six-Strand Flat Braid. In the six-strand braid the cords that move do not double back on themselves, as in the two previous braids. In braiding the six-strand flat braid you alternate between two different movements worked on alternating sides. To begin the braid arrange six cords so there are three dark cords on the left and three light cords on the right. Begin by taking the cord on the left (1) over the second cord (2) and under the third cord (3). Now bring the cord on the right under the next cord (5) and over the following two cords (4 and 1). Continue braiding by alternating between these

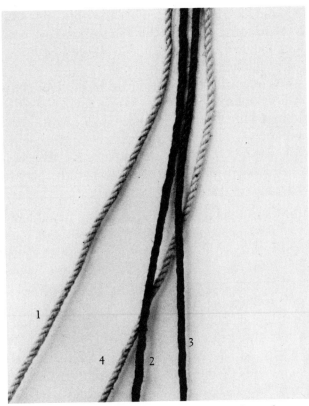

Four-Strand Braid: Step 1. Arrange four cords so there are two dark cords in the center and one light cord on each side. Take cord 4 under cords 3 and 2.

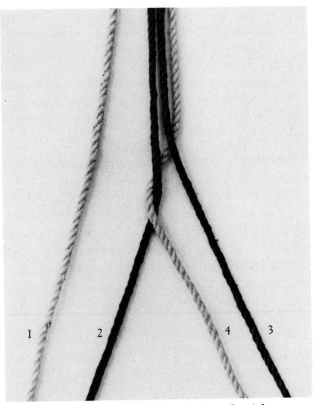

Step 2. Bring cord 4 back over cord 2 to the right.

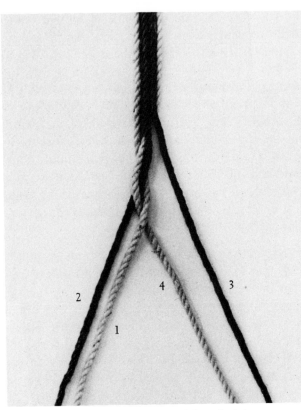

Step 4. Bring cord 1 back over cord 4 to the left.

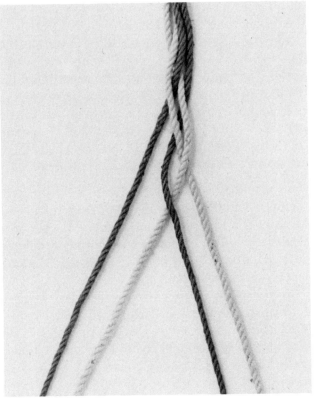

Step 5. Repeat Steps 1 and 2 by taking the right cord under two cords to the left and back over one cord to the right.

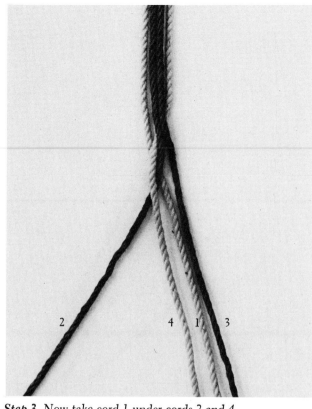

Step 3. Now take cord 1 under cords 2 and 4.

Step 6. Repeat Steps 3 and 4 by taking the left cord under two cords to the right and back over one cord to the left.

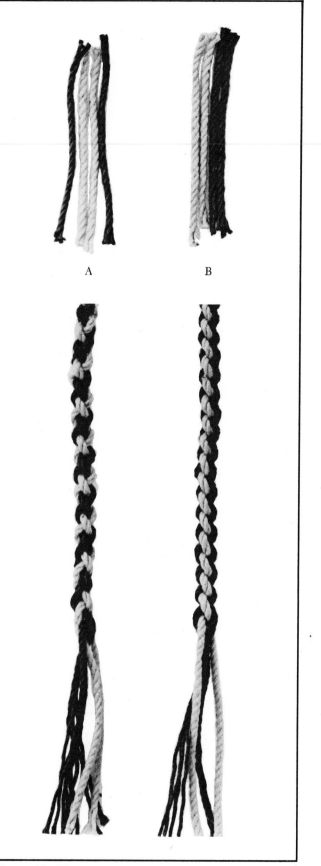

Figure 13. The original color arrangement of the four cords affects the final appearance. In braid A the color arrangement is dark, light, light, dark. In braid B the color arrangement is light, light, dark, dark.

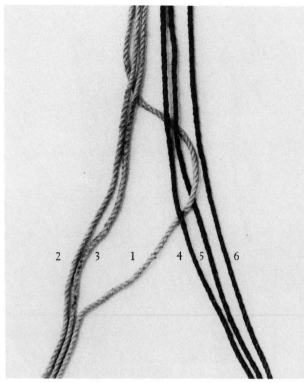

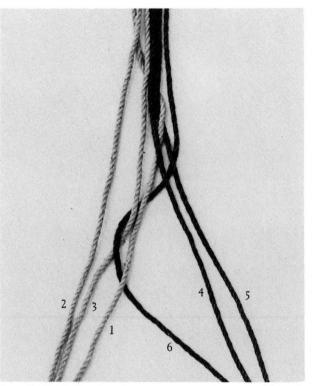

Six-Strand Round Braid: Step 1. Arrange six cords so there are three light cords on the left and three dark cords on the right. Take cord 1 under four cords to the right (2, 3, 4, 5) then back to the left over one cord (5) and under one cord (4).

Step 2. Cord 6 makes the same movement as cord 1, only to the left. To do this, take cord 6 under 5, 4, 1, and 3, back over cord 3 and under cord 1.

Step 3. Continue braiding by alternating between Steps 1 and 2. The braid is shown as it appears after six movements.

Figure 14. Two examples of the same braid with different color arrangements. In braid A the arrangement alternates between light and dark. In braid B the arrangement is equally divided with three light cords on the left and three dark cords on the right.

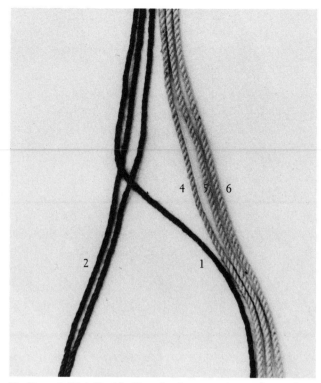

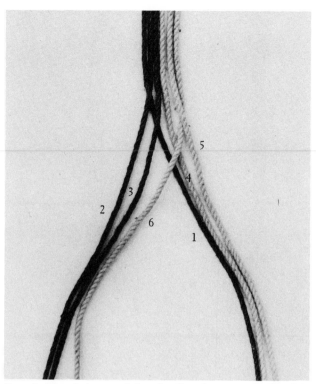

Six-Strand Flat Braid: Step 1. Arrange six cords so there are three dark cords on the left and three light cords on the right. Take cord 1 over 2 and under 3.

Step 2. Now bring cord 6 under 5 and over cords 4 and 1.

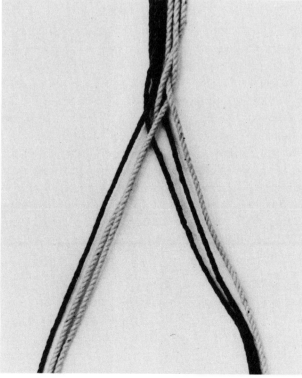

Step 3. Continue braiding by alternating between Steps 1 and 2. The braid is shown as it appears after four movements.

Step 4. The braid after eight movements.

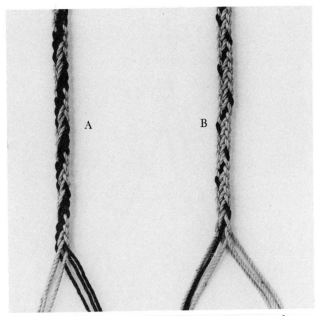

Figure 15. The same braid with two different color arrangements. In braid A the arrangement is equally divided with three light cords on the left and three dark cords on the right. In braid B there are five yellow cords and one red cord. Since the strands move from one side to the other the placement of the single red cord is not important.

two movements. The braid is shown as it appears after six movements and after eight movements. Figure 15 shows the same braid with two different color arrangements. In braid A the original arrangement of colors is equally divided, with three light cords on the left and three dark cords on the right. In braid B there are five yellow cords and one red cord. Since the cords move during braiding from one side to the other and back, the placement of the single red cord is not important.

Seven-Strand Braid. The seven-strand braid is worked to make a flat braid that is concave on one side and convex on the other. There are two movements. The first movement is done with the far right cord, the second with the far left cord. The two movements are different and the braid progresses by alternating between them.

Arrange seven cords so there are five light cords on the left and two dark cords on the right. Take the cord on the left (1) under two cords (2 and 3), and then over two cords (4 and 5). To make the second movement take the far right cord (7) over two cords (6 and 1). Continue braiding by alternating between these two movements. The braid is shown as it appears after six movements. The two braids in Figure 16 show the alternate sides of the seven-strand braid in two different color ar-

rangements. Braid A began with five light cords on the right and two dark cords on the left. In braid B there were four dark cords and three light cords arranged alternately.

Eight-Strand Square Braid. The eight-strand square braid is closely related to the four- and six-strand round braids. The same movement is repeated alternately on each side, and the moving strands double back on themselves.

To begin arrange eight cords so there are four light cords on the left and four dark cords on the right. Begin by taking the cord on the right under five cords to the left and then back to the right over two cords. The same movement is made on the opposite side by taking the far left cord under five cords to the right and then back to the left over two cords. Continue braiding by alternating between the two movements. The braid is shown as it appears after four movements and after eight movements. The eight-strand square braid is shown in Figure 17 in two different color arrangements. In braid A the light and dark cords alternate. In braid B there are four light cords on the left and four dark cords on the right. In each case the braid is a tight square, with two cords showing on each face.

Twelve-Strand Braid. The two movements of the eight-strand braid can be used in working with greater numbers of strands as long as the number is even. The number of cords that the right-hand cord and then the left-hand cord go under and over increases proportionately. The braid can also be worked around a center core. Twelve cords are braided around a central core as follows: take the cord on the left to the right under eight cords and the rope, and then back to the left over three cords and the rope. Then take the cord on the right to the left under eight cords and the rope, then back to the right over three cords and the rope. Continue braiding by alternating between these two movements.

Eight-Strand Chinese Braid. The eight-strand Chinese braid is a loose braid that requires laying one cord at a time—from alternating sides—over a certain number of other cords. Arrange eight cords so that there are three dark cords, two light cords, and then three dark cords. Take the cord on the left over three cords to the right, and then bring the cord on the right over four cords to the left. Repeat the same two movements to continue the braid. Figure 18 shows the completed braid.

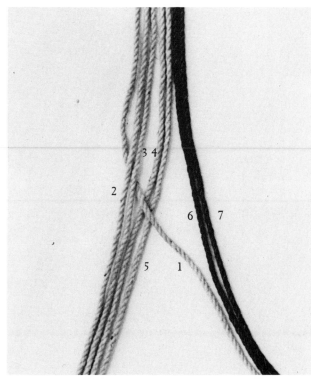

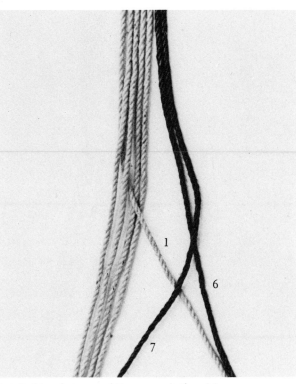

Seven-Strand Braid: Step 1. Arrange seven cords so there are five light cords on the left and two dark cords on the right. Take cord 1 under cords 2 and 3, then over cords 4 and 5.

Step 2. Now bring cord 7 over cords 6 and 1.

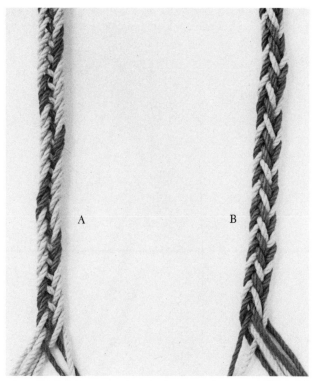

Step 3. Continue braiding by alternating between Steps 1 and 2. The braid is shown as it appears after six movements.

Figure 16. The same braid showing alternate sides with two different color arrangements. In braid A there were five light cords on the right and two dark cords on the left. In braid B there were four dark cords and three light cords arranged alternately.

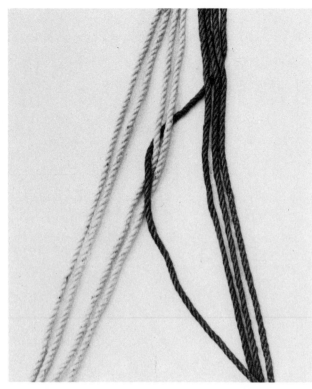

Eight-Strand Square Braid: Step 1. Arrange eight cords so there are four light cords on the left and four dark cords on the right. Begin by taking the cord on the right under five cords to the left and then back to the right over two.

Step 2. Repeat the movement on the opposite side by taking the cord on the left under five cords to the right and then back to the left over two.

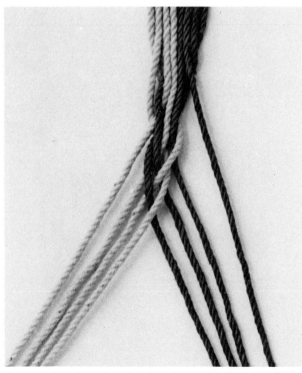

Step 3. Continue braiding by alternating between Steps 1 and 2. The braid is shown as it appears after four movements.

Step 4. The braid after eight movements.

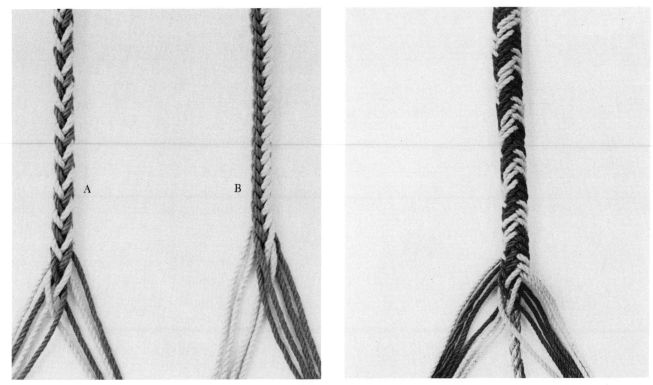

Figure 17. The same braid with two different color arrangements. In braid A light and dark cords alternate. In braid B there were four light cords on the left and four dark cords on the right.

Twelve-Strand Braid. Take the cord on the left to the right under 8 cords and the rope, and then back to the left over three cords and the rope. Next take the cord on the right to the left under eight cords and the rope and then back to the right over three cords and the rope. Repeat these two movements to continue the braid.

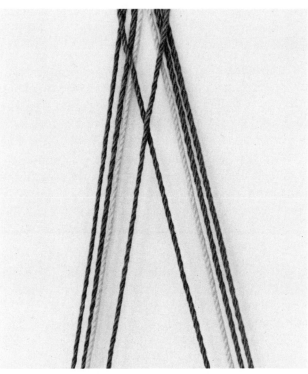

Eight-Strand Chinese Braid: Step 1. Arrange eight cords so there are three dark cords, two light cords, and three dark cords. Take the cord on the left over three cords to the right and then bring the cord on the right over four cords to the left.

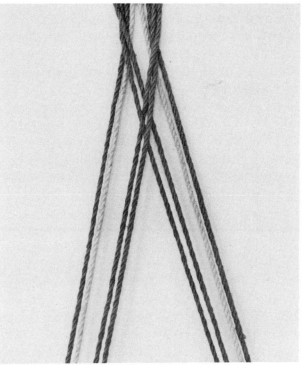

Step 2. Repeat Step 1 by taking the left cord over three cords and then the right cord over four. Continue braiding by repeating Step 1.

Figure 18. A completed eight-strand Chinese braid.

Eleven-Strand Braid. The eleven-strand braid has a simply under-over movement that results in a flat braid similar in structure to the seven-strand braid, but with concave and convex sides. There are six dark cords on the left and five light cords on the right. Begin by taking the far left cord (1) to the right under two cords (2 and 3) and over three cords (4, 5, 6). The second movement repeats the first movement, but it is done with the far right cord (11); take it to the left under two cords (10, 9) and over three cords (8, 7, 1). Continue braiding by alternating the two movements.

SLENTRE BRAID

The word "slentre" is the Danish verb "to stroll or saunter." It is an appropriate name for this braid, since the fingers "walk" back and forth across the working surface, exchanging loops. It is an old Scandinavian braid, and examples exist that were worked by several people, with the several sets of fingers working together. The braid is done with the fingers of both hands, which hold and control a total of five loops. Take two light cords and three dark cords, and form loops in the cords by gathering all the ends together. Arrange the loops so on

the left hand there is a dark loop on finger 1. On the right hand arrange a light loop on finger 2 and a dark loop on finger 3. With the right index finger (1) entering from the top, pull the near side of the loop held by the left-hand finger 3, so the entire loop is shifted to the right-hand finger 1. Then return finger 1 to its original position. Now shift each loop on the left hand over one finger to the left, so that finger 3 takes the loop from 2, and finger 2 takes the loop from 1. Now repeat the same two movements with opposite hands; with the left index finger reach across and enter from the top to take the far loop on the right hand. Now shift each loop on the right hand over one finger to the right. Continue braiding by repeating these four movements as shown in Figure 20.

WOVEN BRAIDS

Woven braids, sometimes referred to as finger weaving or finger plaiting, can be done in a variety of ways, four of which are shown here. The basic principle is that one vertical element becomes a weft thread and proceeds to weave across the other elements, going over and under to produce a flat braid. Different kinds of weaves—plain, twill, and rib—are produced by going over and under different numbers of threads. The finished braid usually shows strong diagonal lines. This type of braiding is frequently used when working with flat strips in basket making.

Three-Strand Woven Braid. This is a simple braid in which the same strand does all the weaving. Arrange two dark cords and one light cord so the light cord is on the left. Weave the light cord back and forth over and under the two dark cords. The loops made by the light cord can be pushed together to form a dense, flat braid, in which the light cord covers the dark cords. The braid can curve by manipulating the two core cords, in this case the dark cords. It can be made wider by using more elements.

Six-Strand Woven Braid. In this braid there are six cords or elements—three cords alternately act as weavers and the other three cords are passive. To begin arrange six cords so they are parallel. The looped horizontal cord (sometimes referred to as a lease cord) holds the six cords in pairs and helps to keep them in order. It is later removed, and it is particularly helpful when using a large number of cords that are closely packed. Begin by weaving the cord on the left (1) to the right by alternately

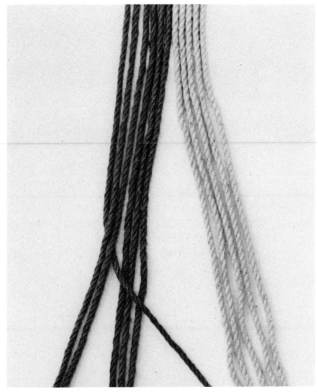

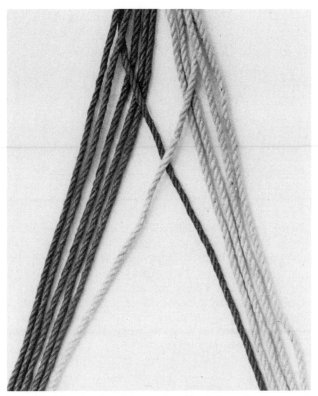

Eleven-Strand Braid: Step 1. Arrange eleven cords so there are six dark cords on the left and five light cords on the right. Begin by taking the far left cord to the right under two cords and over three cords.

Step 2. Take the far right cord to the left under two cords and over three cords.

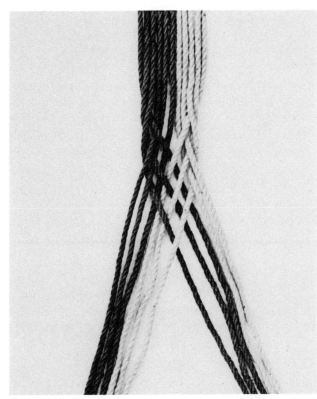

Step 3. Continue braiding by alternating between Steps 1 and 2. The braid is shown here as it appears after completing six movements.

Figure 19. The completed braid showing both sides.

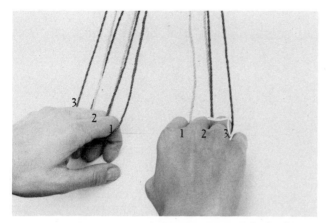

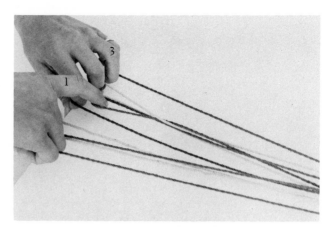

Slentre Braid: Step 1. This braid is done with the fingers, which hold and control five loops. Take two light cords and three dark cords. Form loops in the cords by gathering all the ends together. Arrange the loops so on the left hand there is a dark loop on finger 3, a light loop on finger 2, and a dark loop on finger 1. On the right hand arrange a light loop on finger 2 and a dark loop on finger 3.

Step 2. With the right index finger (1) entering from the top, pull the near side of the loop held by the left-hand finger (3) so that the entire loop is shifted to the right-hand finger 1, and finger 1 is returned to its original position.

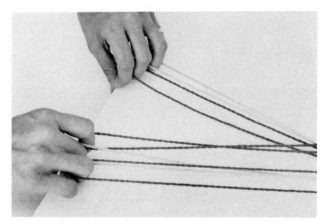

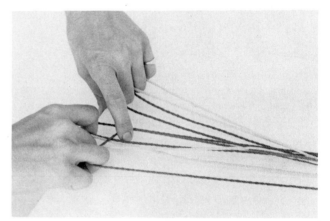

Step 3. Now shift each loop on the left hand over one finger to the left, so that finger 3 takes the loop from 2, and finger 2 takes the loop from 1.

Step 4. The same movements are repeated with opposite hands; the left index finger reaches across the top and enters from the top to take the far loop on the right hand.

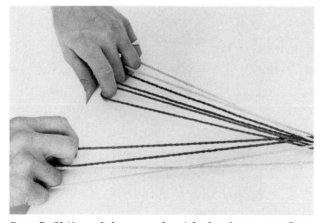

Step 5. Shift each loop on the right hand over one finger to the right. Continue braiding by repeating Steps 2–5.

Figure 20. A completed slentre braid.

Three-Strand Woven Braid: Step 1. Arrange two dark cords and one light cord so the light cord is on the left. Weave the light cord back and forth over and under the two black cords.

Step 2. Continue weaving the light cord back and forth between the two dark cords.

Step 3. The loops made by the light cord can be pushed together to form a dense flat braid in which the light cord covers the dark cords.

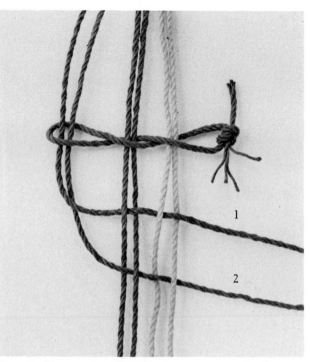

Six-Strand Woven Braid: Step 1. Arrange six cords so they are parallel. The looped horizontal cord shown holds the cords in pairs and helps to keep them in order. Begin by weaving the cord on the left to the right by alternately going over and under the vertical cords. Pull the cord up to the right so it remains in place.

Step 2. Now make the same movement with the new cord on the left by weaving it alternately over and under to the right.

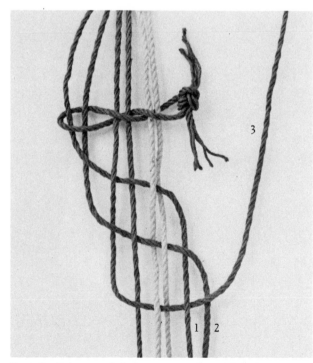

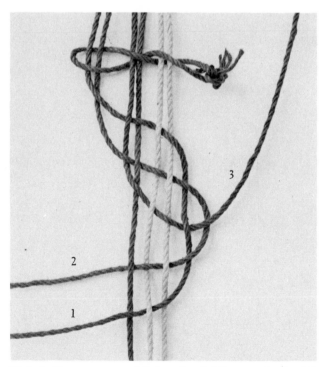

Step 3. Bring cord 1 (woven to the right) down under cord 2 (woven to the right). Now make the same movement as described in Step 1 with the new cord on the left (3) and weave it alternately over and under across. Bring cord 2 down under cord 3. Keep the third cord drawn up so it will remain in place and out of the way.

Step 4. Now weave cord 2 (on the right) across to the left by going alternately over and under, and then weave cord 1 across in the same manner. Cord 2 is brought down over cord 1 to take a vertical position, and cord 3 is woven across. Cord 1 is then brought down over cord 3.

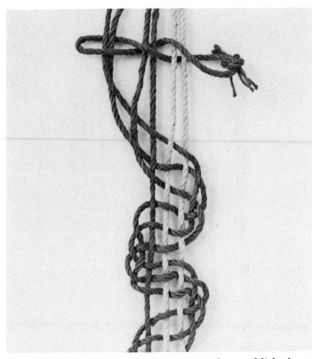

Step 5. To continue weaving, repeat the established pattern, weaving to the right and back to the left with cords 1, 2, and 3.

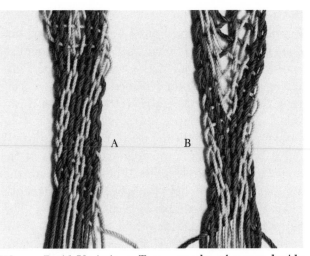

Woven Braid Variations. Two examples of woven braids: cords move across by going, in progression, over and under the other cords. In each braid the top is left loose to show the structure, and the bottom is pulled tight to show the texture and color movement. As each cord weaves across, the other cords are spread out or pushed tightly together. In braid A the weaving moves consistently from left to right. In braid B cords weave over and under from the center out to the sides, with the center strands crossing to maintain the over-under progression.

going over and under the vertical cords. Pull the cord up to the right so it remains in place. Now make the same movement with the new cord on the left (2) by weaving it alternately over and under to the right. Now bring the first cord woven to the right (1) down under the second cord woven to the right (2) to complete the over-under sequence. Now make the same movement with the cord on the left that you made with cord 1, and weave it alternately across. Then bring cord 2 down under cord 3. Keep the third cord drawn up so it will remain in place and out of the way. Now proceed to alternately weave back to the left the three cords that were just woven to the right. First take cord 2, which is on the right, across to the left by going alternately over and under, and then weave cord 1 across. Bring cord 2 down over cord 1 to take a vertical position, and then cord 3 is woven across. Now bring cord 1 down over cord 3. To continue braiding repeat the established pattern, weaving to the right with cords 1, 2, and 3 and then back to the left.

Variations. As more and more elements are used in a braid they can be arranged on a dowel or bar. This helps to keep them in order and when stabi-

lized acts as a firm anchor point to pull against. If you are braiding a long braid, it is possible to work from the center of the braid out. To do this, the strands at the center are temporarily tied around a dowel. The first half is worked pulling from the dowel, then the dowel is removed, the piece anchored, and the second half is braided. The photo shows two examples of such woven braids mounted on a common dowel. The cords in each braid move across by going in progression, over and under the other cords. In each braid the top part is left loose to show the structure, and the bottom part is pulled tight to show the texture and the color movement. As each cord weaves across, the other cords are spread out or pushed tightly together. In braid A the weaving moves consistently from left to right. The cord on the far left is always brought across in the over-under progression. If colors are arranged in groups, strong diagonal stripes will occur. In braid B cords weave one at a time over and under, from the center out to the sides, with the center strands crossing to maintain the over-under progression. If the cords for this braid are arranged in stripes as shown, chevron shapes will appear as braiding progresses.

SPRANG

Sprang is a more complicated form of braiding and is ancient in origin. It has been used continuously since ancient times in both Scandinavia and Peru. Sprang, sometimes called twined plaiting, is a technique in which stretched vertical elements are linked by twisting to form a netlike textile. The linking is formed with the use of fingers and dowels, and it happens simultaneously at both ends of the stretched cords or elements. The twisted construction is ultimately held in place by permanently locking the cords in position at the center. This center locking thread maintains the position of the vertical threads, and prevents the linking from coming undone. Sprang can be worked on any arrangement where the cords are spread out and held taut at both ends. Tension must be adjustable, since the fabric pulls in as the interlinking progresses. Sprang is usually worked on a continuous warp wrapped between two dowels that are secured to a frame. Directions for building a frame with adjustable tension are included in the next section on frame braiding.

Instructions. The photographs demonstrating sprang show a small sampler worked between two dowels held apart by T-pins on a Celotex board. Begin by tying the cord to the bottom dowel on the left. Bring the cord under and around the top dowel and over and around the bottom dowel a number of times. End by tying the cord to the bottom dowel on the right. There should be an even number of warp threads. In this sample there are 16 cords, referred to as warp threads. The first six cords on the left are numbered beginning with number 1 on the left. Now weave a new dowel across all the warp threads by going over and under from the right side to the left side as shown. The cords are picked up in order by the fingers and slipped onto the dowel. This dowel organizes the warp threads. Another dowel (dowel A) is now brought across. This is the first movement of two dowels that will be repeated to form the network. Beginning on the right side bring cord 1 under cord 2, over cord 3, and under cord 4. Draw cord 1 up and slip it over the dowel. Now bring cord 3 under cord 6 and then slip 3 over the dowel, so that cord 6 is under the dowel and cord 3 is over the dowel. Continue working across the warp elements in this manner by taking one cord under another as with cords 3 and 6. Slip the last cord on the left side over the dowel. There should be two cords over the dowel on the left and two cords under the

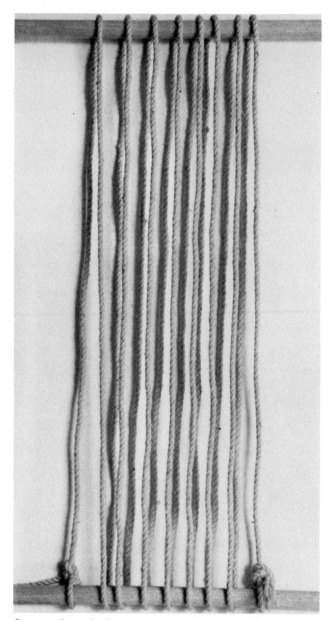

Sprang: Step 1. Sprang is worked on a continuous warp. The continuous warp is wound between two dowels that are secured to make a frame. Tension, which is maintained by the dowels, must be adjustable. The individual warp threads work back and forth with the aid of fingers and dowels to form an interlinking net-like structure. Here the dowels are held apart by T-pins on a Celotex board. Begin by tying the cord to the bottom dowel on the left. Bring the cord around the top dowel and around the bottom dowel a number of times. End by tying the cord to the bottom dowel on the right. There should be an even number of warp threads (here we have used 16).

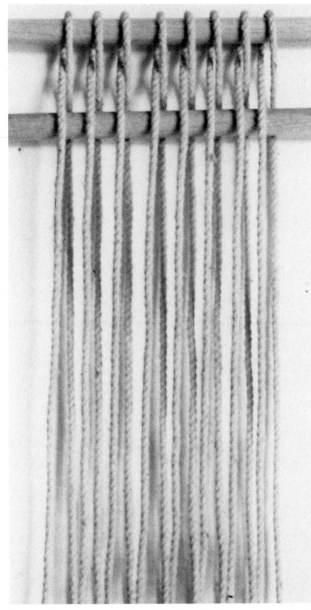

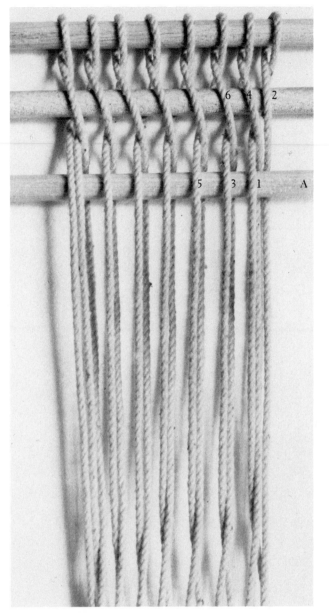

Step 2. Weave a new dowel across all the warp threads by going over and under from the right side to the left side. The cords are picked up in order by the fingers and slipped onto the dowel. This dowel organizes the warp threads.

Step 3. Another dowel (dowel A) is brought across. This is the first step of two that will be repeated to form the network. Beginning on the right side, bring cord 1 under cords 2 and 4 and slip it over the end of the dowel so that cords 2 and 4 are under the dowel and cord 1 over it. Now bring cord 3 under cord 6, then slip 3 over the dowel, so that cord 6 is under the dowel and cord 3 over the dowel. Continue taking one cord under another as with 3 and 6 to the other side. Slip the last cord on the left side over the dowel. Notice how the warp threads are twisting and interlinking at the bottom of the sampler as well as at the top.

Step 4. *A third dowel (dowel B) is brought across; this represents the second step of the two that will be repeated to form the network. Bring the first cord on the right (cord 2) under cord 1 and then over the dowel. Take the next cord (cord 4) under the next cord in line (cord 3) and over the dowel. Continue taking one cord under the next and over the dowel to the other side.*

Step 5. *Continue plaiting by repeating the movements described in Steps 3 and 4. The warp threads will twist and link at both ends. After each dowel is worked across another can be inserted to push the bottom twist tightly into place. As the net grows, remove the first dowels. If all the dowels are removed the linked structure will disappear. When the center is reached, work a cord across to secure the linked structure. The cord can be woven back and forth over and under the individual warp threads, or it can be twined, crocheted, or knotted.*

dowel on the right. Notice how the warp threads are twisting and interlinking at the bottom of the sampler (as well as at the top where the dowels have been inserted). Another dowel can be inserted into the same opening that dowel A occupies and drawn down to pack the interlinking at the bottom.

Another dowel, dowel B, is now brought across. This represents the second step of the two that will be repeated to form the network. Bring the first cord on the right (cord 2) under cord 1 and then over the dowel. Take the next cord (cord 4) under the next cord in line (cord 3) and over the dowel. Continue across to the other side by taking one cord under the next and over the dowel. As before, another dowel can be inserted through the same opening and used to pack the twists at the bottom. Continue plaiting by repeating the movements described in Steps 3 and 4. The warp threads will twist and link at the top and the bottom. After each dowel is worked across another can be inserted to push the bottom twists tightly into place. As the net grows, remove the first dowels. If all the dowels are removed the linked structure will disappear. When the center is reached, work a locking cord across or leave the dowel in to secure the linked structure. The locking cord can be woven back and forth over and under the individual warp threads, or it can be twined, crocheted, or knotted.

In working with large numbers of closely packed threads it is easiest to slip the lifted threads over the right forefinger and after completing the row to slip the dowel across. Large pieces can be worked between two rods so that the top rod is suspended and weights hang on the bottom rod. The weights keep the piece under a constant flexible tension. One way of setting up is to clamp the top bar to the top molding of a doorway and then to weight the bottom bar with bricks.

The two working movements described produce what is called a single twist, the simplest form of sprang. This means that one warp thread twists around one adjacent warp thread. It is also possible to do the single twist in pairs so that two warp threads twist around two other warp threads. More complicated structures with different kinds of openings can be formed by twisting the threads around two or more times. Openings or slits in the sprang network can be made by working individual sections. This is done by not twisting or crossing two threads that would normally cross or twist. The opening is started on an A row. Then in the next

row, which would be a B row, the part of the network on each side of the opening is treated as a separate piece. Then in the next row (A row) the pairs can again be left uncrossed to continue the opening, or a normal row can be done to close the opening.

Sprang is somewhat like knitting. It is highly elastic in the horizontal direction, and the textile or fabric must be stretched and supported to show the structure and to keep it from collapsing. This structure can be highly regular and even, or broken and spread out, depending on the manner of interlinking. A piece can also be varied by changing colors or materials (use a weaver's knot or a weaver's square knot to join the ends of different colors during continuous warping).

FRAME BRAIDING

This method of braiding is done on a frame and is worked in a similar manner as sprang. Historically, the Hopi Indians of Arizona have used this technique for centuries to make a white cotton wedding sash. The sash is woven for the bride by the men of the bridegroom's family. This belt is also used as part of a man's ceremonial costume. Other Indian groups have acquired the sash from the Hopi to use in their ceremonial dances. The traditional Hopi sash is made of two-ply white handspun cotton, braided into a strip from 8" to 10" wide and from 8 to 10 feet long, including a long, twisted fringe at each end.

The technique is especially beautiful for producing the traditional sash, but it also has interesting possibilities for other fabrics and uses.

The demonstration piece is worked on an easily constructed frame. The continuous warp is medium-weight rug wool. A special frame was constructed for it, which can also be used for sprang, but any frame arrangement that keeps the threads spread out and under adjustable tension is satisfactory. Our frame is made of 1½" x 1½" pine and the outside measures 24" x 36", but a frame can be made in any convenient size. The frame must be strong and may be made of any usable material. The corners of the frame shown were dovetailed for strength. The frame is drilled through near the edges on the top and bottom (a total of four holes) and fitted with 6" threaded eye bolts as shown. Wing nuts on the outside of the frame are used to adjust the dowels, which tension the warp.

The warp is continuous and wraps around two anchor dowels. Color changes are made by adding

Frame Braiding: Step 1 (Right). Any frame arrangement with adjustable tension can be used for this braid. As with sprang, the warp is continuous and wraps around the two anchor dowels. Color changes are made in the continuous warp by square knotting the ends together. Unlike the sprang sampler, only the top layer of warp threads are used. The total number of warp threads, counting on the top side, should be divisible by three with the addition of one. The braid shown contains 127 warp threads.

Step 2 (Below). The warp threads are moved by fingers, and a dowel is inserted to hold them in position. The first row begins on the right. Take the first cord under three cords and then lift the first cord over the dowel. Now put the next two cords over the dowel so there are three cords behind the dowel and three cords over the dowel. Repeat this pattern across to the left side. When the row is completed there will be one odd cord on the left side under the dowel. This cord will begin the second row.

Step 3 (Bottom). Work the second row as you did the first row, but begin on the left side. Take the first cord under three cords and over the dowel. Then put the next two cords over the dowel so there are three under and three over. Continue in this manner across to the right side where there will be one odd cord behind the dowel to begin the third row.

Step 4 (Left). Each successive row holds the previous row in place so earlier sticks can be removed. The warp twists and links at the top and at the bottom of the frame as in sprang. A dowel can be inserted to push the bottom twists into place. If all the dowels are removed, the warp threads will revert back. As the two sets of twists meet, a cord must be worked across the center (woven, braided, crocheted, or knotted) to hold the braid in place, or the center can be cut and the resulting fringe knotted. As the rows are twisted, the dowels can be taken over the anchor bar so the twists are moved around to the back warp threads.

Step 5 (Below). A detail of the braiding in progress. The braid gives the appearance of twill weaving.

new-colored warp threads joined by using the weaver's square knot. The total number of warp threads, counting on the top surface only, should be divisible by three with the addition of 1. Unlike the sprang sampler, only the top layer of threads is used in the braiding. The braid in the demonstration uses 127 warp threads. The warp threads are moved by fingers, and a dowel is inserted to hold them in position. Remember that you will be working only on the top layer of threads.

Instructions. The first pattern row begins on the right. Take the first cord under three cords and then lift the first cord over the dowel. Now put the next two cords over the dowel so that there are three cords behind the dowel and three cords over the dowel. Repeat this pattern across to the left side. When the row is completed there will be one odd cord on the left side under the dowel. This cord will begin the second row. Beginning on the left, work the second row just as you did the first row. Take the first cord under three cords and over the dowel. Then put the next two cords over the dowel so that there are three under and three over. Continue in this manner across to the right side, where there will be one odd cord behind the dowel to begin the third row. Continue by braiding alternately between the first and second rows.

Each successive row holds the previous row in place so earlier sticks can be removed. The warp threads move and link at the top and at the bottom of the frame. As in sprang a dowel can be inserted to push the bottom twists into place. If all the dowels are removed, the warp threads will revert back. As the two sets of twists meet, a separate cord must be worked across the center (woven, braided, crocheted, or knotted) to hold the braid, or the center may be cut and the fringe knotted.

In the traditional Hopi method, the top bar of the stretched warp is anchored to the wall of the house or kiva and the other bar to a heavy stone, so the warp is stretched horizontally just above the floor. The braid is worked with the weaver or braider sitting parallel to the bar. The sticks are inserted at the end where he is working, brought toward the body and then pushed away. After a number of sticks have been inserted they are worked all the way around the warp, over and around the other anchor bar and down the underneath side, so the interlinking butts up with the top set of interlinked threads. As braiding continues the entire warp is periodically shifted to move the interlinked fabric to the bottom so the braider does not have to stretch

too far or move out of position. Eventually the warp threads are cut in the center, forming a long braided sash with fringe at each end. There is a kind of seam at the sash center where the two parts of the braid meet, but no separate center cord is worked across.

TWISTED BRAIDING

This braid, which was used by the pre-Columbian Peruvians, is very similar in structure to bobbin lace. It can be worked on a wide scale with many cords in order to construct a fabric, but is shown in the demonstration in its simplest form. Due to the way one cord is brought over another, both the cords and the color move gradually in diagonal progress from one side to the other. Clothespins are handy to hold the cords in position, and each cord length is wound up and held by a rubber band to keep it from tangling.

The smallest number of cords for a complete braid is eight. When worked with more cords it is done in series of eights. To do the braid shown in the demonstration arrange eight parallel cords. To begin take cord 1 over cord 2 and then take cord 4 over cords 3 and 1. The same movement is repeated with the next four cords. In each group of four the cord on the left goes to the right over one cord, and then the cord on the right goes to the left over two cords. The four center cords now form a new group of four, and the same movement is repeated; the cord on the left goes over one and the cord on the right goes over two. Still working with only the four center cords, repeat the movement. Figure 21 shows a braid in progress.

BOBBIN LACE

Bobbin lace is a technique involving vertical, paired threads that use bobbins or similar objects as weights. The bobbins both store and tension the threads. Each element or cord is wound around one bobbin. The fabric is formed by moving the bobbins so the cords twist and interlace. Traditionally bobbin lace is worked with fine threads mounted on a special pillow and using highly ornate bobbins. Today's bobbin lace frequently uses heavy materials and makeshift bobbins, producing open irregular compositions that combine different kinds and weights of materials and patterns. There is a special vocabulary for working with bobbin lace, and although few of the terms will be mentioned, the structure produced and the process are so similar to the other braids that it is easier to think of bobbin lace as being a kind of braiding rather than a unique technique. The bobbin is a handy tool. The particular bobbin used depends on the weight and bulk of the

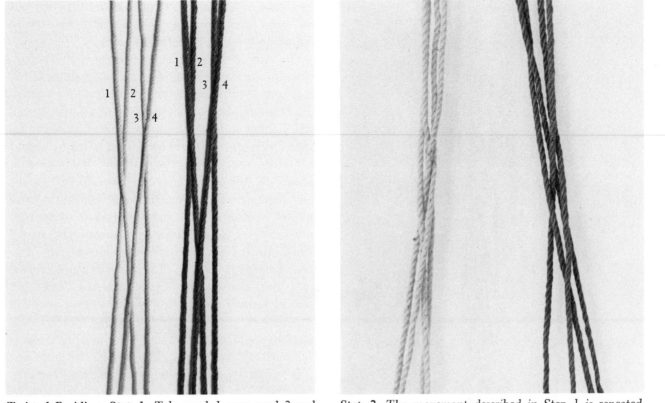

Twisted Braiding: Step 1. Take cord 1 over cord 2 and then take cord 4 over cords 3 and 1. The same step is repeated with the next four cords.

Step 2. The movement described in Step 1 is repeated. In each group of four, the cord on the left goes to the right over one cord, and then the cord on the right goes to the left over two cords.

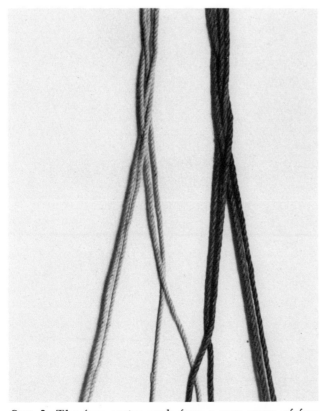

Step 3. The four center cords form a new group of four and Step 1 is repeated; the cord on the left goes over one and the cord on the right goes over two.

Step 4. Still working with only the four center cords, repeat the movement described in Step 1. The braid continues by repeating Steps 1–4.

Figure 21. A completed twisted braid.

cord used. It acts as a kind of handle to the threads and helps in crossing the cords because you pick up and move bobbins rather than cords.

The sample shown is set up using makeshift tools. The white form, traditionally called a pillow, is the back of a styrofoam wig stand. The form is attached to a base-board to reduce movement and is covered with a latex surface to prevent disintegration. Assorted nuts and bolts are used as bobbins to weight and store the cotton seine twine. Each cord is looped to form a pair, or two working elements. The extra length of each element is wound on a bobbin, ending with a half-hitch knot to prevent unwinding. T-pins are used to anchor the paired cords. In bobbin lace the crossing of any two threads forms a "stitch." The two basic movements in bobbin lace are the "cross" and the "twist." A cross is formed by crossing the two inner cords of two adjacent bobbin pairs by taking the left cord over the right cord. A twist is formed by crossing the cords right over left. The process can continue by alternating between these two stitches. Openings are created by giving extra twists. Cords can be pinned and redirected to shape the piece. Bobbins can also act as independent elements and weave over and under other cords.

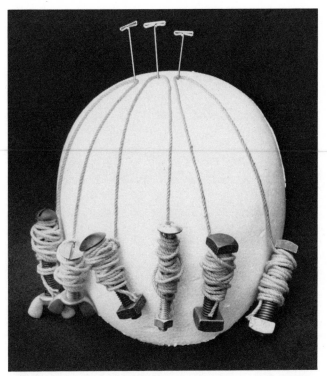

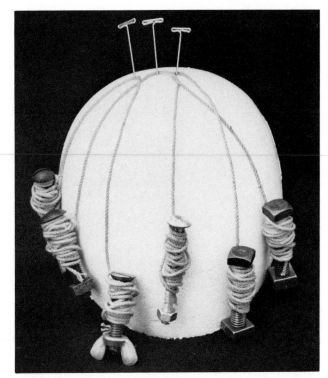

Bobbin Lace: Step 1. This shows a setup for making bobbin lace using makeshift tools. The white form, or pillow, is the back of a Styrofoam wig stand, latexed and attached firmly to a board to reduce movement. Assorted nuts and bolts are used as bobbins to weight and control the cords. Each cord is looped to form a pair, or two working elements. The extra length of cord is wound around a bobbin, ending with a half-hitch to prevent unwinding.

Step 2. A stitch is formed by crossing any two threads. Here three pairs of threads have been anchored to the pillow. The cords at the upper left show a "cross," formed by crossing the two inner cords of two adjacent bobbin pairs by taking the left cord over the right cord. A "twist," shown on the right, is formed by crossing the cords right over left. Lace is formed by repeating these movements in various patterns.

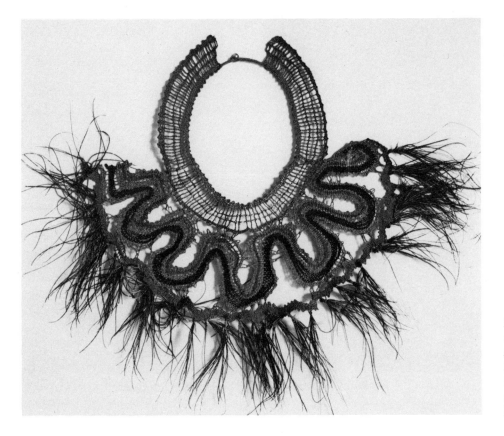

Necklace by Lydia Van Gelder. Mixed yarns, feathers, about 24″ in diameter. The flexible nature of bobbin lace becomes evident in this decorative necklace. Photo by David Donoho.

Victorian Grosspoint Loom. This loom was used as a braiding frame for the Hopi wedding sash technique. The hard wood frame tilts, and tension on the crossbars is adjustable. *Courtesy of Anne Blinks. Photo by Candace Crockett.*

Basket, 3½" x 7". This basket is similar to a woven braid. It is worked dimensionally and the flat wicker material goes over and under a number of strands rather than one. Photo by David Donoho.

Plaited Firehose (Below) by Betty Anne Beaumont, 96" x 9" x 9". Courtesy of the Museum of Contemporary Crafts, New York. Photo by Bob Hanson.

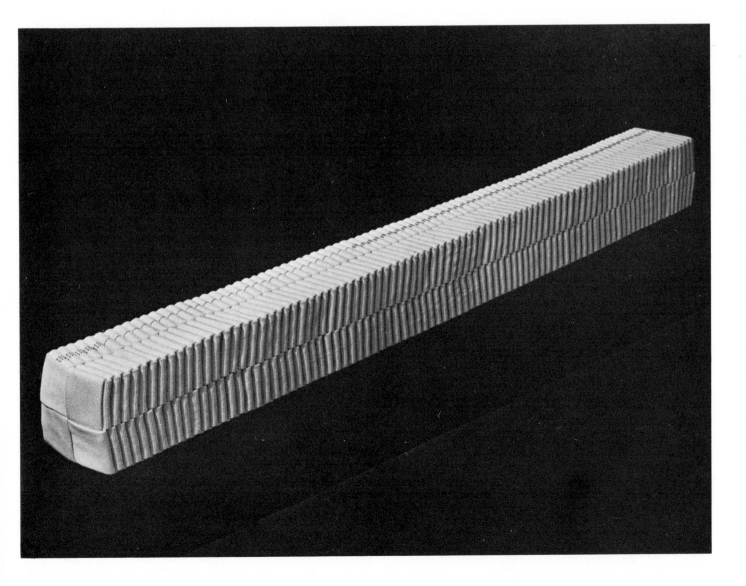

Indonesian Comb. *Bamboo, wood, and wire, 7" x 3¼". Fine wire is twined and looped in various ways to both hold the teeth at regular intervals and to act as a decorative motif. Courtesy of the Museum of International Folk Art, Santa Fe, New Mexico. Photo by Candace Crockett.*

CHAPTER EIGHT

WRAPPING AND COIL CONSTRUCTION

If you coil an element and then wrap that coil, you will be structurally holding the first element in place, enhancing the surface, and increasing the strength of the foundation material. These are facts noticed long ago and practiced by people on every continent. Neither of the materials need be rigid; in fact, it is better if both are flexible. The rigidity comes from the technique.

Each element can be different in color, and there is a choice in covering one completely with the other or letting both show, one through the other. This is, of course, if the coils are to be made into a dimensional form. But, what if we were just to wrap the foundation in some attractive way—or tie a simple knot in the cord and wrap between the knots? It would then be similar to a yarn abacus, an instrument for calculating and keeping records.

We find many variations of wrapping and coil construction as we search through the arts of all people in history. Usually these techniques are associated with basketry but sometimes they are used in constructing other objects. The aforementioned knotted and wrapped cord is an example. It is called a "quipu" and is still in use today in some remote villages of Peru. Historically, a number have been found there, many with very elaborate systems that recorded the statistics of a given community. The community recorder used the quipu to keep his records. It told who was born, who died, how many men and women in a given age group, as well as how many sheep, etc., were owned. Each keeper had his own system of recording, similar to but not duplicated by that of any other village. An example of a quipu can be seen at the American Museum of Natural History in New York City.

WRAPPING AND COIL IN OTHER ARTS

Many techniques associated with textiles are found duplicated in architecture, and in the case of coil construction, in another craft—ceramics. The thesis that coil pottery evolved from coil basketry cannot be supported as well as the one that recognizes coiling as a method of building a strong form. The use of coil in ceramics may have developed separately. This supposition is based on the fact that most traditional basketry is round in form while many ceramic pieces built of coil are not.

Some of the confusion may even come from varying translations of text. For example, the Greek word for basket is "kaneon" from "kanna" (a reed) and is the root of our English word "canister." In Latin text the word was frequently applied to containers of clay, bronze, and gold as well as those of cane.

The helix, or spirally coiled basket, is most common to the Indians of the southwestern United States and is also found in comparable cultures throughout the world. Formed with a foundation coil and wrapped with a second element of flexible vegetable fiber, the coiled basket has served all primitive people as a storing, carrying, cooking, and serving container for millennia.

TOOLS

Tools used for wrapping and coiling are quite simple. Traditionally, they are an awl, a knife, and a needle. Early workmen using these techniques were knowledgeable about selecting their materials in relation to the basket's intended use and their own construction methods. In addition, they knew about waterproofing materials such as piñon gum and as-

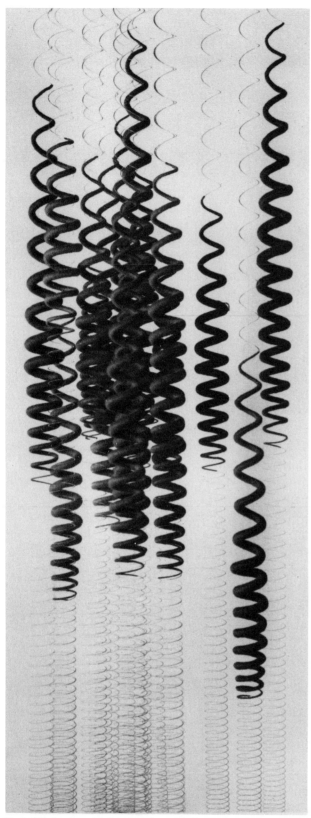

Red Slinky by Claire Zeisler, 1971. Red cotton roving, 52 slinkies, 9 x 4 x 5 feet. Clear, clean, bold, and sensitive, the artist's understanding of the intrinsic nature of the materials is most evident. Courtesy of the Ruth Kaufmann Gallery. Photo by Jonas Douydenas, courtesy of the Museum of Contemporary Crafts, New York.

phalt minerals. They also used soft padding in the foundation coil to help make the work watertight, referred to as chinking.

WRAPPING

If you twist two or more elements together then they become "plied." This increases their strength, as you learned in the chapter on spinning. You have also seen that when you twist in one direction and ply in a counter-direction, the twist of each element counters the twist of the other and further increases the strength. This will hold the larger element fairly straight while at the same time leaving it flexible.

Rigidity is the combined effect of wrapping one element with another. It will not stretch or bend easily. The tighter the wrap, the less give you will have.

Successful wrapping depends on a few basic considerations. The foundation coil is usually larger than the wrapping element. It can be as flexible, but not more so, than the wrapping element. Short lengths of wrapping material can be used making them easier to handle. These can be joined or terminated quite easily.

Exceptions can, of course, be found for any rule. Most notable are the wrapped sculptures in a series by Claire Zeisler. They are based on the "Slinky" and, according to the artist, "It is a child's toy and it's made up of many, many coils that you can do many things with. For some reason or other it interested me because it has motion. The motion element is important. And I feel that my things in the past have been very static and because I felt that, I think that this particular element appealed to me." In her work the foundation is smaller than the wrapping material, and motion as an idea has been pursued rather than minimized by the wrapping.

Another basic is that the wrapping element ends must be securely fastened. Wrapping, itself, is secure, and it is this quality that helps hold the terminal ends in place.

To start, lay the end of your wrapping element parallel to the foundation coil. Bind around, proceeding down the coil toward the end, covering the tail as you wrap. To introduce the next length of wrapping, lay the end toward the completed wraps and bind it into the body of the work. When you reach the end of the first length, lay its tail toward the unwrapped foundation, pick up the now secured second length and continue wrapping. You can change colors in the same way. Do not cut the wrapping element if it is to be a small color area. Lay it against the foundation and cover it with wrapping until you are ready to use it again.

WHIPPING

Whipping is a specific term applied to wrapping the terminal ends of the foundation and is usually associated with securing ends of rope (rope has a tendency to unlay if not whipped).

Whipping can also be a decorative detail; it is useful in binding two or more foundations together. It is also useful in fringing, and can build extra body into a given place in the foundation coil. There are two basic methods of whipping: the first is for terminal ends, the second for an isolated section of wrapping or to introduce a secure branch for wrapping itself. In the second method, the wrapping element would become the foundation coil.

Whipping Terminal Ends. Wrap the foundation, stopping four turns short of the length of wrapping you wish, whipping the tail of the material parallel to the foundation and leaving about 3″ free. Then double the tail back parallel to the foundation, leaving a small loop exposed. Bind this loop to the foundation with three or four turns of the wrapping element. Thread the wrapping element through the loop. Tighten the wrapping element and pull the tail of the loop until the wrapping element is pulled into the body of the wrapping. Cut off the remaining ends.

Alternate Tie-Off. Lay the end of the wrapping element parallel to the foundation to be wrapped. Wrap back, around both the tail and the foundation. After determining how long an area you want to wrap, take a scrap of string and lay a loop of it parallel to the foundation. The loop should lie in the direction you are wrapping, and the two ends should stick out of the wrapped area. Be sure the ends are long enough for you to take hold of later. Wrap the remaining area. Pass the wrapping element through the loop and pull tight.

Then take hold of the string and pull the primary winding element back through the completed wrap. At this point you have secured both ends of the wrapping. You now have available a second foundation growing from the first wrapping and can repeat the steps, or you can cut off all unwanted ends to complete the "tie-off" and discard the pulling loop.

Wrapping can become a total way of constructing an art statement as you can see by the sculpture of

Claire Zeisler. Wrapping is used to increase rigidity, add color, bind units together, create mass, and act as a linear element. Figure 22 shows a number of variations in detail.

COILING

In reference terminology, coiling is frequently used to denote any circular construction. Any method, including a helix construction, is included in coil work in some references. Vantsom netting is often called coiled because it is traditionally assembled in a circular fashion. However, we prefer to use the designation of coiling to specifically identify forms made with a foundation that is wrapped or stitched in some manner to secure it. This definition includes many traditional basket techniques and suggests variations for contemporary forms.

Figure 23 illustrates some considerations in coiled forms: beginning the coil, the size of the foundation, and wrapping. It also illustrates the joining of helix constructions, one of the techniques described later in this chapter.

Coil work usually starts in the center and progresses in a spiral, continually increasing the diameter of the work. This increase continues only until the maximum desired size of the foundation is reached. You have the option of changing directions in the form at this point. All of these considerations are dependent on the rigidity of the foundation and its bending tolerance as well as the bulk of the wrapping element.

Start the coil with only a small amount of foundation and increase it gradually. Unless the foundation coil is very flexible, you should not start with a blunt end. Note the tapering at the beginning of the coil in Figure 23.

This traditional Mexican basket is wrapped with flat, flexible strands of raffia using the Mariposa stitch. This stitch as well as others are discussed later in the chapter. Because the raffia is flat and has a degree of rigidity as well as resistance to bend against its edges, using the Mariposa stitch keeps the coils from touching. The openness of this stitch accounts for its often being referred to as a "lace stitch" in basketry.

JOINING ENDS WITHOUT KNOTS

Securely joining two ends and thus forming a continuous element may be done in a number of ways. A decorative knot is suitable except where the increased bulk of the knot is not acceptable in relation to the form being produced. Glue, or an

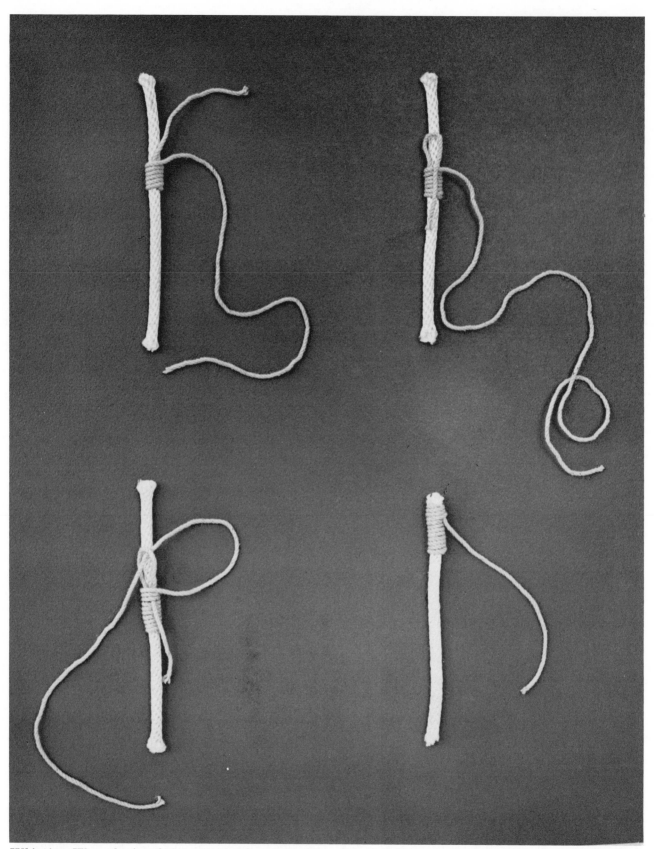

Whipping. Wrap the foundation, stopping four turns short of the length of wrapping you wish, whipping the tail of the material parallel to the foundation after leaving about 3″ free as shown in the upper left. Double the tail back parallel to the foundation, leaving a small loop as shown in the upper right. Bind this loop to the foundation with three or four turns of the wrapping cord. Thread the wrapping cord through the loop as shown in the lower left. Tighten the wrapping cord and pull the tail of the loop until the wrapping cord is hidden under the turns you have just completed. Cut off any remaining ends.

Alternate Tie-off: Step 1. Lay the end of the winding cord parallel to the foundation to be wrapped. Wrap back, around both the tail and the foundation.

Step 2. After determining how long an area you want to wrap, take a second scrap of string and lay a loop of it parallel to the foundation. The loop should lie in the direction you are wrapping. The two ends should stick out of the wrapped area. Be sure the ends are long enough for you to take hold of later. Wrap the remaining area. Pass the winding material through the loop and pull tight.

Step 3. Take hold of the second string and pull the primary winding cord back through the completed wrap. At this point you have secured both ends of the wrapping. You now have available a second foundation growing from the first wrapping and can repeat Steps 1–3 or proceed to Step 4.

Step 4. Cut off all unwanted ends as shown here to complete the "tie-off." Discard the pulling loop.

Figure 22 (Above). This close look at wrapping shows how a very simple, traditional technique can be used in creating a very complex sculptural form. It can be used to increase rigidity, add color, bind units together, create mass, and act as an independent linear element.

Figure 23. A close look at the bottom of this contemporary but traditional Mexican basket shows two points in understanding coil construction. First, note the diminutive coil at the center and beginning of the basket. The beginning foundation material is just a few strands. As the coil fattens and the concentric coils widen in the circle, more strands are added. Second, this is an example of the lace or Mariposa stitch discussed later in the chapter, and it shows how the stitch can be used to form an open pattern.

adhesive appropriate to the material used, is a second method of joining, for example epoxy is often used when joining plied carpet yarns. A third way of joining single-strand materials such as yarn is to simply spin the ends together with your fingers. Splicing is yet another method.

Splicing is used when you have a number of strands making up one working element. It has an advantage over knots in the reduction of bulk and over glue in that it is stronger. Included here are three different splices that are particularly suitable to bulky, plied elements. One is referred to simply as "splicing." The others are an "eye splice" and a "back splice." All are used for splicing two elements together and thus forming a continuous and strong element.

Splicing. Unlay, or untwist, both ends of the plied rope. The length that should lie open depends on the size of the rope. It will be easier to work if you unlay more than you need rather than less. Overlay alternately the two sets of strands. Temporarily secure one set of these to the body of the second rope with wire, string, or tape.

Open out the strands of the second rope. Take the free end of one of the strands and pass it over one of the secured ends and under the next, exiting beyond the rope. Repeat this with each free end and repeat once more with each of the three strands. This is for a short splice. If you want a long splice, repeat once more before going on.

Next remove the temporary binding and pull both sets of ends firmly against the body of rope until the splicing is closed. Cut off the protruding ends. At this point the splice will be slightly larger in diameter than the rope. This thickness can be worked down and tapered by rolling the rope back and forth on a hard surface. By using the ends of one rope length, making a circle, and closing with the first splice here, you can make a hoop.

Eye Splicing. The eye splice forms a loop before being worked back into the rope body. The loop may be made any size and may be worked around another object or used pendant.

Unlay one end of the rope. Make a bend with the rope the size you want the loop. Open the rope slightly at the place you wish to begin closing the loop. Tuck the ends alternately into the main rope body by lifting each strand in sequence. As you proceed around the rope you will return to the first tuck under the strand. Take the strand over one rope strand and tuck into the third. Do this with the other remaining two strands. Pull tightly and trim the ends. This may also be rolled to reduce the thickness if you wish.

Back Splicing. Back splicing is an extension of the crown knot shown in Chapter 6. Both follow the general over and under tucking found in splicing. Start by laying open the rope and tying the crown knot. At this point, each strand will be pointing across another of the rope. Lift one strand and tuck it as you did in the eye splice—over the adjoining strand and under the following one. This may become a long back splice by repeating this a third time. Again, pull all tucks tight against the rope body and trim the ends. Finishing is similar to the other two splices.

EMBELLISHMENTS

The secret of adding embellishments so they become an intrinsic part of the construction lies in anticipating and preparing for their placement. Only one thing must be present: a hole, either natural or artificial.

A bead, for instance, has a natural hole. If you are using short working elements, thread the bead directly and continue wrapping. If you are using a long continuous element as in knitting, thread the bead hole with a loop and pick it up as a working loop.

Feathered Strands. The Peruvians, around 1500 A.D., excelled in their use of feathered textiles. These can be tied to a holding cord in several different ways, thus creating an artificial "eye" with the rachis, or quill end. The photograph shows a detail from one of these feathered strands before it is basted to another fabric.

To tie on feathered strands, first arrange the color sequence of the feathers. Bend the rachis of one feather over a holding cord close to the beginning of the down. On one side of this tie will be two parallel strands and on the other an X. Decide on which side you want the X. Work left to right with your working element. Go over the face of the bent rachis, around, and exit over the top left. Cross down to the right, around the rachis, and exit below the left end. Thread through the diagonal, then exit right. Repeat this process for the next feather.

An alternate knot showing only one strand around the rachis is made by passing from left to right over the face and around the rachis and exiting below the cord. Thread under and through the loop on the right and exit. This may be done once (not too secure) or twice (more secure).

Splicing: Step 1. Unlay both ends of the plied rope or yarn to be spliced. Alternately overlap the two sets of strands. Temporarily secure one set of these ends to the body of the other piece of rope or yarn as shown. This will leave your hands free to work with the second set of strands without losing the first. In this picture we used tape; string will do as well.

Step 2. Open out the strands of the second rope. Take the free end of one of the strands and pass it over one of the secured ends and under the next. Repeat this with each free end.

Step 3. Remove the temporary tape or string. Pull both sets of ends firmly against the body of the plied rope or yarn. Cut off the ends. You have completed a short splice. If you wish to make a longer splice, repeat Step 2 once more before trimming the ends. This splice will be slightly thicker than the main rope; the thickness can be worked down by rolling the spliced area back and forth on a hard surface.

Eye Splicing. Making a permanent eye splice or loop in plied rope or yarn is an extension of splicing. You have only one end to unlay. The strand ends are alternately tucked into the main body by lifting each in sequence as shown here. The strand shown passing under another will pass over the next and under the third. Again, because this adds thickness, the splice may be rolled on a hard surface to reduce it. The loop of the splice can be made any size; it can also go through or around another object.

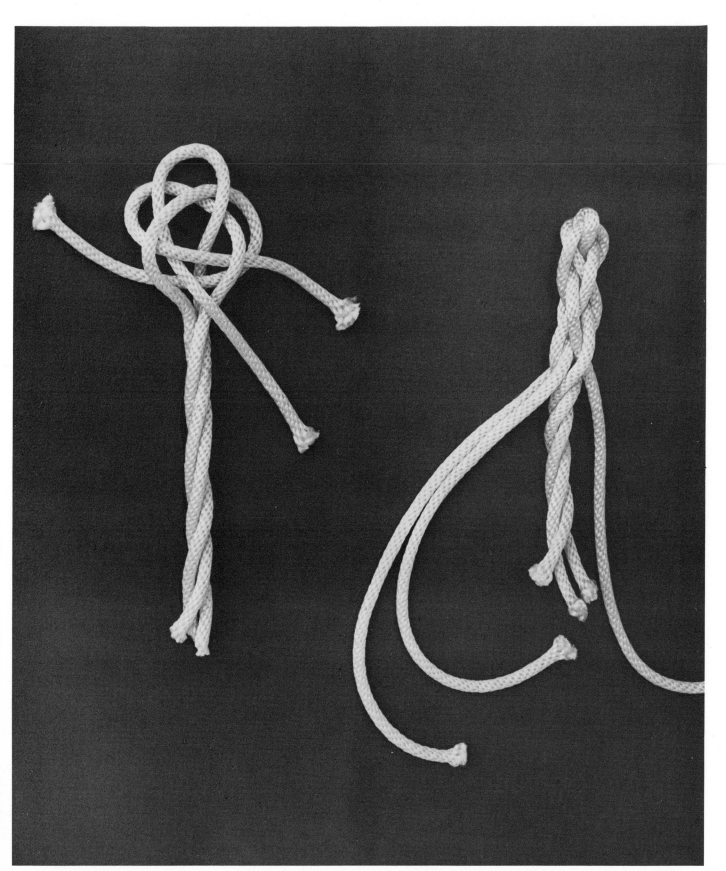

Back Splicing. Back splicing is an extension of the "crown knot." Start by laying open the rope or yarn to be spliced. Tie the crown knot as shown on p. 111. Each end strand will be pointing across another strand in the main body of rope or yarn. Lift the next main strand and tuck an end strand under it. Do this to all strands and repeat at least three times. The example on the left shows the strands opened out as they pass to make the crown and first tuck in the back splice. The view on the right shows the back splice after two tucks and as they are pulled tight.

Tying Feather Strands. This illustration shows one of the methods used by the Incas to tie feathered strands. The feather on the left shows the rachis of the feather as it is bent over the carrying strand. A second strand passes twice around the end of the quill and under the last cross before going on to the next tie. The second rachis is tied so the face of the feather is toward you to show the finished knot. A third thread was occasionally tied on traditional strands of longer feathers.

BASKET STITCHES

Five of the traditional stitches used in sewn basket work are: simple basket, figure eight, Peruvian, Mariposa, and imbricated. These may be interlocked, closed or open, whole or split (furcated). There are numerous variations and combinations found throughout the world that have varying degrees of proficiency and refinement. Basically there is a relationship between the speed with which each can be worked and the use to which the basket is to be put. As today, work intended for a special use or having special meaning required extra care in the preparation of the material and the execution of the work. The directions that follow begin with the simplest and most common basket stitch.

Simple Basket Stitch. This stitch is also called the "Lazy Squaw." Start wrapping the foundation coil at the thinned tip, bending back the end of the wrapping element under the wrapping and parallel to the foundation. When enough of the foundation is wrapped so it can be folded back against itself, secure it with a wrap against itself. Proceed, wrapping and stitching alternately from one coil to the other previous one. One thing to remember—all stitching and wrapping should be tight. You should not be able to push the wrapping down the coil. Do push the stitches together from time to time as you work to be sure they adjoin each other.

Figure Eight Stitch. This stitch is also referred to as "Navaho" because it was so widely used by that American Indian tribe. Each coil is joined with a stitch that resembles a figure eight. The working element passes around a coil and crosses before it is passed around the adjoining coil. Actually, when pulled tight, the wrapping looks as if each coil has been wrapped separately and later stitched together. While a few baskets have been constructed that way, the figure eight stitch is the more universal. The illusion becomes stronger when a fine material is used. The figure eight is more noticeable when a coarse material is used.

Peruvian Stitch. Wrap the base coil several times before casting the connecting stitch. Then cast a stitch around the adjoining coil as you do in the simple basket stitch.

The firmness desired in a piece is a major consideration in your decision to use this stitch. As there are fewer adjoining stitches, there may be a loss in rigidity making it less stable. A slight diagonal or twist may show in the construction if the adjoining stitches are contiguous as shown in the illustration.

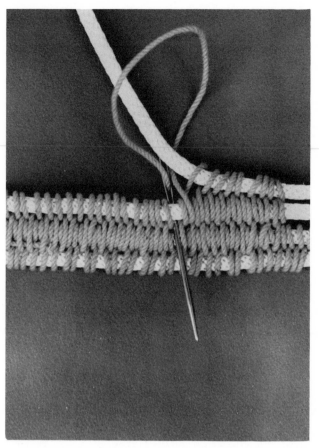

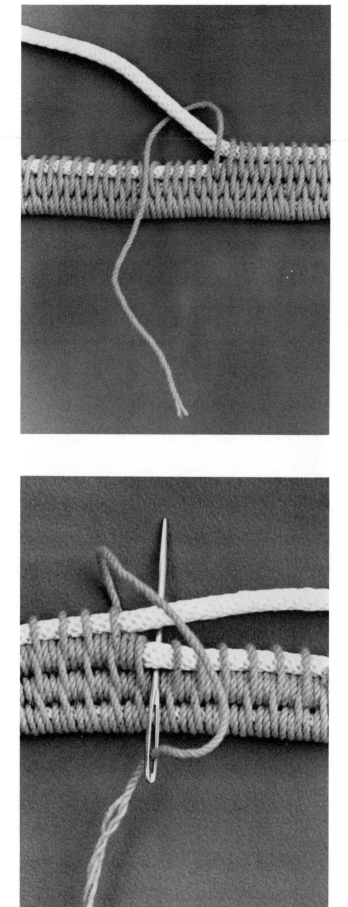

Simple Basket Stitch (Above Left), or the "lazy squaw," this stitch starts by wrapping the starting end or foundation material around and around. The example shown here is not a round form and shows the foundation wrapped straight. Subsequent rows alternate with the beginning wraps. To do this short and long stitch, cast one short around the foundation and then one long going into the previous row beneath. Pulled tight, this gives both a very firm construction and an impacted look to the surface. This is the most widely used stitch in coil work.

Figure Eight (Above Right). Another name for this coil technique is "Navajo." Two foundation coils are joined by the binding in the manner shown here. Note the crossing over with each wrap, which gives it the popular and descriptive name of "figure eight." Actually, when pulled tight, the wrapping looks as if each coil is wrapped separately and then stitched independently. This illusion becomes stronger when fine materials are used, less so with wider or coarse materials where the crossings are more evident.

Peruvian Stitch (Left). Wrapping the single base coil several times before casting the connecting stitch spaces out the surface pattern in this stitch. After the winding cord is pulled through, bring it toward you, between the newly stitched coil and the one just below. Here the foundation coil is wrapped twice before each stitch. Notice the diagonal pattern of the stitch as it is repeated in each consecutive round. Most traditional work is done right-to-left, but we find there is little difference when it is worked in the reverse.

Lace or Mariposa Stitch: Step 1. The interstices found in basketry are popularly referred to as "lace" or "Mariposa" stitches. The smaller wrapping cord shown in this picture is cast over the larger foundation cord. It is then brought back between the foundation coils.

Step 2. Before drawing the stitch tight, pass the wrapping cord across the front of the cast cord and under the wrapping stitch on the previous row. This will hold the stitch when it is pulled closed. In our example one long Mariposa stitch alternates with one short wrapping of the lower foundation cord.

Imbricated Surface: Step 1. This shows a second color being tied over the core strand along with the wrapping cord. Make a loop of the second strand. Then, loop the wrapping cord around both itself and the foundation. Pull it tight against the body of the form. The second color loops may be any length you wish. Note: in the picture the first two rows have short loops, thus showing more of the wrapping material. The loops being tied are much longer. When this surface is complete, more of the looping color will show, but very little of the winding color.

Step 2. After you have pulled the wrapping coil firmly against the completed body, pass the needle under the short loop on the previous coil. This will hold the cord and the second color loop. Proceed around the form repeating Steps 1 and 2. As you work, the second color will settle into the form and the loops will shorten slightly.

Mariposa Stitch. The interstices found in some baskets are the result of using the Mariposa stitch. Wrap or wind several wrappings around the foundation cord before casting a simple binding stitch. Bring the wrapping element between the two foundations.

Before drawing closed, cast the wrapping element across the face of the working element, around the joining cast, and sew under the wrap of the secondary coil. This will lock the stitch in place. The motion is similar to that of sewing on a button and tying off the thread before cutting. Here, you cast only once and you do not cut the working element but continue wrapping until the next Mariposa stitch. In basketry, this cross stitch may be called beading.

The Imbricated Stitch. The imbricated basket stitch is the most complicated and decorative of those included here. It is generally used with flat strips of different-colored material in a fashion similar to plaiting. One colored strip folds over another colored strip, exposing the first and covering part of the second. Our example uses round flexible cording because we wanted to see if it would work as a suitable variation. It also has many characteristics of looped pile textiles such as those using Persian or slip-loop knots, very different from the usual imbricated surface.

In the imbricated stitch you are tying one color strand onto the foundation coil with a second working element. Lay a loop of one color parallel to the foundation coil. With a second element, bind the first to the foundation with a figure eight stitch. Stitch under a previous wrapping stitch to lock the crossing that occurs between the two coils. Pull this stitch tight to hold the loop of the first color. Repeat at intervals depending on how dense you want the looping on the surface. In working with the round cord we found that the loops had a tendency to settle into the space between each coil. The shorter the loop, the more even the distribution of the two colors; the longer the loop, the more likely for that color to prevail. You should cast a longer loop than you anticipate having in the finished design. This settling in does not occur when you use a stiff, flat material. The result is a flat and hard-edged plaited design.

The word imbricated means shingled or shingle-like, so the general effect of this stitch is always overlapping but at the same time, both of the colors used in working the stitch will be exposed to some degree.

SINGLE-WEFT CONSTRUCTION

Wrapped-warp basketry uses one continuous working element that circles the warp once before progressing to the next. The lags between the wrapped warp are usually on one face, thus making an individual warp completely circled. This is referred to as a "hitched weft." A hitched weft is worked on a rigid warp with a more flexible weft, and as a textile technique the method falls somewhere between coiling and twining. It may be worked either flat or in the round.

DOUBLE-WEFT CONSTRUCTION (TWINING)

As mentioned previously, a number of textile techniques found expression in primitive architecture, appropriate to the area and its climatic conditions. For example: in the desert areas of South America the earliest netting, put together with a twining system, was the only "architecture" needed.

Twining is worked on a warp system with two or more weft elements that twist about each other as they pass around progressive warp. It is one of the oldest textile techniques. With 2500 B.C. as a starting date, Dr. Junius Bird describes the division of textile techniques in Peru:

"The breakdown is dominantly, if you take all the techniques (in Peru), some 72% twining. . . . It's an economical way to utilize your yarn. Now with twining, in that pre-ceramic situation, you get some 10% to 12% fabrics where you take a single element and with a succession of loops, interlocking loops, you create a fabric. Then there are a great number of knotted fabrics, the most common of which are fish nets but they also utilize that for the creation of bags and other things just as you have compact knotting with pattern in them. And then when you get down to weaving, less than 3% of the total are woven fabrics. . . . The warps were finger manipulated and I think that the implication we can place on this is that nobody had figured out the simple little heddling, (a) controlling system that was so widely used in later times. But as you come up in time in archaeological material, suddenly, say, after 1200 B.C. the proportion of twine fabrics to woven fabrics is just reversed."

Dr. Bird continues on twining that is done in South America today and the "loom" that holds the warp:

"In the Chaco of Paraguay, people drive two stakes down in the ground with a little Y-shaped fork on top. A cross bar rests in that fork and another rod parallel to that (is) lashed to the two

Simple Twining. This illustrates the simplest form of twining: that done with half turns of the weft elements. While there is no set number of weft strands used for twining, you must have at least two. One weft strand is placed under the first warp strand, the second over the same warp element. Give a half turn to the weft strand. This will place what was the bottom weft strand on top and above the second warp strand. Repeat as you pass to each warp element. If two colors are used, you will have alternating patterns with each color.

Full-Turn Twining. Full-turn twining is an alternate to simple twining. Each warp element is enclosed by the weft strands with a full turn between. In our example one weft element is always on the same side of each warp strand. Using this method, the same color will appear on the face of each warp strand if you use a two-color weft.

Counter Twining. The surface of counter twining resembles knitting. Do a row of half turns; it does not matter whether you work right-to-left or left-to-right. Counter twining means that you reverse the next set of twining threads. Each row mirrors the next.

Alternate-Paired Twining. Twining with a half or full turn can be done using more than one warp strand. In paired twining you enclose two warp elements in each turn. Paired twining is shown here in the top row. The second row of twining separates each pair of warp elements, thus developing an alternate pair. The alternate pair is then used for the second row of twining. The warp is returned to its original position for the next row. A variation would be to cross the warp strands in the second row before twining and then cross a third pairing of warp strands before the next twining. Our example creates an open vertical pattern; the variation would create a diagonal pattern.

rods that come out of the ground, the two poles, then they set the warp over that. It looks like an endless belt warp but actually it turns around a cord which is tied to the two stakes so when you finish weaving you pull that cord out. What looks like an old fashioned towel roller fabric opens out and has selvages at either end or ends that can be finished off. Now, this is as far as we can deduce the oldest warping system used in the Peruvian pre-ceramic (era) and it's still being used down in that area for twine fabrics, not for woven fabrics. Today, they've gone a step in a direction that the pre-ceramic weavers and fabric creators did not do. They compact the weft to create tapestry in twining."

There are two types of twining: warp and weft. Warp twining encompasses many of the techniques in tablet or card weaving, which will be discussed in Chapter 9. In the following references to twining, we are speaking of weft twining. These include: simple twining, full-turn twining, counter twining, and alternate-paired twining.

Playing a Child's Game. The children's game of "Cat's Cradle" is played throughout the world. As you know, it is done with twine joined into a closed loop; it can be played by yourself or with a friend. It is mentioned here because of the similarity in nomenclature and the pairing of the string loop to make a form.

In Korea Cat's Cradle is called Culin and translates into "woof-taking." The Japanese call the game Aya Ito Tori, which means "woof pattern string taking." Germans call it Abheben (taking off), Faden-abheben (taking off string), or Faden-spiel (string game).

There was no similar game known among Central American ethnic groups until modern times and only a few in South America. One of these is found among the Indians of Chaco in Paraguay. The occurrence of twining in a geographical area parallels that of the children's game of Cat's Cradle. There is a notable absence of historical examples of twining on the African continent and there is no evidence of the game occurring there in the past.

Characteristics of Twining. Twining is formed on a warp that may be either rigid or flexible, although it is not usually more flexible than the weft strands. If the warp is flexible, some artificial stiffening is used while it is being worked. This means stretching it on a simple frame loom, hanging it from a support, or temporarily weighting the warp ends. The latter method prevails among the Chilkat tribe of

Northwest Indians. There are no special tools for twining beyond the possible use of a loom frame; all of the work is finger manipulated. There is no counterpart in machine production.

Increasing and decreasing may be achieved in several ways. To decrease, combine more than one warp together during the twining. To increase, introduce an auxiliary warp, enclosing it as you do the regular warp and with the same twining motion. You may also increase the twist. If you are using simple twining, you may introduce full-turn twining.

Simple Twining. This twining is done with a half-turn of the paired weft between each warp element. One of the twining elements will pass behind the warp and the other will pass in front of it. To check the correct twist between the warp, trace one of the elements. It should consistently pass over one warp and under the next warp with a slight twist or screw appearance in between. If you use two colors in the weft, you will develop vertical stripes of alternating colors.

Full-Turn Twining. Each warp is enclosed with a pair of elements as in simple twining. Here, however, a full turn or full twist is given before enclosing the next warp. Full-turn twining will result in having the same color on all the faces. If two colors are used, the reverse side will be in the second color. There will be only slight evidence of a second color between the ribs. Trace one of the elements to see that you have the correct sequence of turns—it will be always on top of or always behind the warp.

Counter Twining. This is simple twining except that one row is twisted in one direction and the next row is counter twisted. If you look at two rows together, it is as if they are mirror images of each other. When the work is counter twined, an impacted surface will be similar in appearance to knitting without the loops. A slight chevron or V (on its side) will show on the surface.

Alternate-Paired Twining. Here, the warp as well as the weft is double. Two warp threads are twined with a simple twining. In the second row the warp pairs are divided to form a second set of warp pairs. The new pair is then twined with simple twining. From here you have a choice of variations. One is to return the warp to its original pair and continue twining as illustrated here. An alternate is to cross the warp to form a third pairing and to twine these. This will make an untied X in the warp that will show between the twining rows. The choices noted here have diverted warps. You may also choose not

Fringe. *This shows the three twists to be considered when making a fringe. Two contrasting colors are used in our example. Notice that on the left the yarns are twisted to the left. In the second group these yarns have been twisted in a counter direction, to the right. The completed two-color fringe is again twisted to the left. While these have been worked very loosely to illustrate the direction or lay of the twist, you should work quite tightly so the fringe will pull against itself and remain in place when it relaxes.*

to manipulate the double warp but use it in the original positions. Also, there are many ways of diverting warp. The warp must be relaxed slightly to work. Within the preceding structural directions are other possible patterns beyond the vertical stripe resulting from simple twining with two colors, for example:

You may also twine, with three colors using two alternately together and the third as a single. This means that you would pass under one warp with two colors (1 and 2) and over the face of that warp with the third (3). Work left to right. Twist, bring 2 to the face, carry 1 and 3 behind. Twist, bringing 1 to the face and carrying 2 and 3 behind. Twist and your original organization of 2 on the face with 1 and 3 behind will reappear. This will develop a three-color vertical stripe.

To develop a diagonal stripe, shift the above sequence one warp to the left at the beginning of each row.

To develop a small herringbone, work one row left to right and the next row right to left. To make a larger one, work two or three rows in one direction before reversing for two or three rows in the other direction.

Braiding, discussed in Chapter 7, is one form of twining. In braiding one of the twining elements is locked between the other two twining elements as the twist is done. When this is not done, three-strand twining has an appearance of twisted cord or fringe.

Tea Kettle. Vegetable fibers, 8½″ in diameter. This American Indian kettle is pitch lined, and hot rocks were dropped into it to make the brew warm for serving. Photo by David Donoho.

FINISHING

Detail finishing is very important on any work regardless of the major construction technique. Ends can be secured in many of the single-element and multiple-element techniques. Some of these, covered in the single-element constructions chapter, provide their own self-edge or method of tying off.

A fringe is one decorative manner of finishing the edge. It can be an added element or result from ends secured in the body of the work. Some techniques you can use are crochet (finger or hooked), macramé, numerous braids, wrapping, winding, or back splicing. One of the simplest fringing methods finds its counterpart in methods used to make rope (as discussed in Chapter 1).

Fringe. Take a pair of elements and determine their twist, S or Z. One end of each of the pair should be secured. Let's say they are the extended warps after you have finished twining. Tie them together with a simple knot, insert a pencil or the equivalent, and twist in a direction counter to their determined twist until they are tightly twisted. Double them against themselves and release the pencil. They should ply together. Sew the ends into the body of the work.

This may be repeated pair by pair, or you may twist a group together making a heavier fringe. This method of fringing becomes its own body of work, too.

Contemporary African Basket (Above). Reed, fine cotton, natural grasses, 9″ x 11″ in diameter. The figure eight stitch is used to tie large coils of reed with fine cotton, giving the appearance of weaving. Collection of Helen Pope. Photo by Candace Crockett.

Peruvian Fan (Right). Cotton cord and feathers, 9½″. We estimate that this fan was made in the late fifteenth century. The colorful feathers were knotted before being wrapped on a thin strand. Collection of Kenneth Shores. Photo by Marcia Chamberlain.

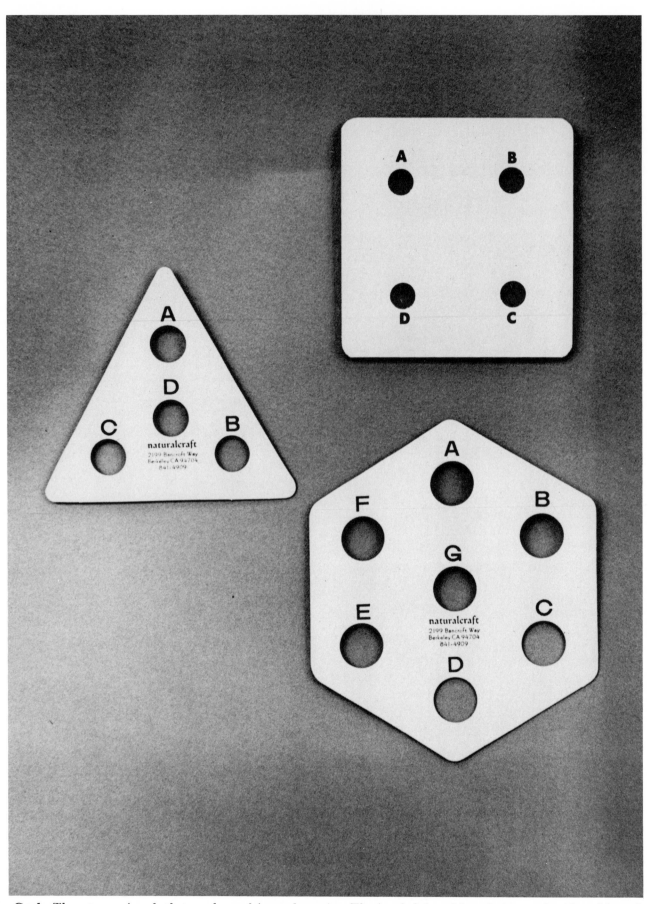

Cards. Three types of cards that can be used for card weaving. The four-holed card is easiest to work with and is used most often.

CHAPTER NINE

CARD WEAVING

Card weaving is a form of weaving that is similar in structure to braiding and twining. The tools and equipment are simple, and once the techniques are learned, the weaving progresses quickly. Highly detailed, changing patterns can be produced with card weaving, and some of the most pleasing results are due to characteristics that are unique to this technique. The designs and patterns can be simple, complex, subtle, or bold. Card weaving has traditionally been a technique for producing patterned, narrow bands, but as the photographs throughout this chapter show, the recent reawakening of interest in weaving has made it into a vigorous contemporary art form.

In card weaving, small cards (most commonly square, 3½″ x 3½″) form a kind of loom. A single card weaving might typically involve from 10 to 50 cards. Each card has a small hole near each corner through which pass the warp threads, with each hole having its own thread as well as an identifying letter. These warp threads are knotted together at each end and anchored under tension. If you were to compare the cards to a loom, the card holes act as heddle eyes. When all the A holes of the cards are lined up they are equivalent to one harness. If four-holed cards are used the card arrangement can be compared to a four-harness loom. The hands turn the cards rather than having treadles to lift the harnesses, in effect turning up a new harness with each turn.

Cards can be made or bought in different sizes and shapes and with different numbers of holes. This chapter is concerned with four-holed square cards, which are most common and most practical. During weaving certain arrangements of the holes

create an open space or weaving "shed" with half the warp threads above and half below this weaving shed. A separate thread, the weft, is passed through this opening, to bind or weave the warp threads together. As the cards are turned, usually as a unit, the holes shift and the threads change position, forming a new shed. The turning cards cause the threads to twist in sets of four, so that a four-ply fabric is formed. Most card weavings are done from patterns, usually drafted or worked out on a grid. These patterns can be very simple or highly complex.

HISTORY

Card weaving, though ancient in origin, has always been less universally known than most techniques discussed in this book. Card weaving was developed and used in ancient and medieval times only in cultures where weaving was already a sophisticated art. It was practiced in Europe, Asia, and North Africa, but not in the Americas. Cards have been found made of stone, wood, leather, bone, ivory, tortoise shell, and parchment. It is possible that card weaving was in use many thousands of years before the Christian era, and that it was brought from Egypt through Rome to western and northern Europe. Whether from Egypt, Scandinavia, or the East, card weaving spread throughout Europe and was in wide use up through the sixteenth century. Although card weaving has continued to be passed on from generation to generation in parts of Asia, Europe, and in North Africa, until recently it was lost as a widely popular craft.

For the Western intellectual world, card weaving was "rediscovered" at the turn of this century by a German scholar, Margarethe Lehman-Filhes. She was studying Icelandic weavings and decided that in order to thoroughly understand them she had to actually weave them. In the process she rediscovered and reconstructed card weaving. Her study led to the publication of *Ueber Brettchenweberei* (About Card Weaving) in 1901. This book marks the beginning of literature on the subject, and also the beginning of a revival that is now being reinterpreted in contemporary ways.

MATERIALS

The tools and materials used in card weaving are simple, available, and of modest cost. Weavers produce very admirable work using nothing more than cards and yarn. Cards can be purchased for pennies each from weaving shops (see Suppliers List) or they can easily be made from sturdy cardboard. This chapter deals with the four-holed square card because it is the one most often used, most generally available for purchase, and by far the easiest shape to work with. The typical card is about 3½″ square, with slightly rounded corners and with four corner-

holes lettered A, B, C, and D. Many types of yarn can be used for card weaving, but the yarn should be strong and relatively smooth. Since the cards turn on the yarn and move back and forth over the strands, weak threads or loosely twisted threads will give way. For the beginner, a medium-weight plied yarn is best. The cards are packed close, so fuzzy threads will catch and bind and prevent the cards from turning. As you become experienced, more delicate yarns can be used. Some weavers have no problem card weaving with single-ply handspun yarns, others would not touch it. Generally speaking the knitting worsted yarn that is available at all dime stores is unacceptable; weaving yarns give the best results. Most of the samples in this chapter were woven with a 3-ply wool weaving yarn of medium weight. Heavier yarns are more difficult to work with, and fine yarns require many more cards to produce a weaving of any width. Wool is pleasant to work with because of its natural resiliency and good color range.

In selecting color remember that the greater the

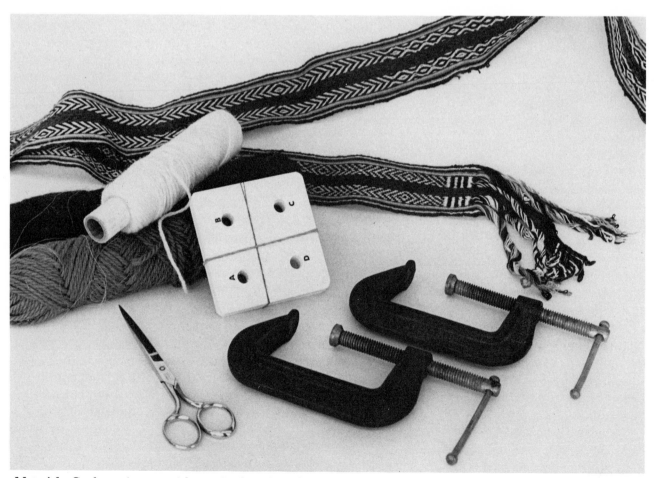

Materials. Card weaving materials are simple and can be easily improvised: yarn, cards, scissors, two C-clamps, and a belt or strap.

contrast between colors the more the pattern will show. A small belt shuttle is helpful for holding the weft thread and for beating it into place. A couple of C-clamps are useful to use for winding warp threads and to use as anchor points, but they are not necessary.

INSTRUCTIONS FOR CARD WEAVING

The following instructions will show you one way of setting up and weaving a card-woven band. Your first card weaving will be the hardest—on you, the yarn, and the cards—and the most difficult. Competence increases with practice and experience.

Pattern Drafting is the first step in card weaving. It is a plan worked out on a grid that tells you what color thread to put through each card hole. It can be simple or complex. Many card weavers do not actually draft their patterns out, but any pattern can be drafted. The form for a pattern draft is shown in Figure 24. The letters A, B, C, D, run down the left-hand side and represent the four individual card holes. The numbers across the bottom stand for individual cards. Each arrow along the bottom indicates the direction the threads take in passing through that particular card. (Threading is discussed in the next section.) The grid bounded by the letters and numbers represents the design area. Each square within that area represents an individual warp thread. Each hole in every card will carry its own thread. A pattern involving 10 cards will require 40 threads. The grid is filled in to indicate the color arrangement of the warp threads. Examples of pattern drafts and their woven bands are shown in the section on designing pattern drafts. The way you arrange the grid pattern (using symbols, colored pencils, or felt tip markers) determines how many warp threads of each color you will need and through which holes they will pass. For your first sampler you may use one of the pattern drafts in this chapter, you may design your own pattern draft, or you may thread the cards arbitrarily.

Threading. Each card must be threaded in one of the two ways shown in Figure 25. It is important to think of the printed side of the card as the "face" or "front" side, and to always keep this side facing to your left during threading and weaving. In example A the threads go through the card from the front to the back. This is indicated on a pattern draft by an arrow pointing to the right. This means that the threads will go through the card from the left to the right. In example B the threads go through the card from the back to the front or right to left. This is indicated on a pattern draft by an arrow pointing to the left. The threading direction is very important in pattern designing, as it influences the direction the threads twist during weaving. If the threading direction has been mixed or confused within an individual card, the threads will bind and the card will not turn. It will be impossible to make a weaving shed. The threading direction is part of the pattern draft. How it affects the woven design can be seen by studying the pattern drafts and the woven bands discussed in the section on designing pattern drafts.

Preparing the Warp. The number of warp threads needed for a card weaving is calculated by multiplying the number of holes times the number of cards. The sample pattern draft (Figure 24) would need 40 warp threads. How many threads of each color will depend on how many of each is called for in the pattern draft. In deciding how long to make your warp threads, take into consideration that they will be knotted at both ends and that weaving can progress only as far as it is possible to turn the cards. Wrap your warp under tension around a stationary anchor point and cut the ends when you have enough. This method is quick and insures that all strands will be the same length. C-clamps work well and are easily adjustable, but anything from table legs, to nails on the wall, to sticks in the ground will work. It is best to avoid knots in the warp, since movement of the cards will cause them to come loose. In measuring yarn be aware that if the yarn stretches and is wrapped under tension, it will be much shorter when it is cut and tension released. After warping you should have the exact number of threads in the right colors that are required by the pattern draft.

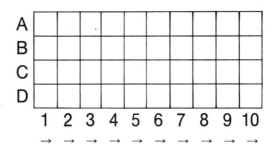

Figure 24. A pattern draft is best worked out on a grid to indicate color placement and threading direction. The letters on the left designate the lettered card holes. The numbers across the bottom stand for individual cards. The arrows indicate the direction of threading.

Threading the Cards. Count out the number of cards you will be using and number them consecutively in pencil (cards can be reused later). Stack the cards so that number 1 is on top. Pick up this first card, hold it so the lettered side faces left, and thread it according to your pattern draft. Be sure the threading direction is correct, and remember that each warp thread goes through only one hole. Draw the four threads going through card 1 out about 10″ and place the card face down. Some weavers like to knot these four strands at the end to help keep the threads in order. Continue threading each card and placing it face down on top of the preceding card. When all the cards are threaded and stacked, knot together all the just-threaded loose ends, and put a rubber band around the cards to keep them from getting mixed or tangled.

Preparing to Weave. The next step is to tie the knot to a secure anchor point. Tie a strong piece of cord under the knot and then tie the cord to something solid: C-clamp, door knob, fence post, piano leg, tree, hook, nail, etc. Slip the rubber band off the cards and begin pulling the cards away from the anchor point. Gradually and gently draw the cards down to the other end of the warp. This combs the warp and puts it in order. If the threads are par-

ticularly tangled, stop, put the rubber band back on, and comb out the strands with your fingers. Pull the cards to within about 10″ of the other end. Be careful—if the cards get too close to the end the threads will come out of the holes and all will be lost. When the cards reach the other end, hold all the threads taut and even the tension. Then knot the threads together near the end just as you did at the other end. A weft thread must be prepared before weaving can begin. The weft thread is a separate thread that goes through the opening (weaving shed) that resulted from turning the cards. The weft thread will not show in the weaving, but it will show where it "goes around the corner" along each edge. The weft thread is usually the same color and kind of yarn as the threads that go through the first and last (border) cards. Wind the weft thread into a small ball or around a small shuttle. Now anchor the second knot so the cards are suspended and the warp is under tension. Most card weavers find it comfortable to anchor the second knot to a belt around the waist. Tension can be easily adjusted by shifting the body toward or away from the weaving. Others like to be free, and prefer to devise some means of securing both ends to stationary anchor points (see Figure 26). Any means for achieving

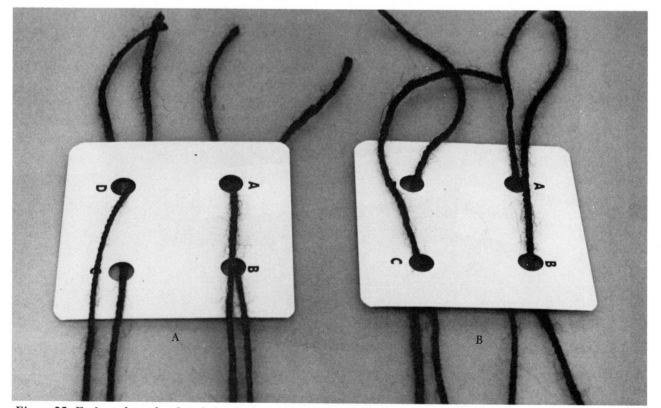

Figure 25. *Each card can be threaded one of two ways: from the front of the card to the back (indicated in a pattern draft by an arrow to the right), or from the back of the card to the front (indicated by an arrow to the left).*

tension will be satisfactory. Before weaving begins, check the cards to make sure that they face to the left and are in correct numerical order. Then turn the cards so that all holes A and D are on the top. Pull the cards toward your body, then push them firmly but gently away to open up the weaving shed. If the cards have been threaded properly, the pull-push movement will open up the weaving shed. When you pass the weft thread through the shed (allowing the weft end to hang out about 8″) your actual weaving will have begun.

Weaving. The conventional way to card weave is to turn the cards as a unit one quarter-turn at a time. Each quarter-turn creates a new weaving shed through which the weft thread passes. Weaving progresses by turning the cards in sequences of eight quarter-turns: four quarter-turns toward the body and four quarter-turns away from the body.

The beginning or neutral position is with holes D and A in the top position. The first four quarter-turns are toward the body, and the weft thread is brought across after each quarter-turn. Use both hands to turn or rotate the cards. Turn 1 brings hole C to the top so the threads that pass through holes C and D form the top layer of the weaving shed. Turn 2 brings B to the top, so that B–C form the top layer. Turn 3 brings A to the top so that A–B form the top layer. Turn 4 brings D to the top so that D–A (the neutral position) form the top layer of the weaving shed. Remember that after each turn of the cards the deck should be pulled toward the body and then pushed away. Pass the weft thread through after each quarter-turn, and push it into place with a finger, shuttle, or edge (a kitchen knife, letter opener, or ruler). The cards will turn easily if even, taut tension is maintained on the warp threads. Hold the deck of cards loosely together, keeping each card slightly apart so it will turn easily.

The second four quarter-turns, which complete the sequence of eight, are away from the body. Turn 1 brings hole B to the top, so the threads that pass through holes A–B form the top layer of the weaving shed. Turn 2 brings hole C to the top so that B–C form the top layer. Turn 3 brings D to the top so that C–D form the top layer. Turn 4 brings A to the top so that D–A form the top layer of the weaving shed. Weaving progresses by repeating this sequence of eight turns. As the cards are turned toward the body the pattern appears as it is drafted on the grid. As the cards are turned away from the body, the mirror image of the drafted pattern appears. Weaving does not have to progress in the conven-

tional sequence of four turns toward the body and four turns away. The cards can turn any number of turns in either direction, and any two holes can be used as a neutral point. Single cards or groups of cards can be turned to vary and change the pattern.

If you are using your body as an anchor point, untie and retie the woven band as weaving progresses, moving closer and closer to the first anchor point. If you run out of weft thread, begin a new one by overlapping the old and new threads in the shed. When the band is woven to the required length, or the cards reach the knot, simply untie the knot and slip the cards off.

Moving the Cards Laterally. During card weaving individual cards can be picked up and moved to a new position within the deck so the order of the cards is changed. This lateral movement of cards changes the pattern, and brings warp threads across the face of the weaving. This movement of the warp threads, particularly when cards threaded in the same color are moved simultaneously, creates a linear flow and movement that has tremendous design potential.

DOUBLE-FACE WEAVING

Double-face weaving with four-holed cards produces a two-face fabric; the threads that go through two holes of each card appear on the top surface of the weaving and the threads that go through the other two holes appear on the bottom surface of the weaving. For example, if all A and B holes in a card weaving carry white threads and all C and D holes carry black threads, a band can be woven in which the top surface is white and the bottom surface is black. Double-face weaving involves a sequence of just four quarter-turns rather than the usual sequence of eight turns. The double-face technique does not require special setting up, since it results simply from a particular card turning sequence.

With the cards in the D–A or neutral position, the sequence explained here will produce a double-face weaving in which the warp threads that pass through holes A and B will form the top surface of the fabric, and the threads that pass through holes C and D will form the bottom surface of the fabric. Turn two quarter-turns away from your body, then two quarter-turns toward your body. Bring the weft thread across after each quarter-turn. This sequence of four quarter-turns is repeated to extend the weaving. The double-face technique is sometimes used to form letters and large designs on the fabric surface. You may change the design by turning individ-

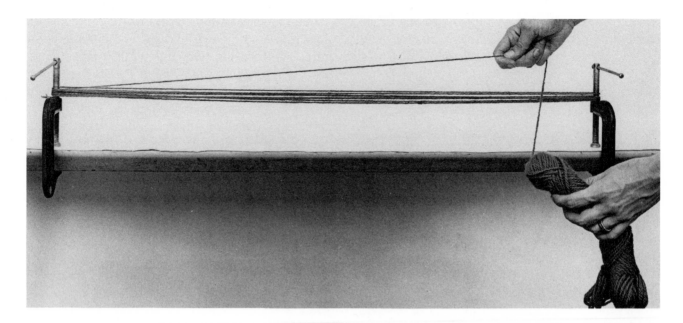

Card Weaving: Step 1 (Above). A warp can be measured by winding threads between two C-clamps.

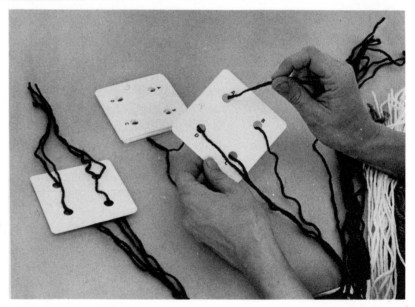

Step 2. Number the cards to be used, stack them face up in order with card 1 on top, and begin threading. As each card is threaded (and the warp pulled through about 10″) it is placed face down on top of the preceding card.

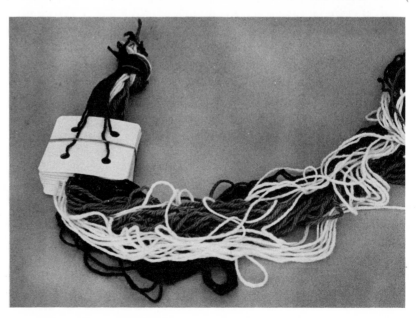

Step 3. After threading the cards, knot the ends that have just been threaded and place a rubber band around the cards.

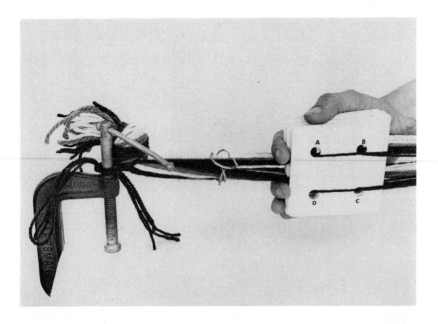

Step 4. Anchor the knot, slip the rubber band off, and pull the cards along the warp to the other end.

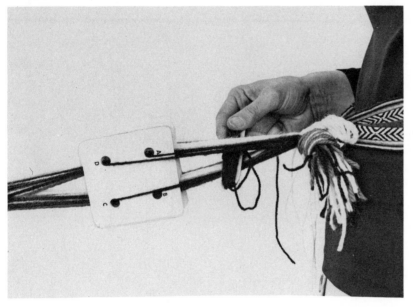

Step 5. Even up the tension of the warp threads, knot the ends, prepare the weft, and anchor the second knot to your waist. You are ready to begin weaving. The cards are usually turned in quarter-turn sequences of four turns toward the body and four turns away from the body. After each turn the weft thread is passed through the opening, or shed, formed by the turning of the cards.

Figure 26 (Below). The warp threads can also be anchored between two C-clamps.

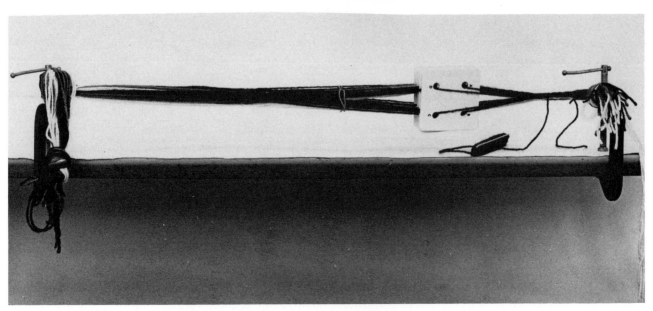

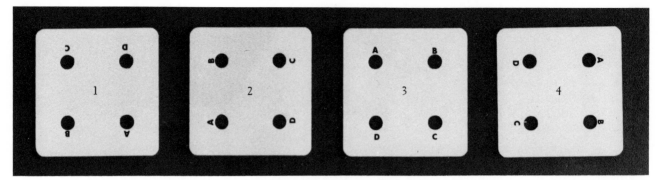

1. *The card positions as they appear when turned toward the body four quarter-turns.*

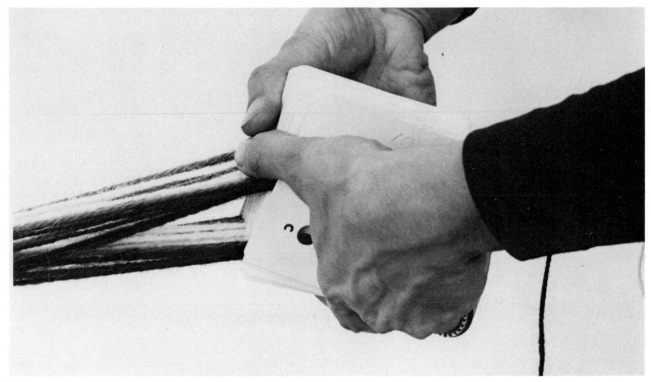

2. *The position of the hands while turning the cards toward the body.*

ual cards two quarter-turns in order to bring the color on the bottom surface to the top surface.

DOUBLE WEAVING

The double-weave technique produces two separate woven layers, and like the double-face technique may be integrated into the normal weaving sequence at any time. The shed for double weaving is formed in a special way to create two spaces; the weft thread makes a complete circle, going through both openings before the cards change position. Two holes weave the top layer and the other two holes weave the bottom layer. The cards are angled, with one hole in the top position and one hole in the bottom position. Two weaving sheds are formed. The weft thread is taken through the top shed and then through the bottom shed, so it makes a complete circle. If the threads that pass through holes A and B are to form the top layer of the open shed and threads C and D the bottom layer, hole A should be on top for one turn, and hole B should be on top for the next. Double weaving involves rocking the cards back and forth between these two holes. If one weft thread is used, and it is brought consistently through the top shed and then through the bottom shed after each changing of the cards, a flat tubelike woven structure is formed. Two weft threads can also be used, one going through the top shed and the other through the lower shed, to create two strips not joined at the edges. When you resume the normal turning sequence the two layers will again become one.

1. *The card positions as they appear when turned away from the body for four quarter-turns.*

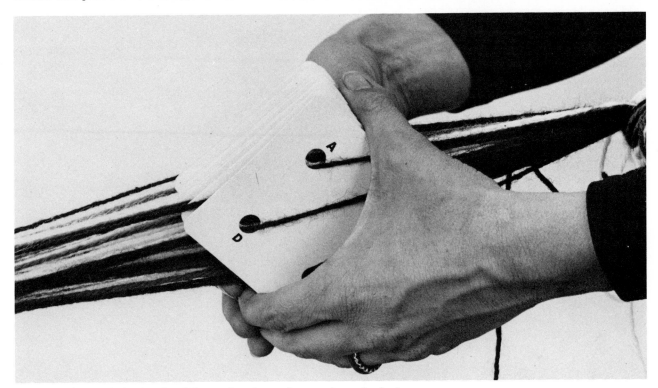

2. *The position of the hands while turning the cards away from the body.*

Tubular Weaving

It is possible to make a tube with double weaving, but "tubular weaving" refers to a technique in which the weft is threaded through the shed in a way that pulls the weaving into a tubular form. In tubular weaving the weft thread always enters the shed from the same side (normal weaving shed), goes under the weaving, and after each quarter-turn of the cards is passed through the next new shed in the same way, and so on. If the weft thread is pulled tight after each passage, the tube will form as weaving progresses by drawing the two edges together.

Designing Pattern Drafts

The pattern draft tells you how to thread your cards for card weaving. It tells you which color thread goes through each card hole, and it tells you the direction from which each card should be threaded. In many cases it is not necessary to draw the pattern draft, but when working with complicated patterns that involve many colors it is very helpful. The form for a pattern draft is shown in Figure 24. Each card can be threaded in one of two ways and this can greatly affect the woven design. Border cards are frequently threaded in the same color as the weft thread, so the weft thread does not show along the edges. In drawing a pattern draft it can be helpful to work in colored pencils. There are no color rules, but as in all warp face weaves, the more contrast between colors the more visible the pattern. Many weavers prefer to use symbols to determine the design and to decide on individual colors later.

Moving Warp Threads. In order to move warp threads laterally, pick up one or more cards and move it or them to the new position in the deck.

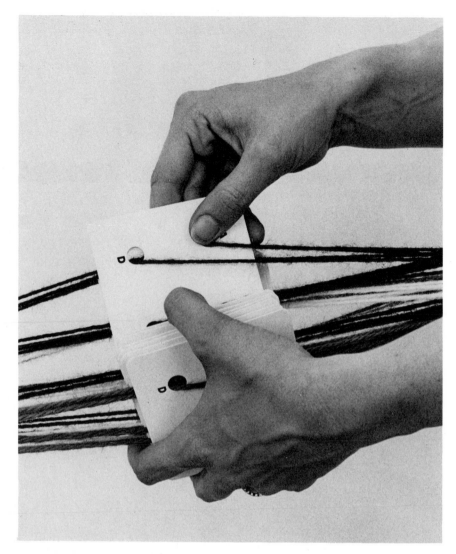

Double Weaving (Below) is done by angling the cards so two weaving sheds are formed simultaneously.

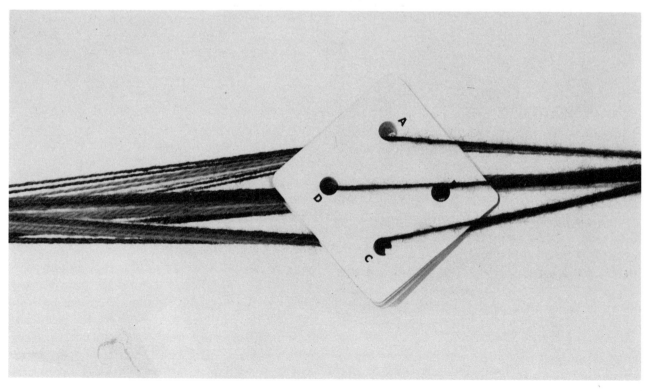

If the cards are turned toward the body during weaving the pattern as drafted will appear. The mirror image of the drafted pattern appears when the cards are turned away. It can be helpful in visualizing the complete pattern to draw or draft the full eight turns so that each row of the weaving, as indicated by the letters on the side, are repeated in sequence to show the mirror image (from the bottom up, D, C, B, A, A, B, C, D).

The best way to understand how threading affects the design is to look at a pattern draft and then to examine the woven band. For example, the colors in Figure 27, with the exception of the four border cards, were picked randomly. The cards were threaded in what is called "alternate threading." The threading direction changes with each card. The resulting woven band is shown. Alternate threading gives a surface appearance similar to knitting. As the cards turn the threads in groups of four, a twist occurs in alternating directions. In weaving the band the cards were turned in one direction for many turns before reversing. In Figure 28 the symbols on the grid are arranged symmetrically in a chevron or half-diamond design with the apex between cards 8 and 9. The threading direction changes at the apex, so half of the cards, 1 through 8, are threaded in one direction and the rest, 9 through 16, in the opposite direction. When the cards are turned four turns toward the body and four turns away, diamond-like shapes are formed. When the cards are turned continuously in one direction half-diamonds or chevrons appear. If the threading direction was just the opposite, the shapes would have broken edges rather than smooth edges. The two bands in Figure 29 were woven from the same pattern with the same color arrangement, but with different threadings. In band A the threading direction was all one way. In band B alternate threading was used.

Figure 30 is a simple regular pattern of oblique stripes in which each card (with the exception of the border cards) carries two dark threads and two light threads. The two different threadings indicated on the pattern draft are shown worked up nearby. Threading 1 produces smooth lines on the top surface. Threading 2 produces broken lines on the top surface. In this case the bottom side of band A is identical to the top side of band B and vice versa. When cards are threaded as indicated in Figure 30, the oblique angles will go to the right when the cards are turned in one direction and to the left when turned in the other direction. It is possible to construct many exciting linear patterns by turning

Card Weaving (detail) by Candace Crockett. Wool and sheep's fleece, 120" x 30". This hanging combines loom weaving with card weaving. The photograph shows the result of decreasing warp threads by cutting the thread at the anchor point and slipping off the cards. The cut threads were woven across to the edge to make fringe. Photo by David Donoho.

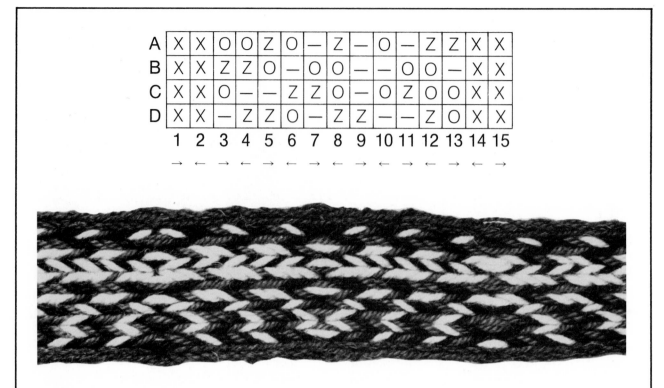

	1	2	3	4	5	6	7	8	9	10	11	12	13	14	15
A	X	X	O	O	Z	O	—	Z	—	O	—	Z	Z	X	X
B	X	X	Z	Z	O	—	O	O	—	—	O	O	—	X	X
C	X	X	O	—	—	Z	Z	O	—	O	Z	O	O	X	X
D	X	X	—	Z	Z	O	—	Z	Z	—	—	Z	O	X	X

→ ← → ← → ← → ← → ← → ← → ← →

Figure 27. A band with random color threading woven from the pattern draft shown. On the draft O = black, Z = brown, — = white, and X = blue.

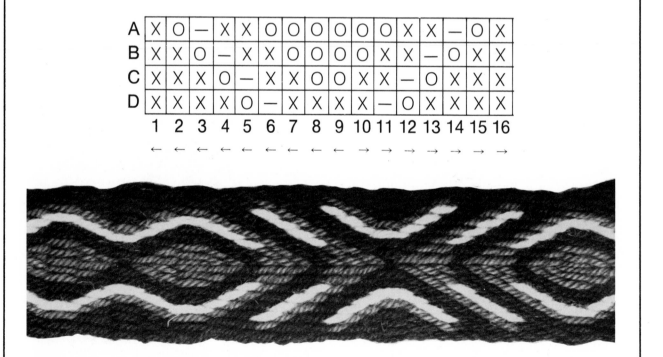

	1	2	3	4	5	6	7	8	9	10	11	12	13	14	15	16
A	X	O	—	X	X	O	O	O	O	O	X	X	—	O	X	X
B	X	X	O	—	X	X	O	O	O	O	X	X	—	O	X	X
C	X	X	X	O	—	X	X	O	O	X	X	—	O	X	X	X
D	X	X	X	X	O	—	X	X	X	—	O	X	X	X	X	X

← ← ← ← ← ← ← ← ← → → → → → → →

Figure 28. A band woven from a pattern draft designed with predetermined lines and shapes. Each card was threaded according to the grid pattern, which was designed to produce strong linear patterns. X = black, O = brown, and — = white.

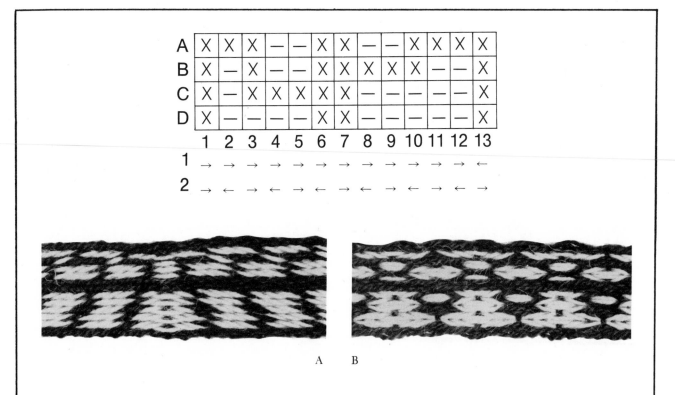

	1	2	3	4	5	6	7	8	9	10	11	12	13
A	X	X	X	—	—	X	X	—	—	X	X	X	X
B	X	—	X	—	—	X	X	X	X	X	—	—	X
C	X	—	X	X	X	X	X	—	—	—	—	—	X
D	X	—	—	—	—	X	X	—	—	—	—	—	X

1 → → → → → → → → → → → → ←

2 → ← → ← → ← → ← → ← → ← →

A   B

Figure 29. These two bands were woven from the same pattern draft, but threading 1 was used for band A and threading 2 for band B. X = purple and — = white.

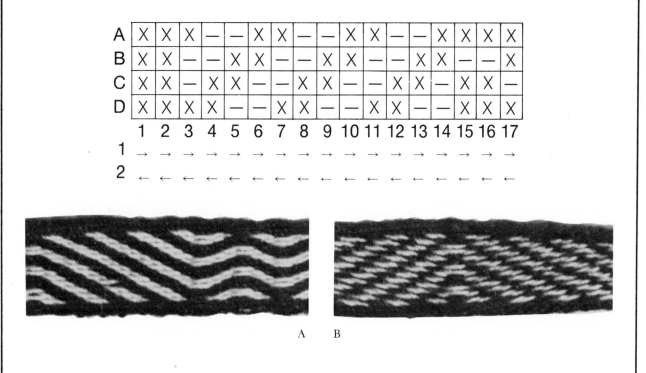

	1	2	3	4	5	6	7	8	9	10	11	12	13	14	15	16	17
A	X	X	X	—	—	X	X	—	—	X	X	—	—	X	X	X	X
B	X	X	—	—	X	X	—	—	X	X	—	—	X	X	—	—	X
C	X	X	—	X	X	—	—	X	X	—	—	X	X	—	X	X	—
D	X	X	X	X	—	—	X	X	—	—	X	X	—	—	X	X	X

1 → → → → → → → → → → → → → → → → →

2 ← ← ← ← ← ← ← ← ← ← ← ← ← ← ← ← ←

A   B

Figure 30. Another example of weaving two bands from one pattern draft. Threading 1 was used in band A and threading 2 used in band B. X = blue and — = white.

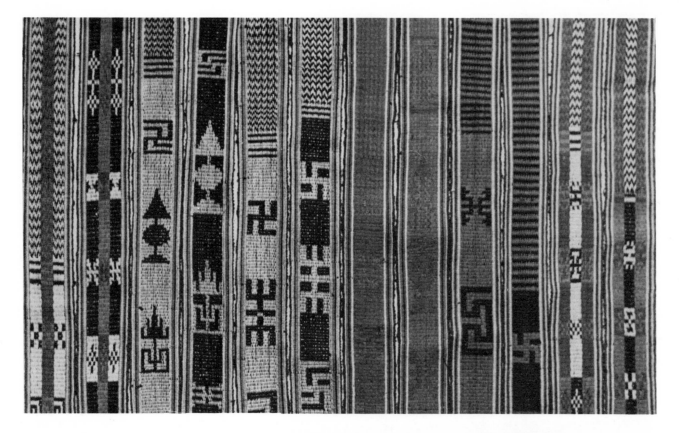

Tibetan Belts (Above). Fine cotton, 2″ in diameter. These contemporary belts were woven by refugee monks living in Nepal. The larger patterns were woven in the double-face technique. Photo by Candace Crockett.

Open-Ended Card Weaving (Right) by Dolores Levin. Plastic-coated wire, 33″ x 23″. In this example of free-form weaving the warp threads become weft threads and meander in different directions. Photo by Candace Crockett.

Bands (Opposite Page) by Flora Milligan. Fine cotton, each 1½″ wide. The two bands had the same threading, with two dark and two light threads going through each card (except the border cards). The cards were arranged to weave oblique angles, then groups of cards were turned in different directions to control whether the angles went to the right or the left. Photo by Candace Crockett.

some cards in one direction and others in the opposite direction.

Many other things besides color and threading will affect and change the pattern during weaving: moving cards laterally, use of double-face weaving, double weaving, turning individual cards, turning the cards in different ways, turning the cards without weaving, working with different weights and kinds of yarn, and using different neutral points.

FINISHING

A card-woven fabric is dense, and due to the twisting of the strands, the warp threads are completely intertwined with the weft thread. No special binding or tying need be done to secure either the warp or weft ends. Although it is not generally necessary, the ends of the weft thread can be taken through the fabric with a blunt-ended tapestry needle. If the weaving does not lie flat after weaving it can be pressed. Some weavers like to braid, knot, or bind the warp ends. Strips can be sewn together easily and smoothly to make larger pieces by butting the edges and whip-stitching them together on the back side. A tapestry needle should be used with the same color and kind of yarn used in the border cards during weaving.

Beads and other objects can be sewn on afterwards, or actually woven in as the weaving progresses. Beads are woven in by stringing the beads on a second weft thread (it can be a very fine thread) that follows along with the normal weft thread. The beads are then pushed along the thread and "dropped" into place. The normal weft thread keeps the weaving tight and compact. The photograph shows a band in progress in which beads are being dropped on the borders.

Warp threads can also be decreased during weaving to shape the fabric. This is done by cutting the four threads that go through an individual card, slipping the card off, and taking the cut warp ends through the weaving shed along with the normal weft thread.

SCULPTURAL CARD WEAVING

Card-woven strips can be combined with techniques such as knotting, braiding, wrapping, and loom weaving to produce dimensional and sculptural pieces. Open-ended or free-form card weaving is a technique that is inherently sculptural. In this process, weaving goes on between the cards and the first anchor point, with the other end being allowed to remain free and open. The cards can be separated and broken down into smaller groups, allowing a great deal of freedom in spacing and shaping the piece. Groups of cards can be pulled and manipulated at will. Warp threads can become weft threads and the directional flow of the weaving can change at will. With this method the ends that are usually tied to the body are left dangling, and tension problems are usually solved by having a number of temporary anchor points. Some weavers find that they can hold the loose warp ends in one hand and turn the cards with the other.

Whether used as a traditional belt weaving technique or as a means of creating complex fabric sculpture, card weaving is a particularly pleasing weaving method: inexpensive, portable, highly variable, and uniquely beautiful.

BIBLIOGRAPHY

BOOKS

American Fabrics Magazine. *Encyclopedia of Textiles.* New Jersey: Prentice-Hall, 1972.

Anchor Manual of Needlework. London: B.T. Batsford, 1958.

Ashley, Clifford. *The Ashley Book of Knots.* New York: Doubleday and Co., 1944.

Atwater, M.M. *Byways in Handweaving.* New York: Macmillan Co., 1954.

Backer, Stanley. *Yarn.* From *Scientific American,* December, 1972.

Birrell, Verla. *The Textile Arts.* New York: Schocken Books, 1973.

Bolton, Eileen. *Lichens for Vegetable Dyeing.* London: Studio Books, 1960.

Colton, M., and Ferrell, R. *Hopi Dyes.* The Museum of Northern Arizona (Flagstaff), 1965.

Conley, Emma. *Vegetable Dyeing.* North Carolina: Penland School of Handicrafts, Inc.

Cook, J. Gordon. *Handbook of Textile Fibers.* Herts., England: Merrow Publishing, 1959.

Crockett, C. *Card Weaving.* New York: Watson-Guptill Publications, 1973. London: Pitman, 1973.

Crowfoot, Grace. *Methods of Handspinning in Egypt and the Sudan.* Halifax, England: The Bankfield Museum, 1931.

Davenport, Elsie. *Your Handspinning.* Pacific Grove, California: Craft & Hobby Book Service, reprint, 1964.

D'Harcourt, Raoul. *Textiles of Ancient Peru and Their Techniques.* Seattle: University of Washington Press, 1962.

Diderot, Denis. *Pictorial Encyclopedia of Trades and Industry.* New York: Dover Publications.

Edson, N., and Stimmel, A. *Creative Crochet.* New York: Watson-Guptill Publications, 1973. London: Pitman, 1973.

Emery, Irene. *The Primary Structure of Fabrics.* Washington, D.C.: The Textile Museum, 1966.

Fairseruis, W.A. *Wool Through the Ages.* New York: The Wool Bureau, 1955.

Fannin, Allen. *Handspinning, Art and Technique.* New York: Van Nostrand Reinhold, 1970.

5000 Years of Fibers and Fabrics. New York: The Brooklyn Museum, 1946.

Forbes, R.J. *Studies in Ancient Technology,* Vol. IV. New York: W.S. Heinman, 1964.

Graumont, R., and Hensel, J. *Encyclopedia of Knots and Fancy Rope Work.* Cambridge, Maryland: Cornell Maritime Press, 1943.

Hall, Eliza C. *A Book of Handwoven Coverlets.* Boston: Little, Brown and Co., 1931.

Harvey, Virginia. *Macramé.* New York: Van Nostrand Reinhold, 1967.

Harvey, V., and Tidball, H. *Weft Twining.* Pacific Grove, California: Craft & Hobby Book Service, 1969.

Henderson, P. *William Morris—His Life, Work and Friends.* New York: McGraw-Hill, 1967.

Hess, K.P. *Textile Fibers and Their Use.* Philadelphia: J.B. Lippincott, 1954.

Hollen, N., and Saddler, J. *Textiles.* New York: Macmillan Co., 1973.

Indian Handcraft Series. U.S. Dept. of the Interior, Bureau of Indian Affairs. Listings and purchase available through the Haskell Institute, Lawrence, Kansas.

James, George W. *Indian Basketry.* Republication of work by H. Malkan, 1909. New York: Dover Publications, 1972.

Kiewe, Heinz E. *The Sacred History of Knitting.* Oxford, England: Art Needlework Industries, 1967.

LaBarge, Lura. *Do Your Own Thing with Macramé.* New York: Watson-Guptill Publications, 1972. London: Pitman, 1972.

Lesch, Alma. *Vegetable Dyeing.* New York: Watson-Guptill Publications, 1970.

Little, Frances. *Early American Textiles.* New York: the Century Co., 1931.

Maile, Anne. *Tie and Dye.* New York: Taplinger Publishing Co., 1963.

Marein, Shirley. *Off the Loom: Creating with Fiber.* New York: Viking Press, 1972.

Mauersberger, H.R., ed. *Matthew's Textile Fibers*. New York: John Wiley and Sons, 1954.

Means, Phillip A. *A Story of Peruvian Textiles*. Boston: the Museum of Fine Arts, 1932.

Meilach, Dona. *Batik and Tie-Dye*. New York: Crown Publishers, 1973.

Meilach, Dona. *Macramé*. New York: Crown Publishers, 1971.

Morron, Mable. *Magic in the Dye Pot*. New Mexico: Santa Fe Natural Dye Workshop, 1966. (Available through M. Morrow, 1001 E. Alameda, Santa Fe, N.M.)

Norbury, J., and Aqutter, M. *Odhams Encyclopedia of Knitting*. London: Odhams Press, 1957.

Nordland, Odd. *Primitive Scandinavian Textiles in Knotless Netting*. Oslo, Norway: Oslo University Press, 1961.

Olschki, Leonardo. *The Myth of Felt*. Berkeley: the University of California Press, 1949.

Phillips, Mary Walker. *Creative Knitting*. New York: Van Nostrand Reinhold, 1971.

Phillips, Mary Walker. *Step-by-Step Macramé*. New York: Golden Press, 1970.

Priestman, Howard. *Principles of Worsted Spinning*. New York: Longmans, Green, 1906.

Robinson, Stuart. *A History of Printed Textiles*. London: Studio Vista, 1969.

Rossbach, E. *Baskets as Textile Art*. New York: Van Nostrand Reinhold, 1973.

Schetky, E.J., ed. *Dye Plants and Dyeing*. New York: Brooklyn Botanical Gardens, 1964.

Square Knot Booklets 1, 2, and 3. New York: P.C. Herwig Co., 1968.

Thomas, Mary. *Mary Thomas's Knitting Book*. London: Hodder and Stoughton, 1938.

Threads of History. The American Federation of Arts, 1965.

Thurstan, Violetta. *A Short History of Ancient Decorative Textiles*. London: Favil Press, 1972.

Thurstan, Violetta. *The Use of Vegetable Dyes*. Leicester, England: Dryad Press, 1965.

Weir, Shelagh. *Spinning and Weaving in Palestine*. London: the British Museum, 1970.

Wool Education Center, 200 Clayton Street, Denver, Colorado, will send various pamphlets free of charge.

DIRECTORIES

The Canadian Textile Directory, Davison's Textile Blue Book, and *Davison's Textile Catalogues and Buyers' Guide*: all industrial in nature, covering all aspects of the textile industry. A number of the sources will deal directly with craftsmen for both equipment and supplies.

International Handspinning Directory and Handbook. Edited by Doloria M. Chapin.

Journal of the Society of Dyers and Colourists. P.O. Box 244, Perkin House, 82 Grattan Road, Bradford, Yorks., BD1 2JB, England.

Textile History. Published annually by David and Charles, Devon, England.

JOURNALS

Professional journals such as *The American Anthropologist* (American Anthropological Association), *Publications in American Archaeology and Ethnology* (University of California, Berkeley), and the *Southwestern Journal of Archaeology* (University of New Mexico, Albuquerque) contain a number of definitive articles. Authors include Junius Bird, M.D.C. Crawford, Mary Lois Kissell, Alfred L. Kroeber, and Lila M. O'Neale.

PERIODICALS

Major among the periodicals devoted to textiles are: *American Dyestuff Reporter, American Fabrics, Craft Horizons, Modern Textiles, Quarterly Journal of The Guilds of Weavers, Spinners, and Dyers* (England), *Shuttle, Spindle and Dyepot*, and *Textile World Magazine*.

CIBA Review is unfortunately no longer being published, however most major libraries have the series for reference. The following articles relate to subjects discussed in this book:

1961: 1. "Medieval Dyeing"; 2. "India, its Dyers and its Color Symbolism"; 4. "Purple"; 7. "Scarlet"; 9. "Dyeing and Tanning in Classical Antiquity"; 10. "Trade Routes and Dye Markets in Middle Ages"; 11. "The Early History of Silk"; 12. "Weaving and Dyeing in Ancient Egypt and Babylon"; 18. "Great Masters of Dyeing in 18th Century France"; 21. "Weaving and Dyeing in North Africa"; 28. "The Spinning Wheel"; 30. "The Essentials of Handicrafts and the Craft of Weaving among Primitive Peoples"; 33. "Bark Fabrics of the South Seas"; 84. "Maori Textile Techniques"; 85. "Indigo"; 95. "Cotton"; 106. "The Stocking"; 108. "Jute and its Substitutes"; 111. "Spun Silk"; 113. "The Wool Fiber"; 115. "Sir William Henry Perkin"; 116. "Coil"; 117. "Tablet Weaving"; 123. "Ramie"; 129. "Felt"; 136. "Peruvian Textile Techniques."

1962: 5. "Hemp."

1963: 5. "Glass Fibers."

1964: 2. "Dyeing Theory"; 6. "Knitting Techniques."

1965: 1. "Nonwovens"; 2. "Flax"; 3. "Yarn and Thread."

1967: 4. "Japanese Resist Dyeing"; 35. "The Hat"; 39. "Madder and Turkey Red"; 44. "Ikats"; 45. "The Crafts of the Puszta Herdsmen"; 49. "Flax and Hemp"; 53. "Silk Moths"; 54. "Basketry and Woven Fabrics of the European Stone and Bronze Age"; 63. "Basic Textile Techniques"; 68. "Dyeing among Primitive Peoples."

1968: 2. "Textiles in Biblical Times."

Handweaver and Craftsman contains information relating to techniques discussed in this book that cannot be easily found elsewhere. Write to the magazine at 220 Fifth Avenue, New York, N.Y. 10001 for information on obtaining back issues and reprints. A list of pertinent articles follows in order of publication date:

1950. Vol. 1 #3: "Commercial Dyes for Handweaving," E.A. Lucey.

1951. Vol. 2#1: "Preparing Plant Fibers for Handweaving," T. Ford. Vol. 2#3: "Wool—Most Versatile of Fibers" (Part I), R.H. Kiessling; "A Spinning Lesson," A. Muller; "Mixing and Matching Colors in Dyeing," E.A. Lucey. Vol. 2#4: "Common Plants Yield Dyes for Homespun Yarn"; "Weaving with Native Materials," R. Fuchs; "Wool —Most Versatile of Fibers" (Part II), R.H. Kiessling.

1952. Vol. 3#2: "Flax—From Seed to Yarn," V. Parslow. Vol. 3#3: "Before Heddles Were Invented," J.B. Bird; "Cotton Plays a Vital Role," W. Hausner. Vol. 3#4: "It's in the Cards," H.G. Thorpe.

1954. Vol. 5#1: "A New Man-made Fiber," K. Laurell. Vol. 5#3: "An Old Wheel Spins Again," C.M. Wetter.

1955. Vol. 6#2: "Raw Silk for the Handweaver," M. Wehrlin. Vol. 6#3: "Characteristics of Man-made Yarns," W. Hausner.

1956. Vol. 7#2: "Spinning Wheels," V.D. Parslow. Vol. 7#3: "New Developments in Man-made Fibers," W. Hausner.

1957. Vol. 8#1: "Learning to Spin," V.D. Parslow.

1958. Vol. 9#3: "Developments in Man-made Yarns and Fibers," W. Hausner.

1959. Vol. 10#2: "Textile Fiber and Dye Garden." Vol. 10#3: "New Zealand Spinners," M. Robinson.

1960. Vol. 11#1: "Developments in Man-made Fibers," W. Hausner.

1961. Vol. 12#1: "Developments in Man-made Fibers," W. Hausner. Vol. 12#2: "Cardweaving Translated to a Handloom," A.R. Priest.

1963. Vol. 14#3: "Handspun Yarns from Black Sheep," P. Simmons.

1964. Vol. 15#1: "Raw Wool Values," J.A. Innes. Vol. 15#2: "Sprang, an Ancient Technique," P. Collingwood.

1965. Vol. 16#2: "Mary Walker Phillips, A New Approach to Knitting." Vol. 16#3: "Cardweaving, A New Approach," E. Regensteiner.

1966. Vol. 17#1: "Handspinning in New Hampshire," T. Brackett; "From Sheep to Shawl," S. Thorne. Vol. 17#2: "Spinning Wheels," G. Martin; "When You Begin to Spin," P. Simmons. Vol. 17#4: "Weaving with Handspun Yarns," P. Simmons.

1967. Vol. 18#2: "Spinning Flax," A.A. Fannin. Vol. 18#3: "Qiviut from the Musk Ox"; "Cardweaving," B. Frey; "Macramé," V.I. Harvey. Vol. 18#4: "On Repairing Spinning Wheels," A.A. Fannin.

1968. Vol. 19#1: "Pueblo Weaving—an Ancient Art"; "Overtwist, A Spinner's Problem," P. Simmons. Vol. 19#2: "Weaving with Handspun Linen Yarn," A.A. Fannin; "Revival of Ikat," J.M. Rushfelt. Vol. 19#3: "Indian Fingerweaving," J. White; "Home Dyeing," J.F. Langton. Vol. 19#4: "Indigo," W. and F. Gerber; "Macramé," V.I. Harvey; "Decorative Braids," M.B. Sober.

1969. Vol. 20#1: "Hella Skowronski Experiments with Sprang"; "Raising Silkworms," F. Pentler; "Brooks Lace and Weaving," O.G. Tod. Vol. 20#2: "Dyeing with Lichens," W. and F. Gerber; "Twined Bags and Pouches," J.K. White; "Carding by Machine," P. Simmons; "Preparation of Fibers for Spinning," A.A. Fannin. Vol. 20#4: "Irregularity in Handspun" (Part I), P. Simmons.

1970. Vol. 21#1: "Plaiting," C. Schira; "Modern Twined Bags," E.H. Spencer; "Irregularity in Handspun" (Part II), P. Simmons. Vol. 21#2: "Irregularity in Handspun" (Part III), P. Simmons. Vol. 21#3: "Assumption Sash," A. Whitelaw; "Spinning in New Zealand," J. Ashford. Vol. 21#4: "Nez Perce Indians," A. Connette.

1971. Vol. 22#1: "Tie-dyeing in Sumba," M. Adams; "Wool—Plants—Color," P. Mercer. Vol. 22#2: "Arctic Handknitted," H.M. Griffiths; "Tied Up in Knots," P. Mercer; "Dip Dyeing," W. Hausner; "Handspinning," D. Senders; "How to Raise Sheep," P. Simmons. Vol. 22#3: "Considering Cardweaving," C. Crockett; "Milkweed and Balduinea in the Dyepot," F. and W. Gerber; "Fundamentals of Basketry," R. Rippy. Vol. 22#4: "Splicing from Central America," M.B. Sober; "Tips on Home Dyeing," G. Hurry.

1972. Vol. 23#1: "The Spinning Wheel," I. Mathieson; "Weaving in Africa," L. Cragholm. Vol. 23#3: "Notes on Vegetable Dyeing," F. and W. Gerber; "Three-dimensional Macramé," E. and G. Andes. Vol. 23#6: "African Textiles," R. Sieber; "Cochineal as Domestic Dyestuff," W. and F. Gerber.

1973. Vol. 24#1: "Collecting Spinning Wheels," W. Ralph; "Tyrian Purple," J. P. Robinson Jr.; "Attu Basketry," L. McIver. Vol. 24#2: "Bobbin Lace and the Linen Stitch," K. and J. Kliot. Vol. 24#3: "Handspinning Technique," L.E. Rees; "Fiber Preparation," V.K. Fraser; "Traditional Ikat"; "A Basketry Workshop," D. Hamsen and B. Morris. Vol. 24#4: "Two Treadle Spinning Wheels," J. Houston.

U.S. Museum Collections

The following museums include permanent collections of textiles (both loomed and non-loomed). We have not attempted to evaluate their size, quality, or specific content. There are also some noteworthy collections not mentioned here that fall under the auspices of various State Historical Societies.

Adena State Memorial, Chillicothe, Ohio 45601
American Museum of Natural History, New York, New York 10024
Berea College Museum, Berea, Kentucky 40403
Brooklyn Museum, Brooklyn, New York 11238
Buffalo Bill Historical Center, Cody, Wyoming 82414
Busch-Reisinger Museum, Cambridge, Massachusetts 02138
Cincinnati Art Museum, Cincinnati, Ohio 45202
City Art Museum of St. Louis, St. Louis, Missouri 63110
Cleveland Museum of Art, Cleveland, Ohio 44106
Colorado Springs Fine Arts Center, Colorado Springs, Colorado 80903
Cooper-Hewitt Museum, New York, New York 10028
Corcoran Gallery of Art, Washington, D.C. 20006
Denver Art Museum, Denver, Colorado 80204
Detroit Institute of Arts, Detroit, Michigan 48202
De Young Memorial Museum, San Francisco, California 94418
Drexel Museum, Drexel University, Philadelphia, Pennsylvania 19104
DuPont Winterthur Museum, Winterthur, Delaware 19735
Field Museum of Natural History, Chicago, Illinois 60605
Hafenreffer Museum of Anthropology, Bristol, Rhode Island 02883
Heard Museum, Phoenix, Arizona 85004
Helen Geier Flynt, Fabric Hall, Deerfield, Massachusetts 01342
Honolulu Academy of Arts, Honolulu, Hawaii 96814
Illinois State Museum, Springfield, Illinois 62706
Kelsey Museum of Archaeology, Ann Arbor, Michigan 48104
Lauren Rogers Library and Museum of Art, Laurel, Mississippi 39440
Los Angeles County Museum of Art, Los Angeles, California 90036
Lowie Museum of Anthropology, Berkeley, California 94720
Maxwell Museum of Anthropology, Albuquerque, New Mexico 87103
Merrimack Valley Textile Museum, North Andover, Massachusetts 01845
Metropolitan Museum of Art, New York, New York 10028
Minneapolis Institute of Art, Minneapolis, Minnesota 55404
Museum of American Folk Art, New York, New York 10019
Museum of the American Indian, Heye Foundation, New York, New York 10032
Museum of the Chicago Art Institute, Chicago, Illinois 60603
Museum of Early Southern Decorative Arts, Winston-Salem, North Carolina 27101
Museum of Fine Arts, Boston, Massachusetts 02115
Museum and Laboratories of Ethnic Arts and Technology, Los Angeles, California 90024
Museum of New Mexico, Santa Fe, New Mexico 87501
Museum of Primitive Culture, Peace Dale, Rhode Island 02883
Nelson Gallery and Atkins Museum of Fine Arts, Kansas City, Missouri 64062
Norwegian-American Museum, Decorah, Iowa 52101
Oakland Art Museum, Oakland, California 94607
Old Economy Village, Ambridge, Pennsylvania 15003
Old Slater Mill Museum, Pawtucket, Rhode Island 02865
Old Woolen Mill Museum, Barrington, Nova Scotia
Peabody Museum of Archaeology and Ethnology, Cambridge, Massachusetts 02138
Rockefeller Folk Art Collection, Williamsburg, Virginia 23185
Scalamandre Museum of Textiles, New York, New York 10022
Smithsonian Institution, Washington, D.C. 20560
Southwest Museum, Los Angeles, California 90065
Textile Museum, Washington, D.C. 20008
University of Washington, Textile Study Center, Seattle, Washington 98105
Watkins Woolen Mill, Lawson, Missouri 64062

SUPPLIERS LIST

Card Weaving Cards

Naturalcraft
2199 Bancroft Way
Berkeley, California 94704

School Products Company, Inc.
312 East 23rd Street
New York, New York 10010

Dyes, Natural

Charles F. Bailey
St. Aubyn, 13 Dutton Street
Bankstown N.S.W. 2200, Australia

Dominion Herb Distributors
61 Saint Catherine Street West
Montreal 18, Quebec, Canada

Nature's Herb Company
281 Ellis Street
San Francisco, California 94102

Dyes, Procion

Glen Black
1414 Grant Avenue
San Francisco, California 94133

Hand Cards

E.B. Frye and Sons
Wilton, New Hampshire 03086

Hand Carding Machine

Made Well Manufacturing Co.
Box 44, Sifton
Manitoba, Canada

Spinning Equipment and Fibers

Greentree Ranch
Route 3, Box 461
Loveland, Colorado 80537

The Mercantile
3375½ Mt. Diablo Blvd.
Lafayette, California 94549

Straw Into Gold
5509 College Avenue
Oakland, California 94618

Spinning Oil

Paula Simmons
Suquamish, Washington 98392

Yarns and Weaving Equipment

Berga/Ullman
P.O. Box 831, 1 Westerly Road
Ossining, New York 10562

Craft Yarns
603 Mineral Springs Avenue
Pawtucket, Rhode Island 02862

Frederick J. Fawcett, Inc.
129 South Street
Boston, Massachusetts 02111

The Mannings
R.D. East Berlin
Pennsylvania 17316

The Yarn Depot
545 Sutter Street
San Francisco, California 94102

British Suppliers

Dryad
Northgates
Leicester LE1 4QR, England

The Handweavers Studio and Gallery
9 Haroldstone Road
London E17, England

Matheson Dyes and Chemicals
Marion Place
London E8 1CP, England

Needlewoman Shop
146 Regent Street
London W1, England

Texere Yarns
9 Peckover Street
Bradford 1, Yorks., England

William Hall & Co.
177 Stanley Road
Cheadle Hulme, Cheshire, England

INDEX